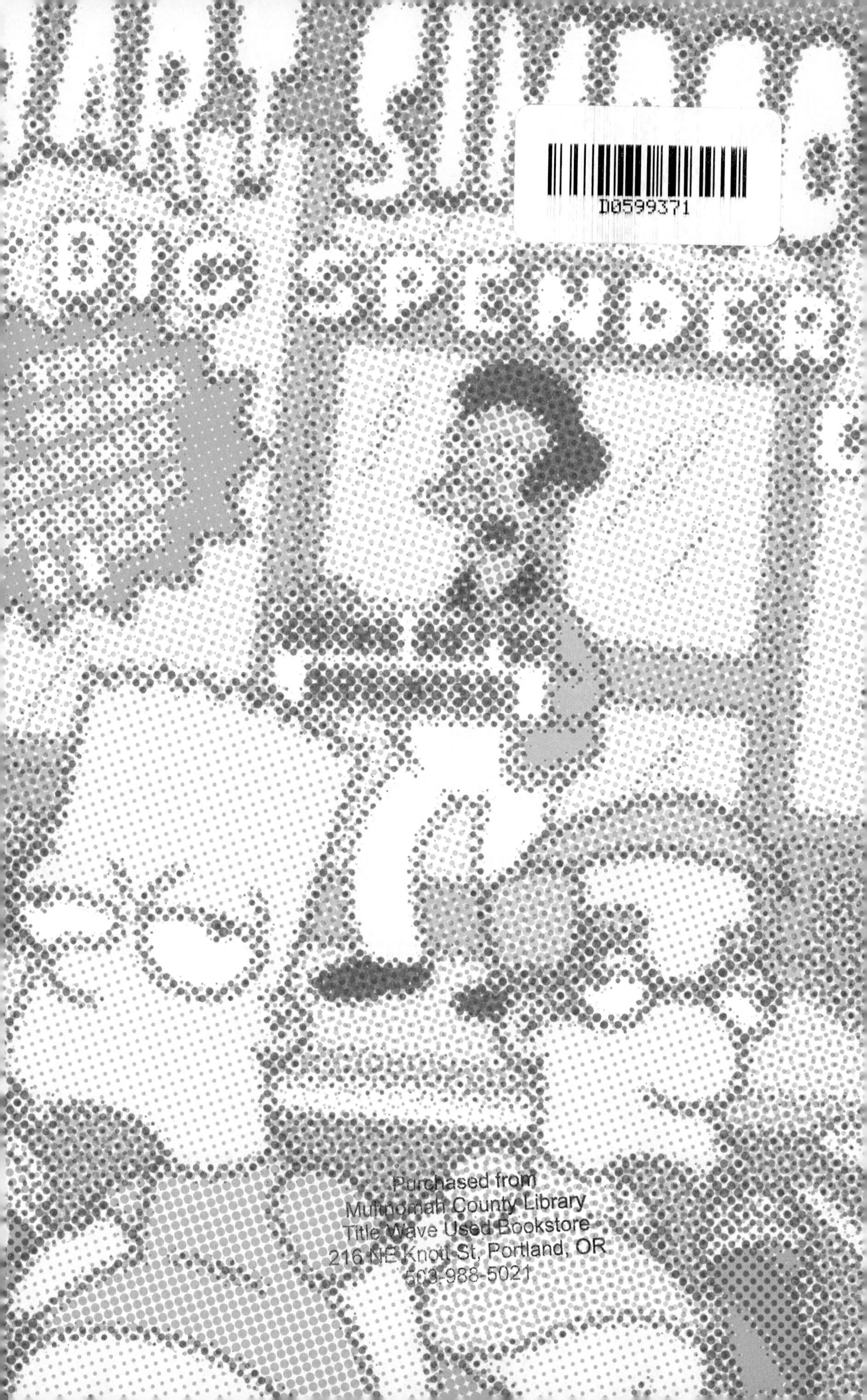

BIG BRILLIANT BOOK OF BART SIMPSON™

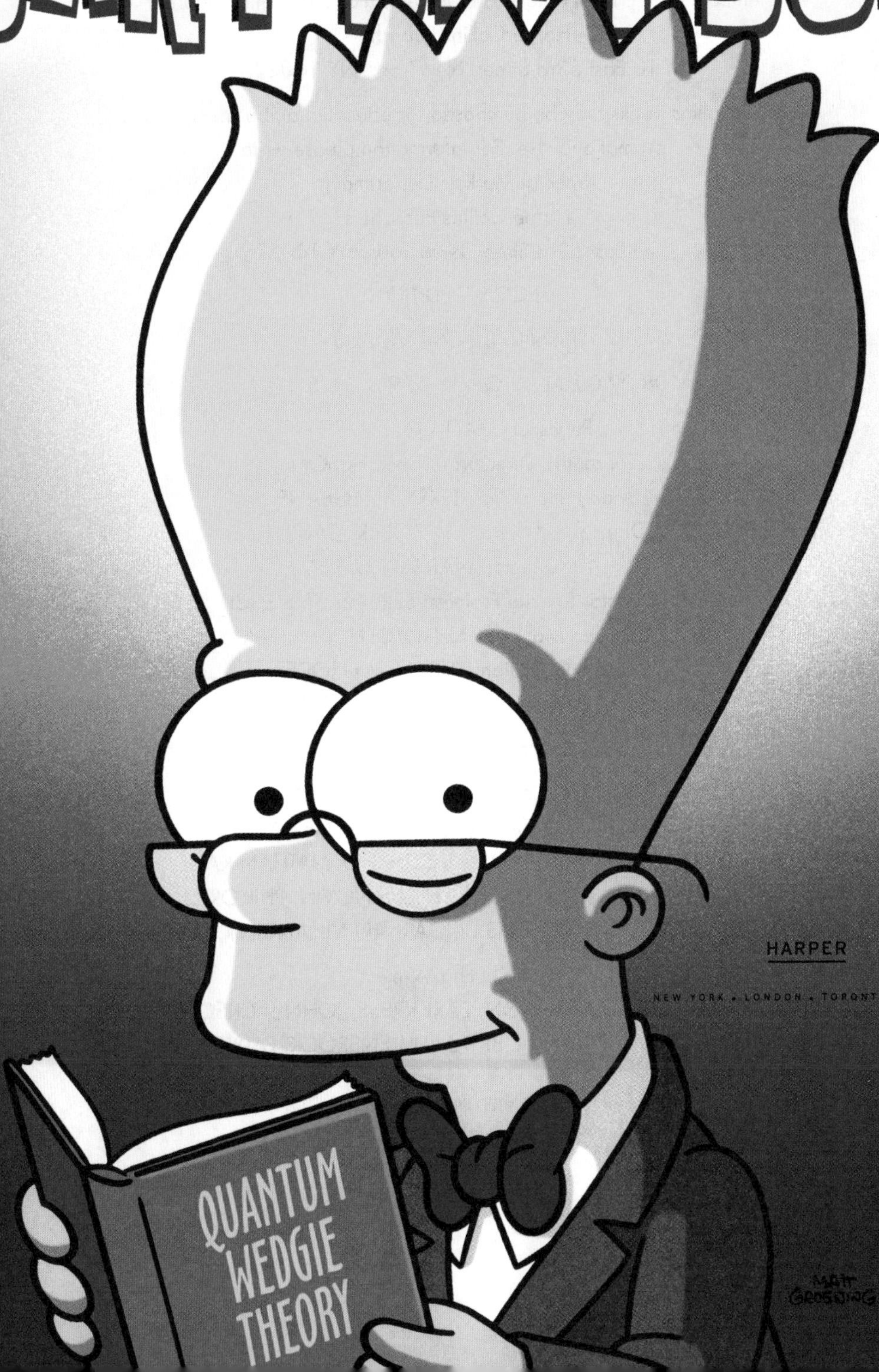
QUANTUM
WEDGIE
THEORY
MATT GROENING

HARPER

NEW YORK • LONDON • TORONTO • SYDNEY

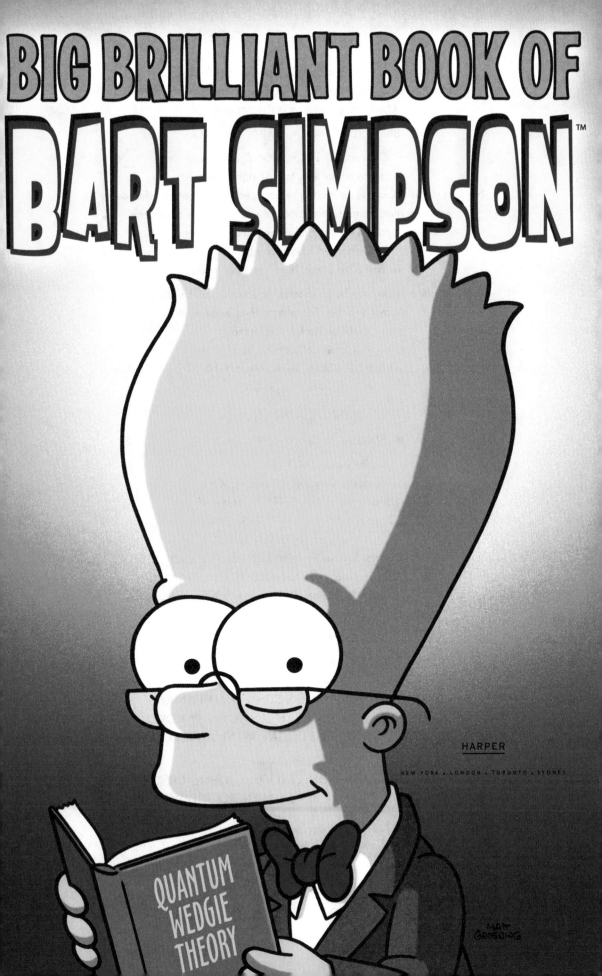

BIG BRILLIANT BOOK OF BART SIMPSON

HarperCollins books may be purchased for educational, business, or sales
promotional use. For information please write
Special Markets Department,
HarperCollins Publishers,
10 East 53rd Street, New York, NY 10022.

SECOND EDITION

ISBN 978-0-06-145022-8

08 09 00 11 12 QWM 10 9 8 7 6 5 4 3 2

Publisher: MATT GROENING
Creative Director: BILL MORRISON
Managing Editor: TERRY DELEGEANE
Director of Operations: ROBERT ZAUGH
Art Director: NATHAN KANE
Art Director Special Projects: SERBAN CRISTESCU
Production Manager: CHRISTOPHER UNGAR
Legal Guardian: SUSAN A. GRODE
HarperCollins Editors: HOPE INNELLI, JEREMY CESAREC

Trade Paperback Concepts and Design: SERBAN CRISTESCU

Contributing Artists:
KAREN BATES, JOHN COSTANZA, JOHN DELANEY, MIKE DECARLO,
CLAY & SUSAN GRIFFITH, NATHAN HAMILL, JASON HO, NATHAN KANE, JAMES LLOYD,
JOEY MASON, BILL MORRISON, JOEY NILGES, PHYLLIS NOVIN, PHIL ORTIZ, ANDREW PEPOY,
MIKE ROTE, HOWARD SHUM, CHRIS UNGAR, ART VILLANUEVA, MIKE WORLEY

Contributing Writers:
JAMES W. BATES, CHUCK DIXON, EARL KRESS, JOHN JACKSON MILLER,
TOM PEYER, DAVID SEIDMAN, BRYAN UHLENBROCK, PATRIC VERRONE

PRINTED IN CANADA

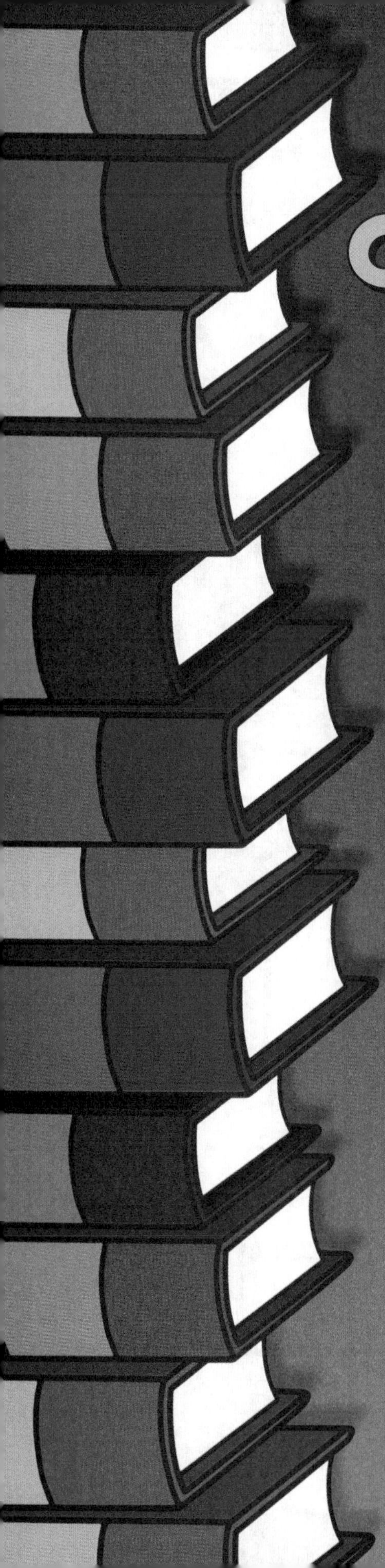

TABLE OF CONTENTS

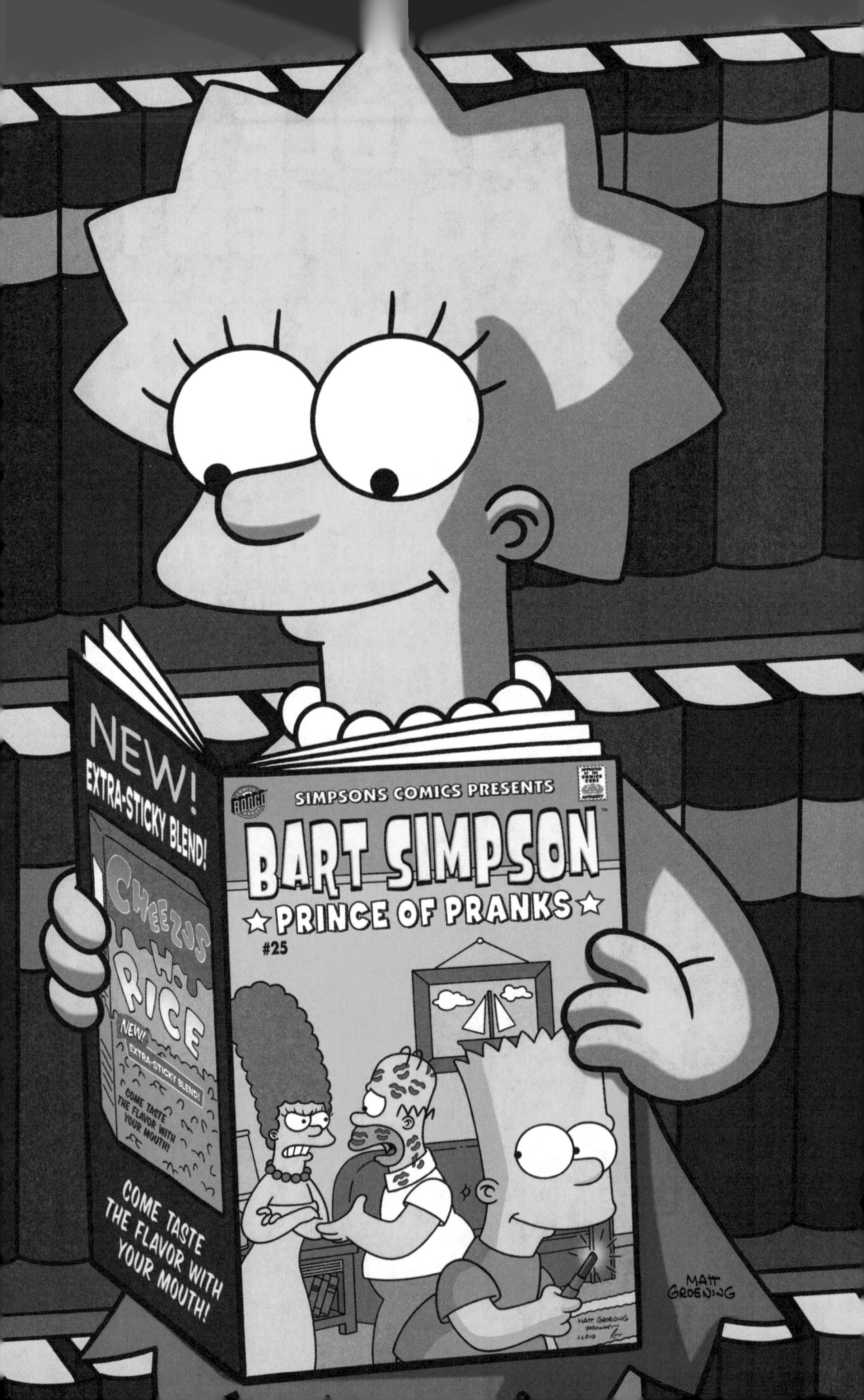

NEW!
EXTRA-STICKY BLEND!
RICE
NEW!
EXTRA-STICKY BLEND!
COME TASTE THE FLAVOR WITH YOUR MOUTH!
COME TASTE THE FLAVOR WITH YOUR MOUTH!
SIMPSONS COMICS PRESENTS
BART SIMPSON
PRINCE OF PRANKS
#25
MATT GROENING

MATT GROENING PRESENTS

the UNDERACHIEVING BART SIMPSON

"COMICS FAN NO MORE!"

TOM PEYER	JOHN COSTANZA	HOWARD SHUM	JOEY MASON	KAREN BATES	BILL MORRISON
WRITER	PENCILS	INKS	COLORS	LETTERS	EDITOR

I AM A COMICS FAN *NO MORE*...

...SINCE WORKING FOR YOU AT THIS CONVENTION MAKES ME A *PRO*!

RIGHT, COMIC BOOK GUY? *RIGHT*?

SPRINGGRAPHNOVSEQARTCOMTRACARDCON
THE SPRINGFIELD GRAPHIC NOVEL, SEQUENTIAL ART, COMICS AND TRADING CARD CONVENTION
JUNE 7TH & 8TH

HARDLY, SIMPSON...

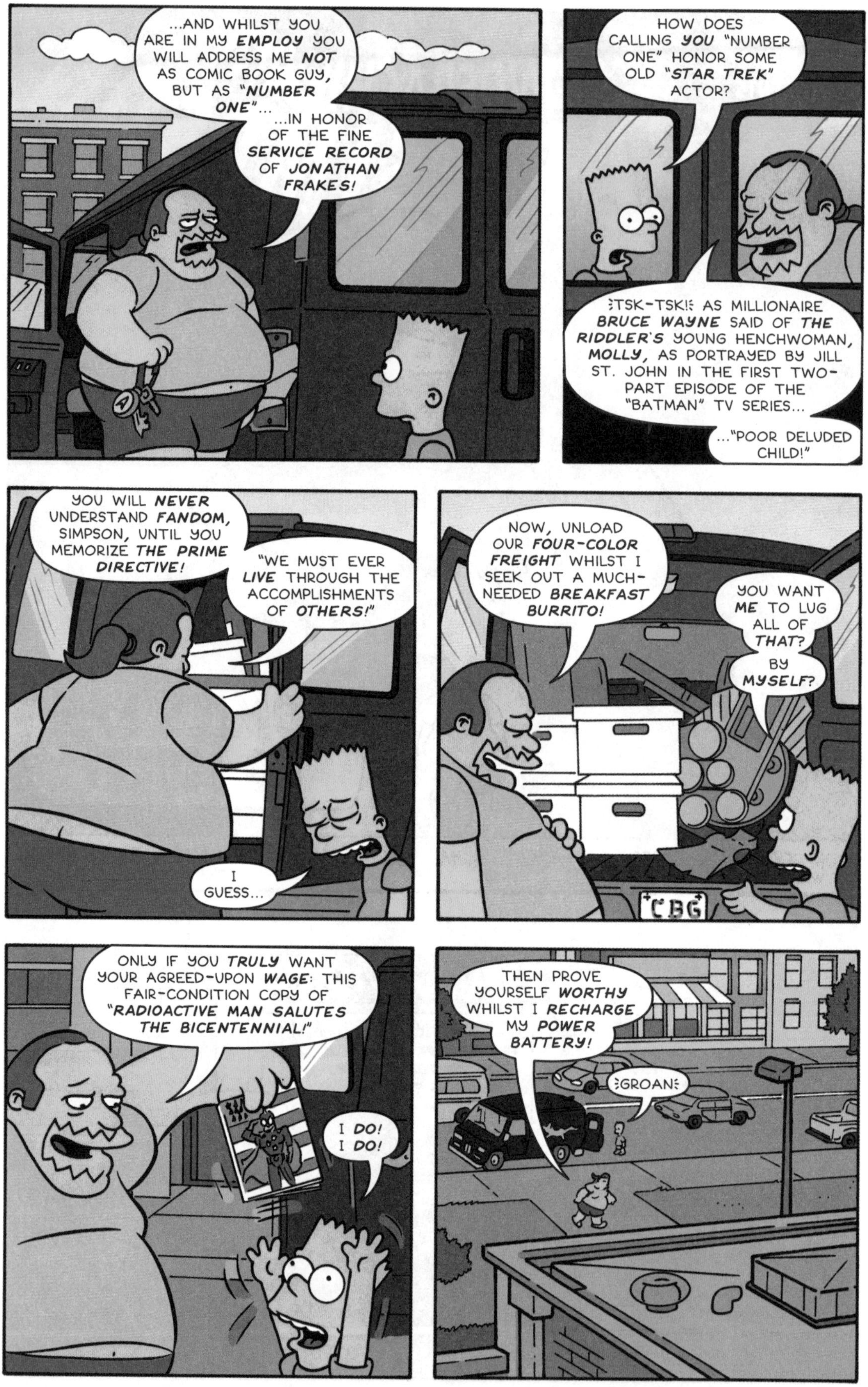
...AND WHILST YOU ARE IN MY EMPLOY YOU WILL ADDRESS ME NOT AS COMIC BOOK GUY, BUT AS "NUMBER ONE"...
...IN HONOR OF THE FINE SERVICE RECORD OF JONATHAN FRAKES!
HOW DOES CALLING YOU "NUMBER ONE" HONOR SOME OLD "STAR TREK" ACTOR?
TSK-TSK! AS MILLIONAIRE BRUCE WAYNE SAID OF THE RIDDLER'S YOUNG HENCHWOMAN, MOLLY, AS PORTRAYED BY JILL ST. JOHN IN THE FIRST TWO-PART EPISODE OF THE "BATMAN" TV SERIES...
..."POOR DELUDED CHILD!"
YOU WILL NEVER UNDERSTAND FANDOM, SIMPSON, UNTIL YOU MEMORIZE THE PRIME DIRECTIVE!
"WE MUST EVER LIVE THROUGH THE ACCOMPLISHMENTS OF OTHERS!"
I GUESS...
NOW, UNLOAD OUR FOUR-COLOR FREIGHT WHILST I SEEK OUT A MUCH-NEEDED BREAKFAST BURRITO!
YOU WANT ME TO LUG ALL OF THAT?
BY MYSELF?
CBG
ONLY IF YOU TRULY WANT YOUR AGREED-UPON WAGE: THIS FAIR-CONDITION COPY OF "RADIOACTIVE MAN SALUTES THE BICENTENNIAL!"
I DO! I DO!
THEN PROVE YOURSELF WORTHY WHILST I RECHARGE MY POWER BATTERY!
GROAN

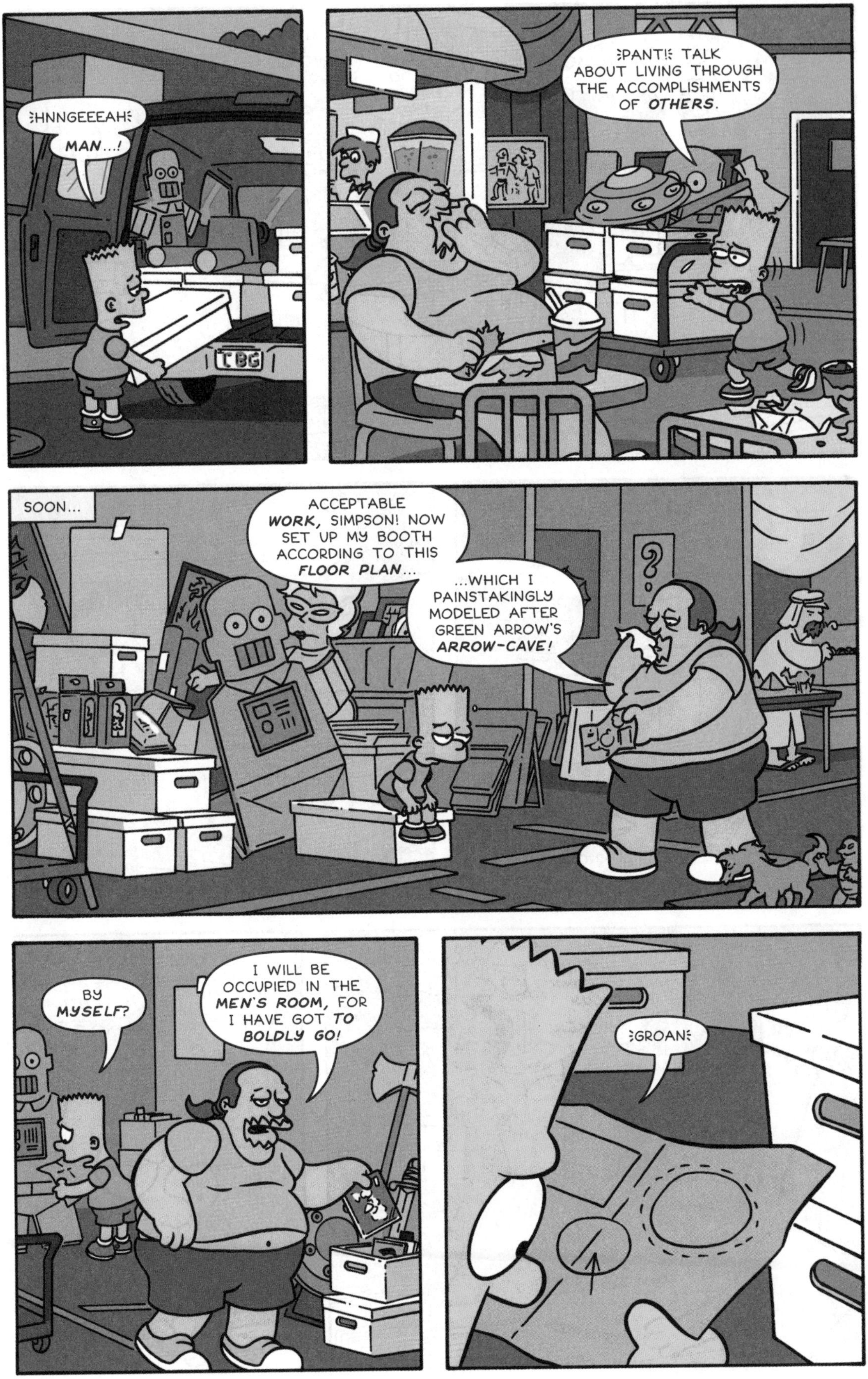

HNNGEEEAH
MAN...!
PANT! TALK ABOUT LIVING THROUGH THE ACCOMPLISHMENTS OF OTHERS.
SOON...
ACCEPTABLE WORK, SIMPSON! NOW SET UP MY BOOTH ACCORDING TO THIS FLOOR PLAN...
...WHICH I PAINSTAKINGLY MODELED AFTER GREEN ARROW'S ARROW-CAVE!
BY MYSELF?
I WILL BE OCCUPIED IN THE MEN'S ROOM, FOR I HAVE GOT TO BOLDLY GO!
GROAN

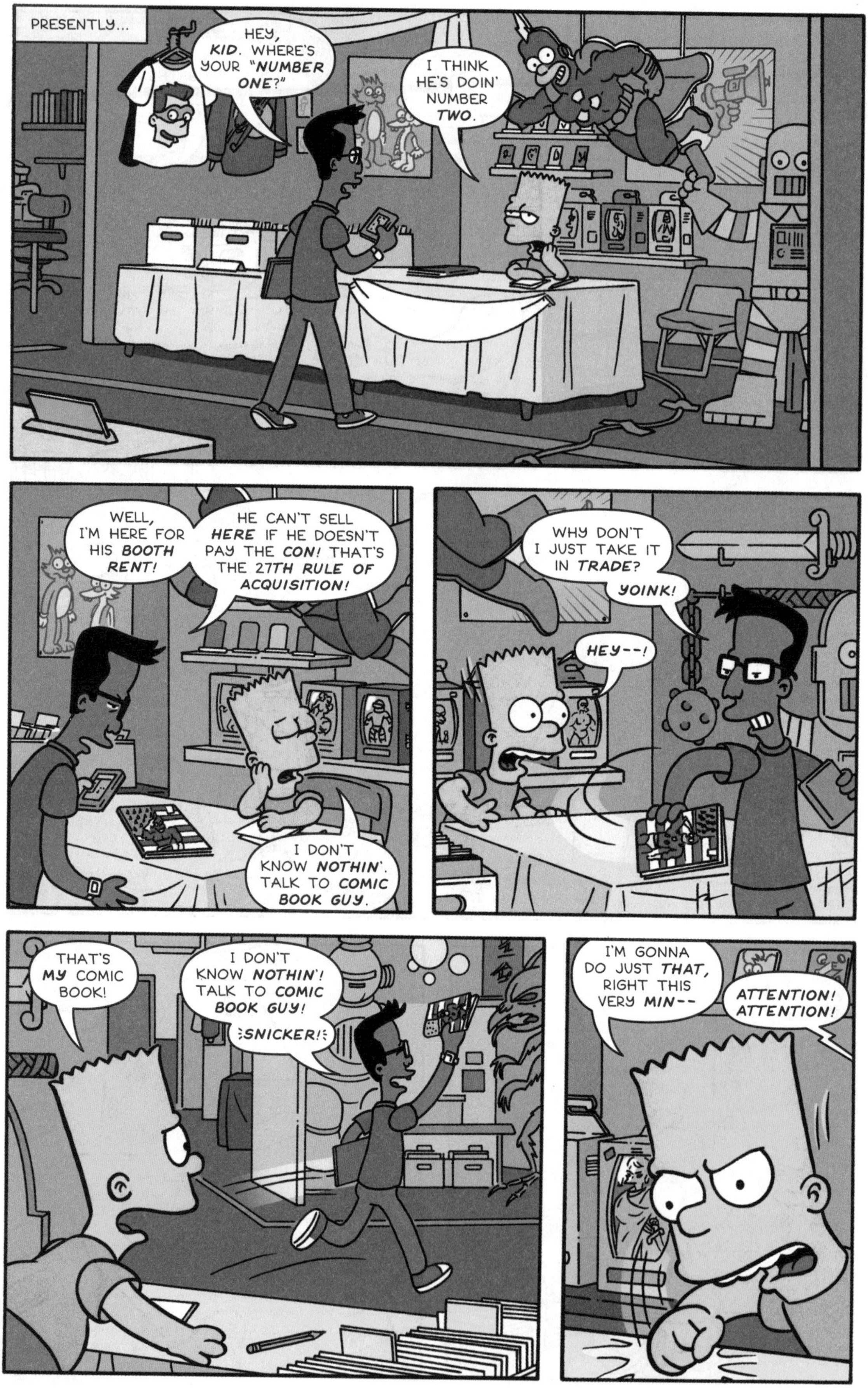
PRESENTLY...
HEY, KID. WHERE'S YOUR "NUMBER ONE?"
I THINK HE'S DOIN' NUMBER TWO.
WELL, I'M HERE FOR HIS BOOTH RENT!
HE CAN'T SELL HERE IF HE DOESN'T PAY THE CON! THAT'S THE 27TH RULE OF ACQUISITION!
I DON'T KNOW NOTHIN'. TALK TO COMIC BOOK GUY.
WHY DON'T I JUST TAKE IT IN TRADE?
YOINK!
HEY--!
THAT'S MY COMIC BOOK!
I DON'T KNOW NOTHIN'! TALK TO COMIC BOOK GUY!
SNICKER!
I'M GONNA DO JUST THAT, RIGHT THIS VERY MIN--
ATTENTION! ATTENTION!

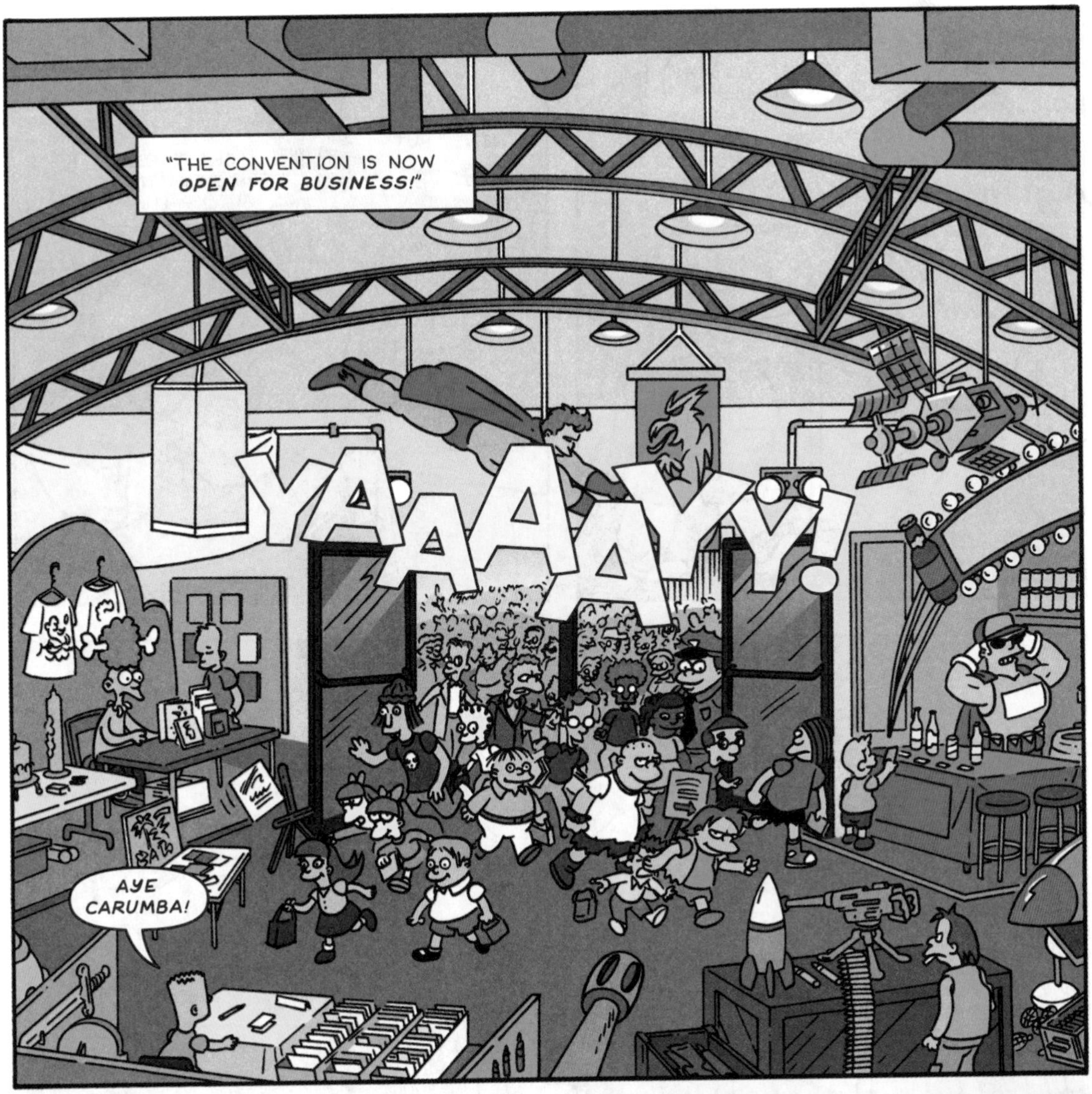
"THE CONVENTION IS NOW OPEN FOR BUSINESS!"
YAAAAY!
AYE CARUMBA!

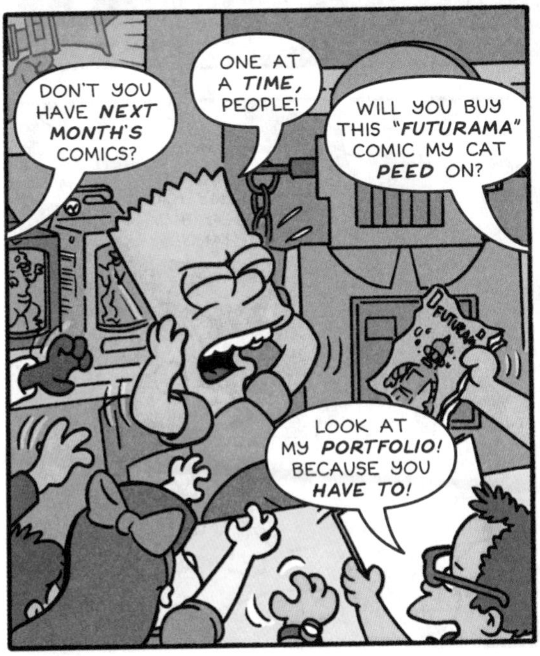
DON'T YOU HAVE NEXT MONTH'S COMICS?
ONE AT A TIME, PEOPLE!
WILL YOU BUY THIS "FUTURAMA" COMIC MY CAT PEED ON?
FUTURAMA
LOOK AT MY PORTFOLIO! BECAUSE YOU HAVE TO!

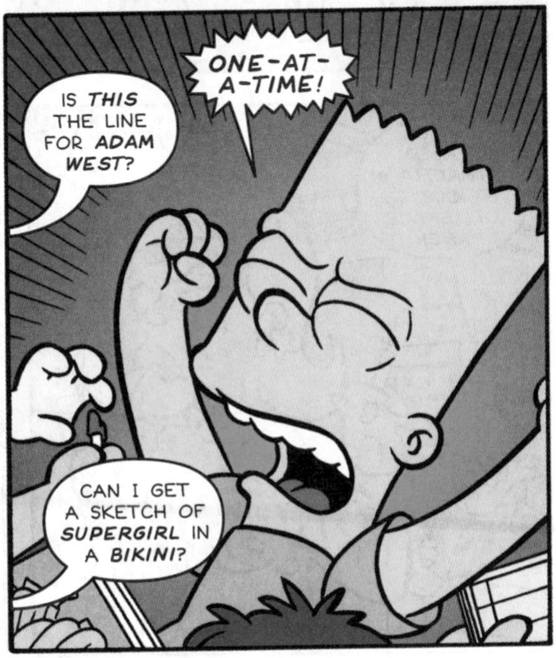
IS THIS THE LINE FOR ADAM WEST?
ONE-AT-A-TIME!
CAN I GET A SKETCH OF SUPERGIRL IN A BIKINI?

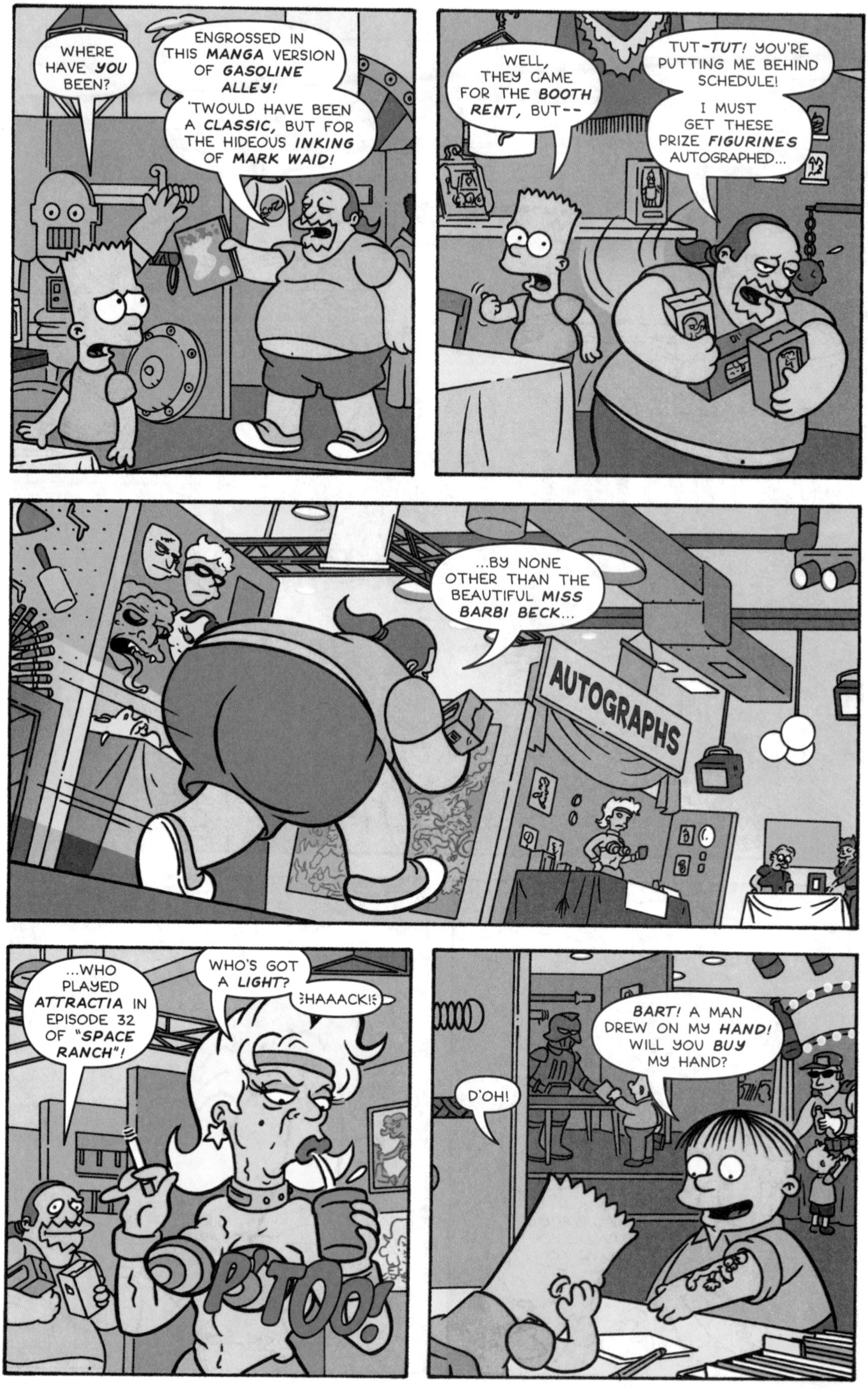
WHERE HAVE YOU BEEN?
ENGROSSED IN THIS MANGA VERSION OF GASOLINE ALLEY!
'TWOULD HAVE BEEN A CLASSIC, BUT FOR THE HIDEOUS INKING OF MARK WAID!
WELL, THEY CAME FOR THE BOOTH RENT, BUT--
TUT-TUT! YOU'RE PUTTING ME BEHIND SCHEDULE!
I MUST GET THESE PRIZE FIGURINES AUTOGRAPHED...
...BY NONE OTHER THAN THE BEAUTIFUL MISS BARBI BECK...
AUTOGRAPHS
...WHO PLAYED ATTRACTIA IN EPISODE 32 OF "SPACE RANCH"!
WHO'S GOT A LIGHT?
HAAACK!
P'TOO!
BART! A MAN DREW ON MY HAND! WILL YOU BUY MY HAND?
D'OH!

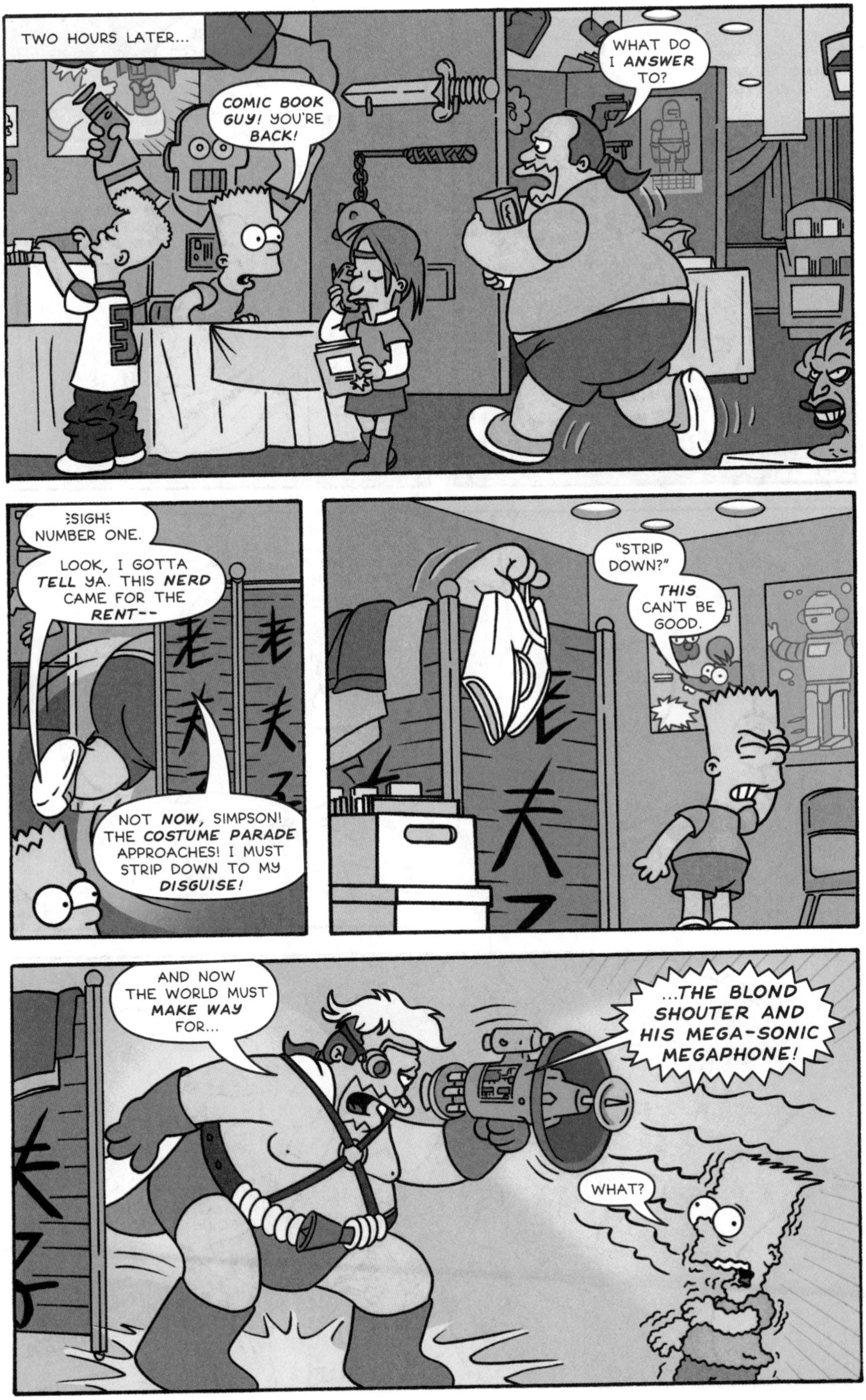
TWO HOURS LATER...
COMIC BOOK GUY! YOU'RE BACK!
WHAT DO I ANSWER TO?
:SIGH: NUMBER ONE.
LOOK, I GOTTA TELL YA. THIS NERD CAME FOR THE RENT--
NOT NOW, SIMPSON! THE COSTUME PARADE APPROACHES! I MUST STRIP DOWN TO MY DISGUISE!
"STRIP DOWN?"
THIS CAN'T BE GOOD.
AND NOW THE WORLD MUST MAKE WAY FOR...
...THE BLOND SHOUTER AND HIS MEGA-SONIC MEGAPHONE!
WHAT?

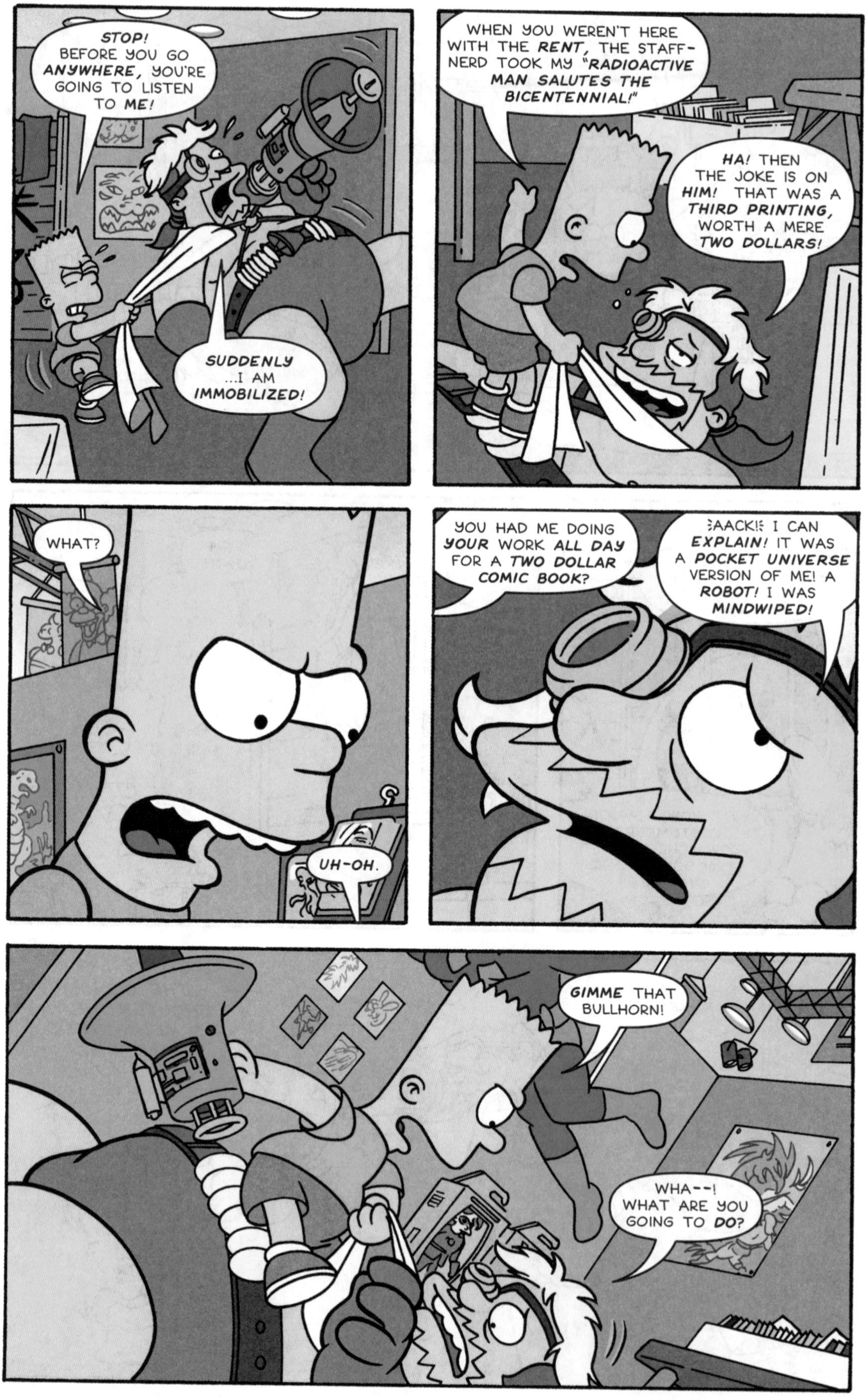
STOP! BEFORE YOU GO ANYWHERE, YOU'RE GOING TO LISTEN TO ME!
SUDDENLY ...I AM IMMOBILIZED!
WHEN YOU WEREN'T HERE WITH THE RENT, THE STAFF-NERD TOOK MY "RADIOACTIVE MAN SALUTES THE BICENTENNIAL!"
HA! THEN THE JOKE IS ON HIM! THAT WAS A THIRD PRINTING, WORTH A MERE TWO DOLLARS!
WHAT?
UH-OH.
YOU HAD ME DOING YOUR WORK ALL DAY FOR A TWO DOLLAR COMIC BOOK?
AACK!! I CAN EXPLAIN! IT WAS A POCKET UNIVERSE VERSION OF ME! A ROBOT! I WAS MINDWIPED!
GIMME THAT BULLHORN!
WHA--! WHAT ARE YOU GOING TO DO?

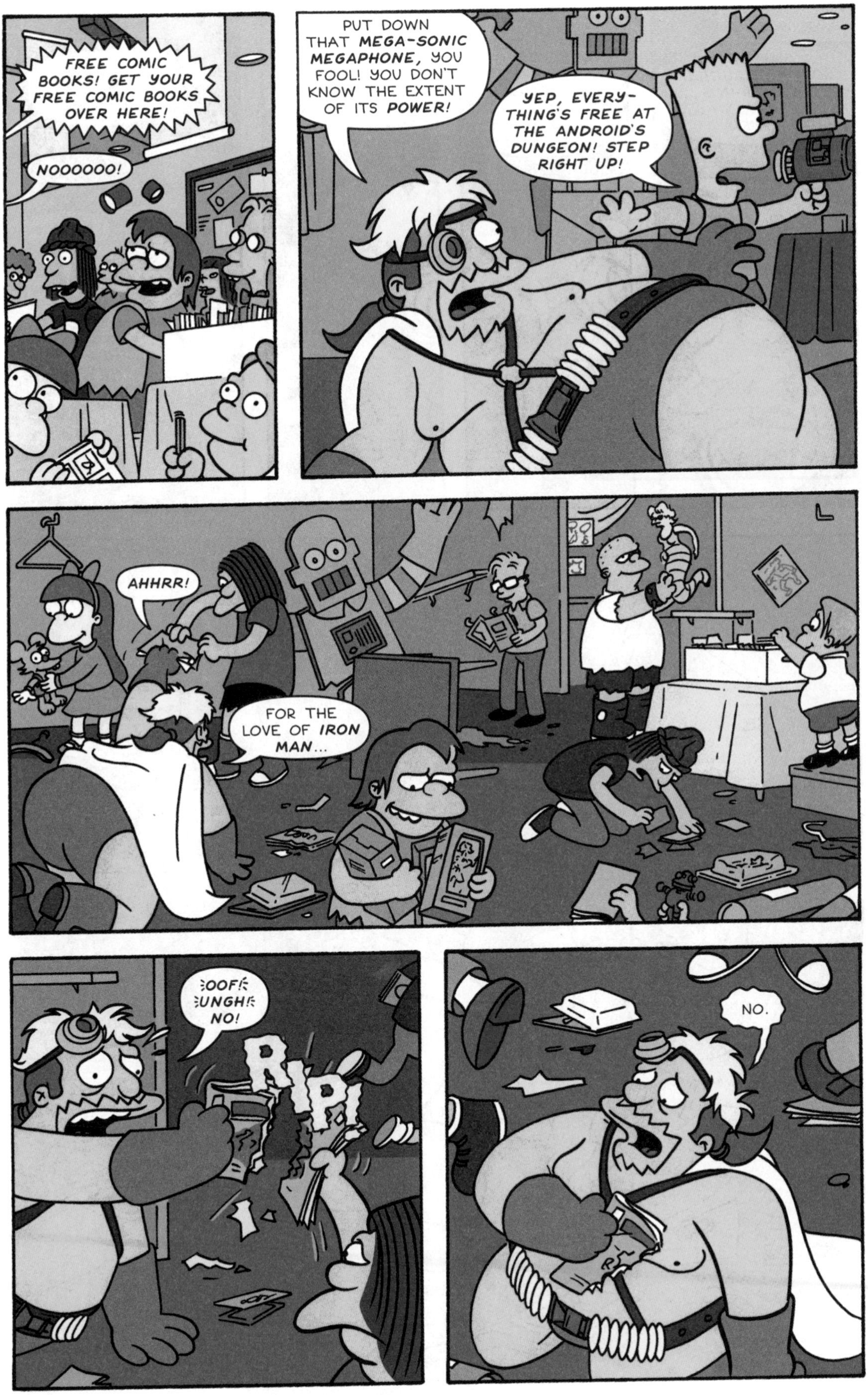
FREE COMIC BOOKS! GET YOUR FREE COMIC BOOKS OVER HERE!
NOOOOOO!
PUT DOWN THAT MEGA-SONIC MEGAPHONE, YOU FOOL! YOU DON'T KNOW THE EXTENT OF ITS POWER!
YEP, EVERY-THING'S FREE AT THE ANDROID'S DUNGEON! STEP RIGHT UP!
AHHRR!
FOR THE LOVE OF IRON MAN...
OOF! UNGH! NO!
RIP!
NO.

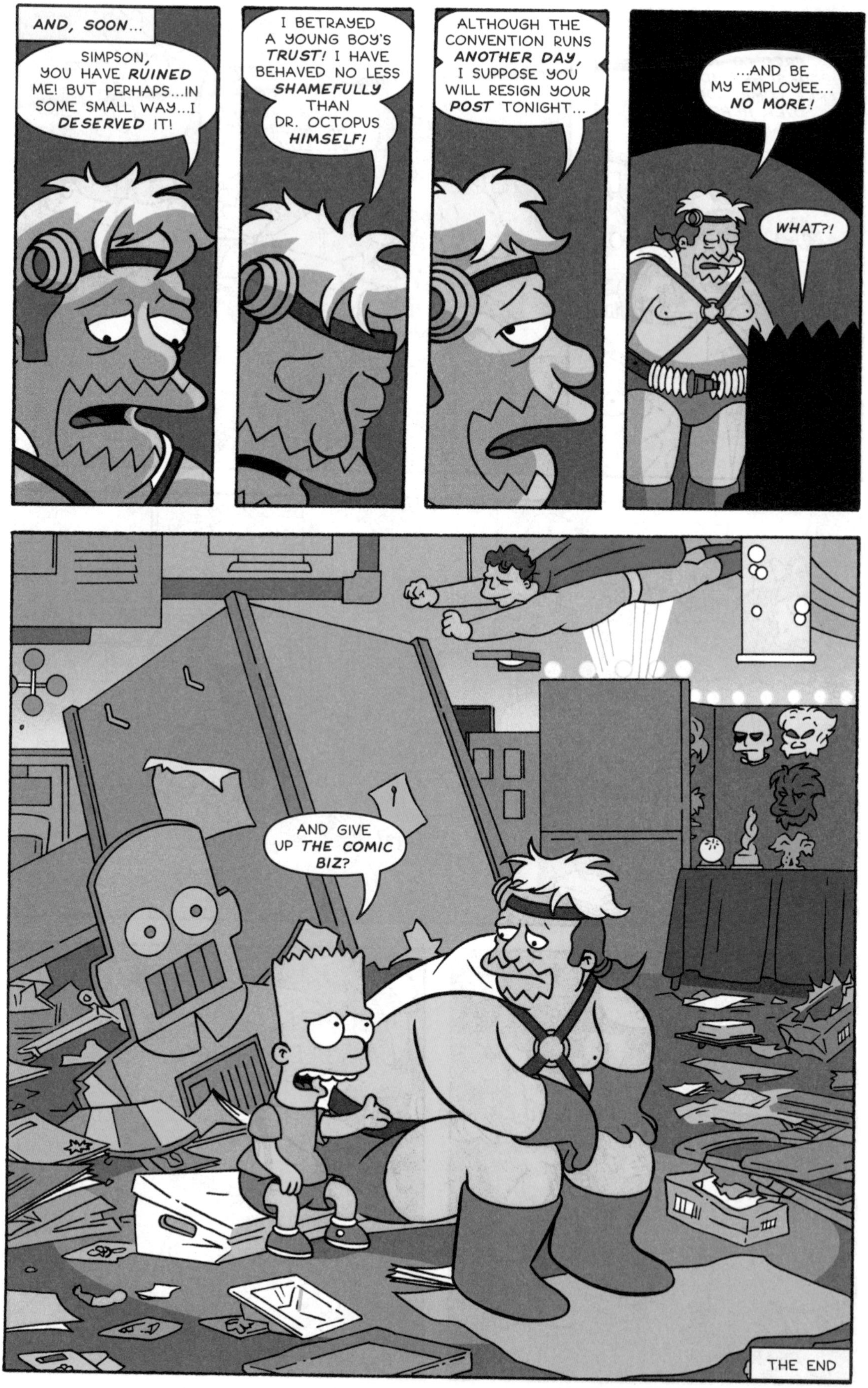
AND, SOON...
SIMPSON, YOU HAVE RUINED ME! BUT PERHAPS...IN SOME SMALL WAY...I DESERVED IT!
I BETRAYED A YOUNG BOY'S TRUST! I HAVE BEHAVED NO LESS SHAMEFULLY THAN DR. OCTOPUS HIMSELF!
ALTHOUGH THE CONVENTION RUNS ANOTHER DAY, I SUPPOSE YOU WILL RESIGN YOUR POST TONIGHT...
...AND BE MY EMPLOYEE... NO MORE!
WHAT?!
AND GIVE UP THE COMIC BIZ?
THE END

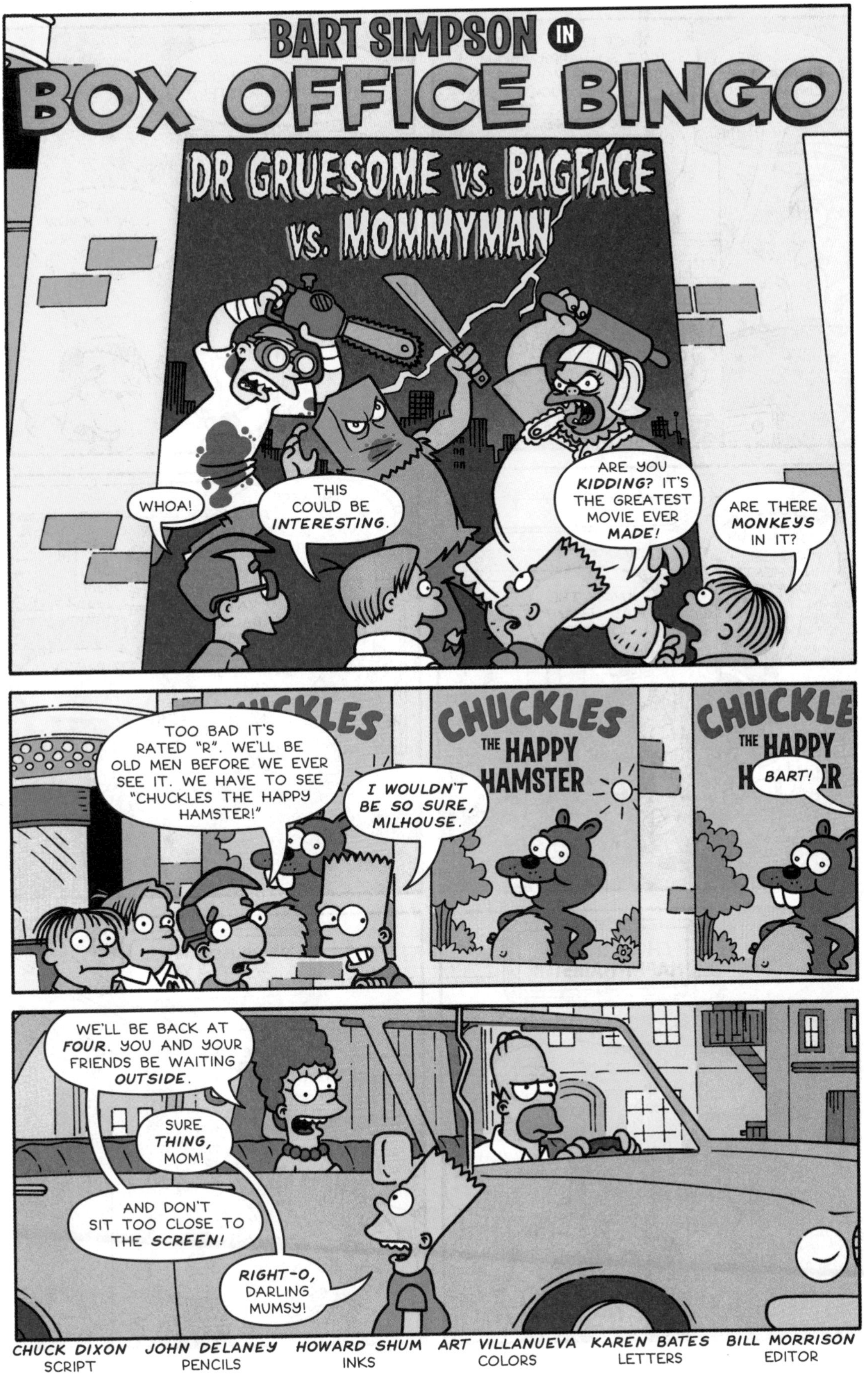
BART SIMPSON IN
BOX OFFICE BINGO
DR GRUESOME VS. BAGFACE VS. MOMMYMAN
WHOA!
THIS COULD BE INTERESTING.
ARE YOU KIDDING? IT'S THE GREATEST MOVIE EVER MADE!
ARE THERE MONKEYS IN IT?
CHUCKLES THE HAPPY HAMSTER
TOO BAD IT'S RATED "R". WE'LL BE OLD MEN BEFORE WE EVER SEE IT. WE HAVE TO SEE "CHUCKLES THE HAPPY HAMSTER!"
I WOULDN'T BE SO SURE, MILHOUSE.
BART!
WE'LL BE BACK AT FOUR. YOU AND YOUR FRIENDS BE WAITING OUTSIDE.
SURE THING, MOM!
AND DON'T SIT TOO CLOSE TO THE SCREEN!
RIGHT-O, DARLING MUMSY!

CHUCK DIXON SCRIPT · JOHN DELANEY PENCILS · HOWARD SHUM INKS · ART VILLANUEVA COLORS · KAREN BATES LETTERS · BILL MORRISON EDITOR

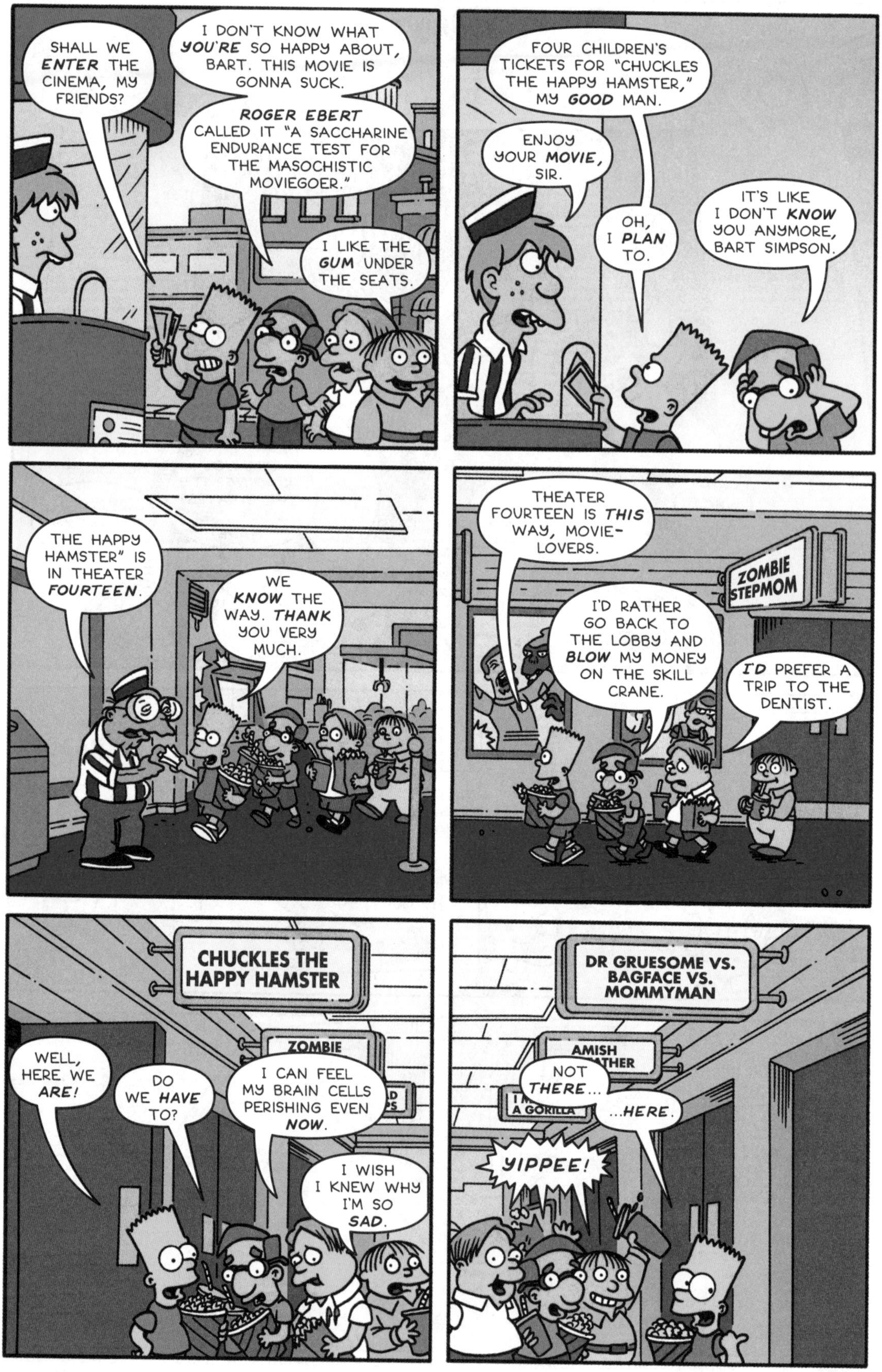
SHALL WE ENTER THE CINEMA, MY FRIENDS?
I DON'T KNOW WHAT YOU'RE SO HAPPY ABOUT, BART. THIS MOVIE IS GONNA SUCK.
ROGER EBERT CALLED IT "A SACCHARINE ENDURANCE TEST FOR THE MASOCHISTIC MOVIEGOER."
I LIKE THE GUM UNDER THE SEATS.
FOUR CHILDREN'S TICKETS FOR "CHUCKLES THE HAPPY HAMSTER," MY GOOD MAN.
ENJOY YOUR MOVIE, SIR.
OH, I PLAN TO.
IT'S LIKE I DON'T KNOW YOU ANYMORE, BART SIMPSON.
THE HAPPY HAMSTER" IS IN THEATER FOURTEEN.
WE KNOW THE WAY. THANK YOU VERY MUCH.
THEATER FOURTEEN IS THIS WAY, MOVIE-LOVERS.
ZOMBIE STEPMOM
I'D RATHER GO BACK TO THE LOBBY AND BLOW MY MONEY ON THE SKILL CRANE.
I'D PREFER A TRIP TO THE DENTIST.
CHUCKLES THE HAPPY HAMSTER
ZOMBIE
WELL, HERE WE ARE!
DO WE HAVE TO?
I CAN FEEL MY BRAIN CELLS PERISHING EVEN NOW.
I WISH I KNEW WHY I'M SO SAD.
DR GRUESOME VS. BAGFACE VS. MOMMYMAN
A GORILLA
NOT THERE...
...HERE.
YIPPEE!

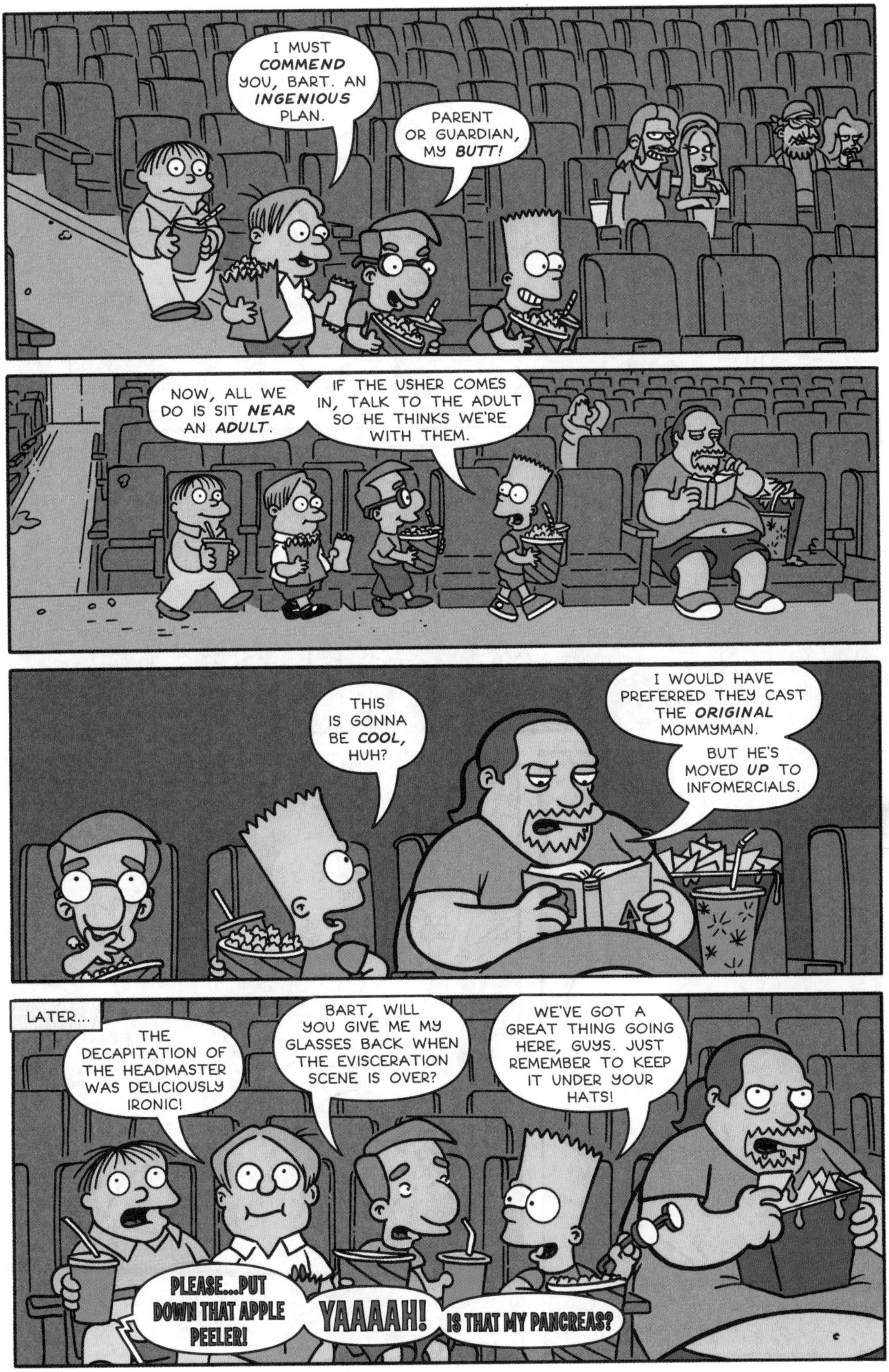
I MUST COMMEND YOU, BART. AN INGENIOUS PLAN.
PARENT OR GUARDIAN, MY BUTT!
NOW, ALL WE DO IS SIT NEAR AN ADULT.
IF THE USHER COMES IN, TALK TO THE ADULT SO HE THINKS WE'RE WITH THEM.
THIS IS GONNA BE COOL, HUH?
I WOULD HAVE PREFERRED THEY CAST THE ORIGINAL MOMMYMAN.
BUT HE'S MOVED UP TO INFOMERCIALS.
LATER...
THE DECAPITATION OF THE HEADMASTER WAS DELICIOUSLY IRONIC!
BART, WILL YOU GIVE ME MY GLASSES BACK WHEN THE EVISCERATION SCENE IS OVER?
WE'VE GOT A GREAT THING GOING HERE, GUYS. JUST REMEMBER TO KEEP IT UNDER YOUR HATS!
PLEASE...PUT DOWN THAT APPLE PEELER!
YAAAAH!
IS THAT MY PANCREAS?

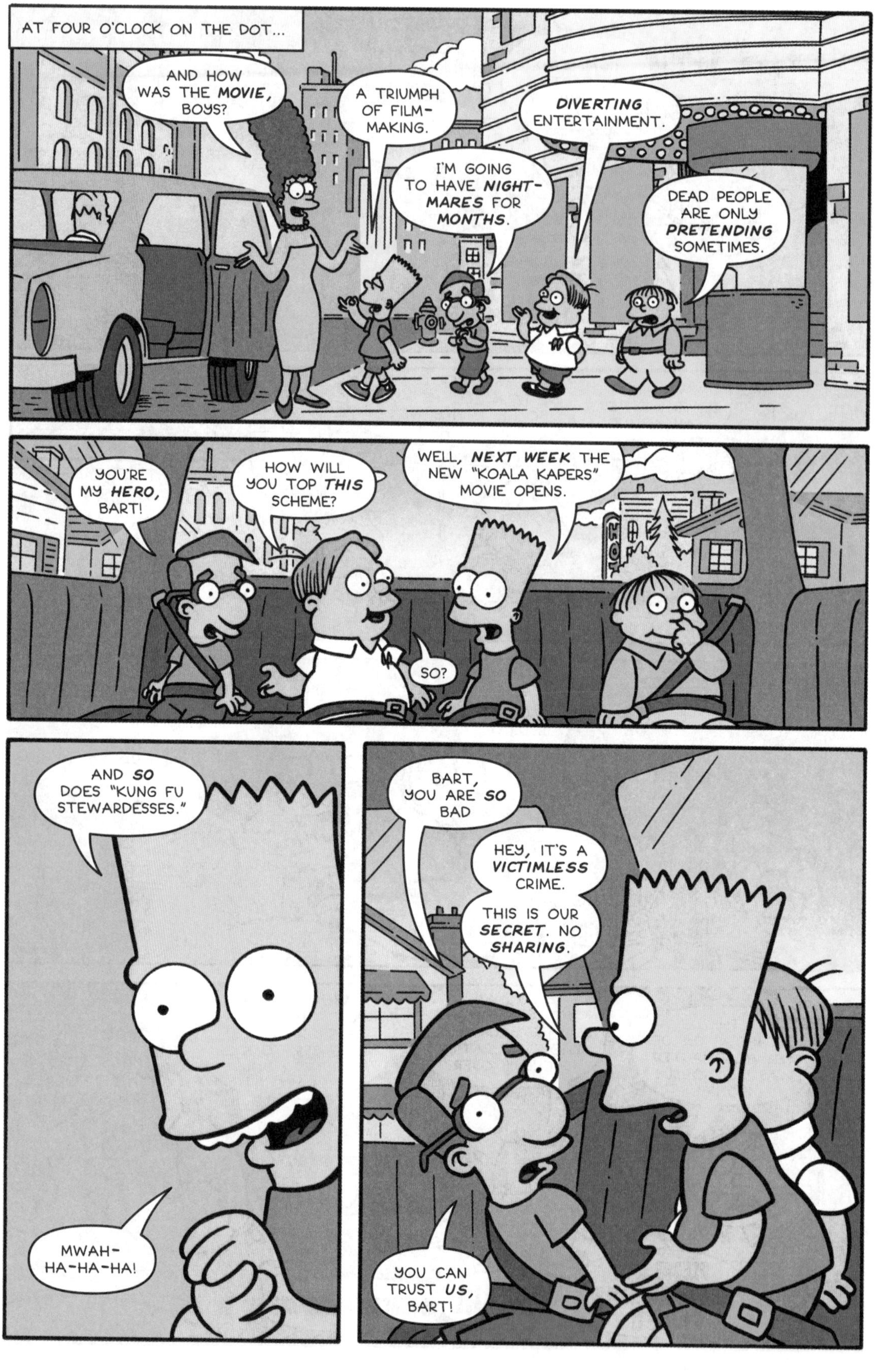
AT FOUR O'CLOCK ON THE DOT...
AND HOW WAS THE MOVIE, BOYS?
A TRIUMPH OF FILM-MAKING.
I'M GOING TO HAVE NIGHTMARES FOR MONTHS.
DIVERTING ENTERTAINMENT.
DEAD PEOPLE ARE ONLY PRETENDING SOMETIMES.
YOU'RE MY HERO, BART!
HOW WILL YOU TOP THIS SCHEME?
WELL, NEXT WEEK THE NEW "KOALA KAPERS" MOVIE OPENS.
SO?
AND SO DOES "KUNG FU STEWARDESSES."
MWAH-HA-HA-HA!
BART, YOU ARE SO BAD
HEY, IT'S A VICTIMLESS CRIME.
THIS IS OUR SECRET. NO SHARING.
YOU CAN TRUST US, BART!

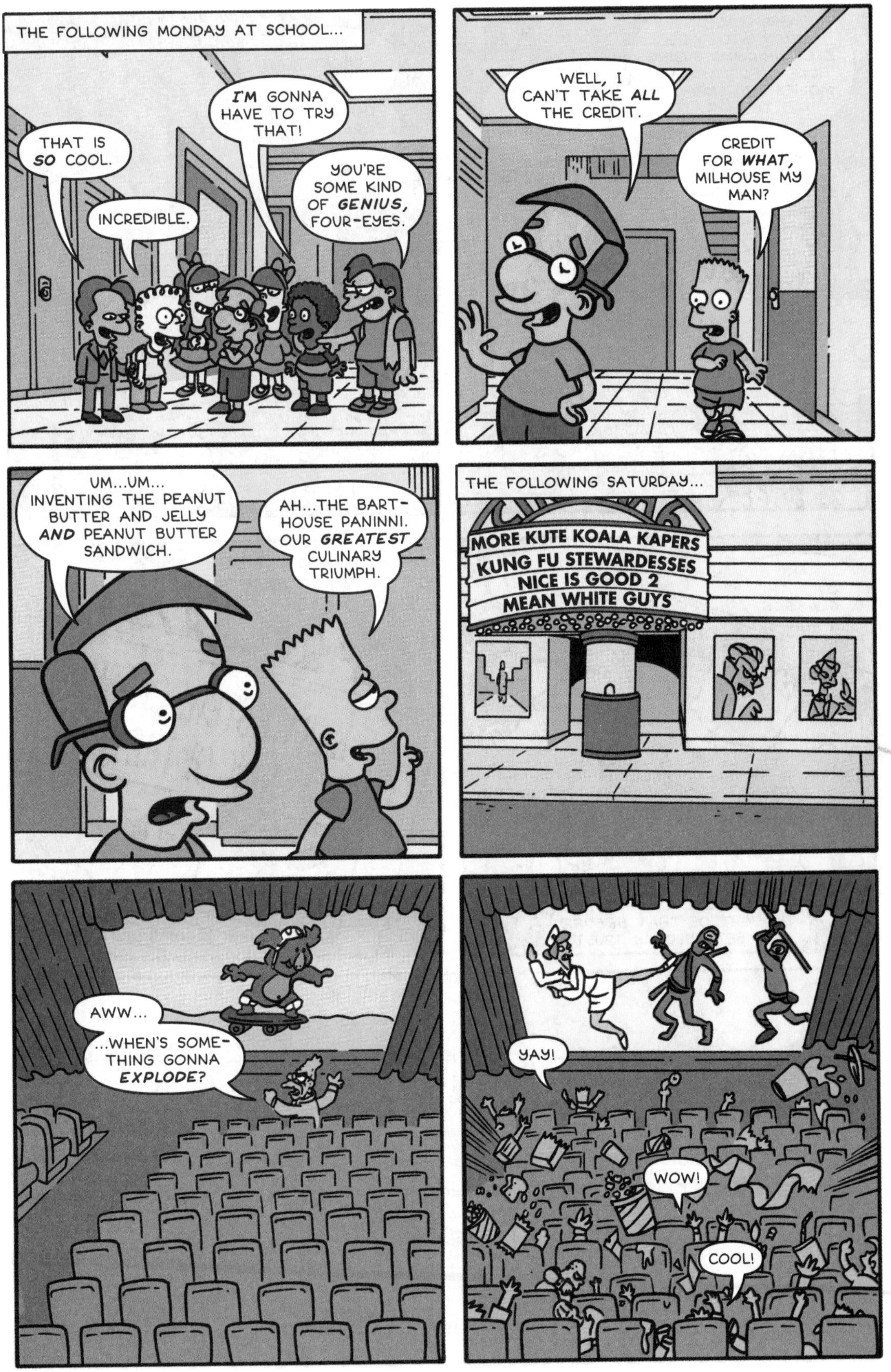

THE FOLLOWING MONDAY AT SCHOOL...
THAT IS SO COOL.
INCREDIBLE.
I'M GONNA HAVE TO TRY THAT!
YOU'RE SOME KIND OF GENIUS, FOUR-EYES.
WELL, I CAN'T TAKE ALL THE CREDIT.
CREDIT FOR WHAT, MILHOUSE MY MAN?
UM...UM... INVENTING THE PEANUT BUTTER AND JELLY AND PEANUT BUTTER SANDWICH.
AH...THE BART-HOUSE PANINNI. OUR GREATEST CULINARY TRIUMPH.
THE FOLLOWING SATURDAY...
MORE KUTE KOALA KAPERS
KUNG FU STEWARDESSES
NICE IS GOOD 2
MEAN WHITE GUYS
AWW...
...WHEN'S SOME-THING GONNA EXPLODE?
YAY!
WOW!
COOL!

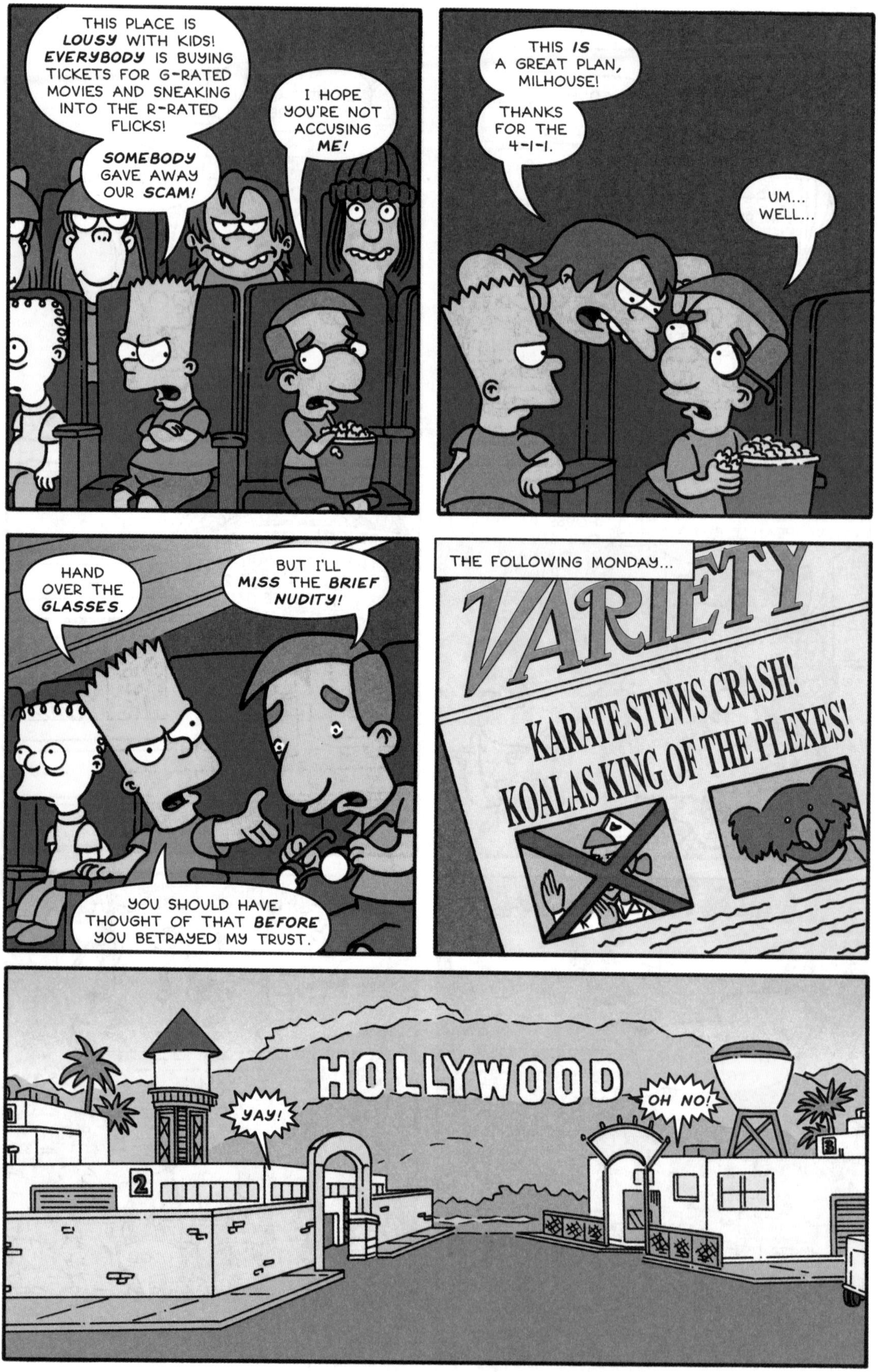
THIS PLACE IS LOUSY WITH KIDS! EVERYBODY IS BUYING TICKETS FOR G-RATED MOVIES AND SNEAKING INTO THE R-RATED FLICKS!
SOMEBODY GAVE AWAY OUR SCAM!
I HOPE YOU'RE NOT ACCUSING ME!
THIS IS A GREAT PLAN, MILHOUSE!
THANKS FOR THE 4-1-1.
UM... WELL...
HAND OVER THE GLASSES.
BUT I'LL MISS THE BRIEF NUDITY!
YOU SHOULD HAVE THOUGHT OF THAT BEFORE YOU BETRAYED MY TRUST.
THE FOLLOWING MONDAY...
VARIETY
KARATE STEWS CRASH!
KOALAS KING OF THE PLEXES!
HOLLYWOOD
YAY!
OH NO!
2
3

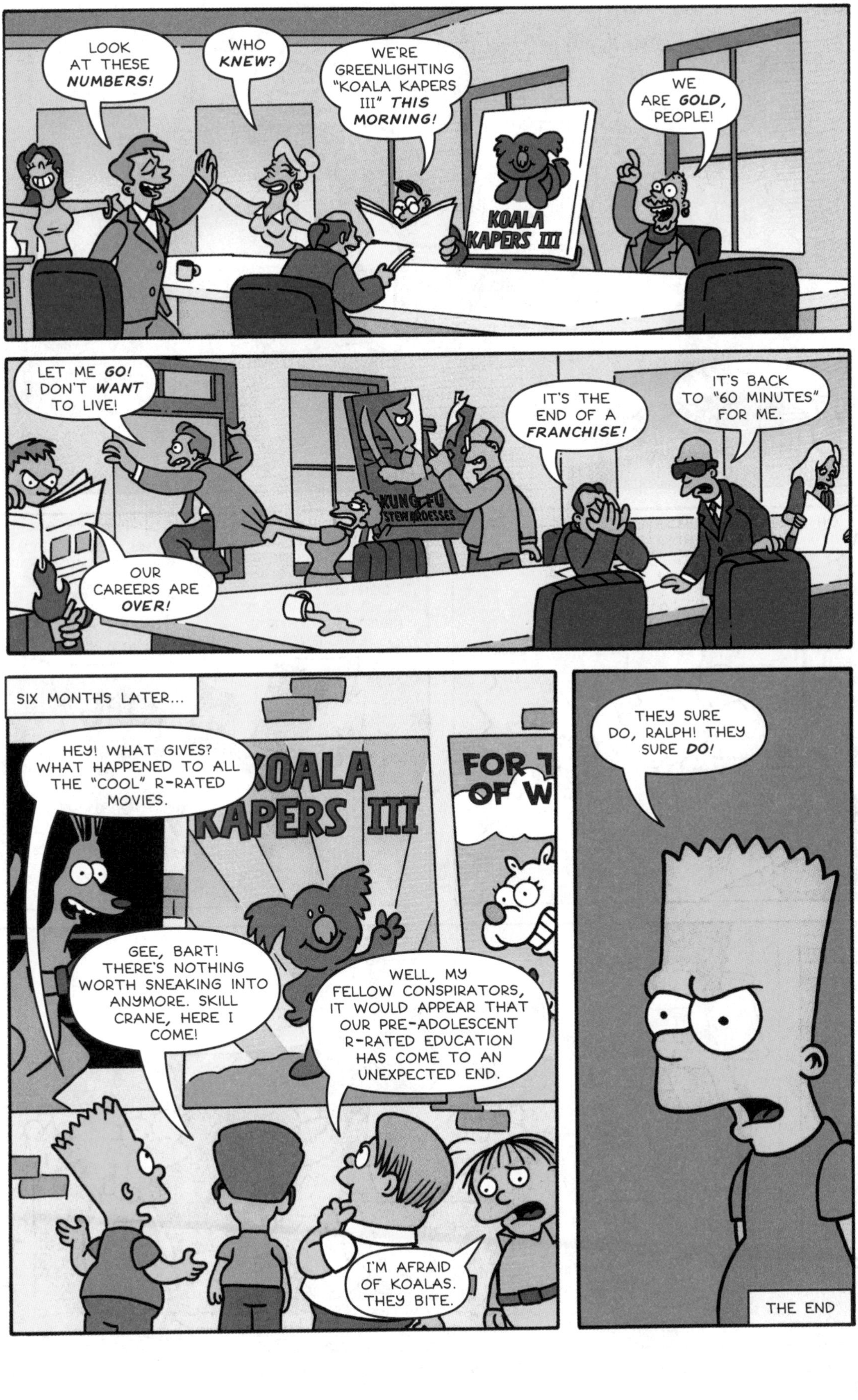
LOOK AT THESE NUMBERS!
WHO KNEW?
WE'RE GREENLIGHTING "KOALA KAPERS III" THIS MORNING!
KOALA KAPERS III
WE ARE GOLD, PEOPLE!
LET ME GO! I DON'T WANT TO LIVE!
KUNG FU STEWARDESSES
IT'S THE END OF A FRANCHISE!
IT'S BACK TO "60 MINUTES" FOR ME.
OUR CAREERS ARE OVER!
SIX MONTHS LATER...
HEY! WHAT GIVES? WHAT HAPPENED TO ALL THE "COOL" R-RATED MOVIES.
KOALA KAPERS III
GEE, BART! THERE'S NOTHING WORTH SNEAKING INTO ANYMORE. SKILL CRANE, HERE I COME!
WELL, MY FELLOW CONSPIRATORS, IT WOULD APPEAR THAT OUR PRE-ADOLESCENT R-RATED EDUCATION HAS COME TO AN UNEXPECTED END.
I'M AFRAID OF KOALAS. THEY BITE.
THEY SURE DO, RALPH! THEY SURE DO!
THE END

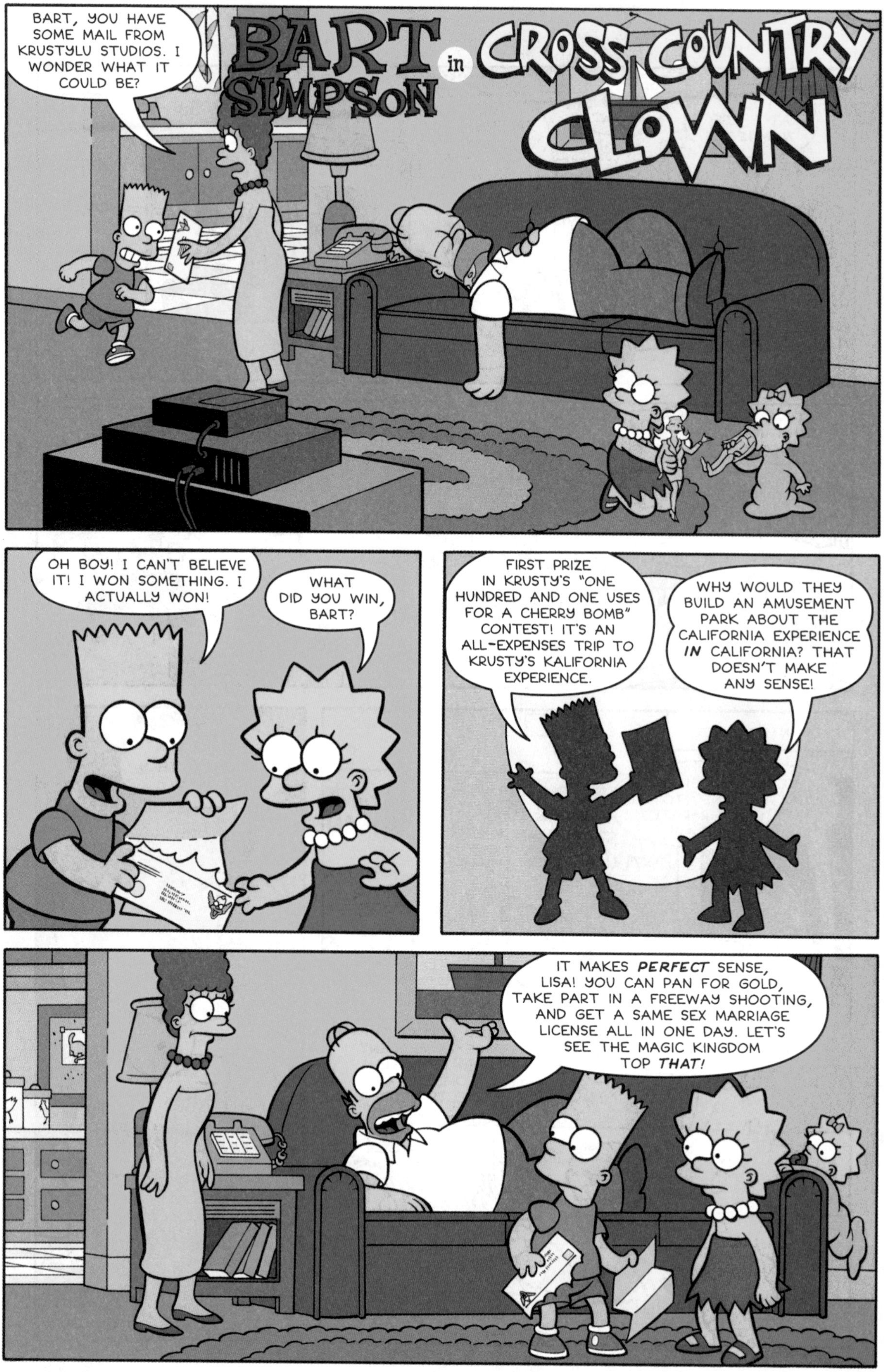
BART, YOU HAVE SOME MAIL FROM KRUSTYLU STUDIOS. I WONDER WHAT IT COULD BE?
BART SIMPSON in CROSS COUNTRY CLOWN
OH BOY! I CAN'T BELIEVE IT! I WON SOMETHING. I ACTUALLY WON!
WHAT DID YOU WIN, BART?
FIRST PRIZE IN KRUSTY'S "ONE HUNDRED AND ONE USES FOR A CHERRY BOMB" CONTEST! IT'S AN ALL-EXPENSES TRIP TO KRUSTY'S KALIFORNIA EXPERIENCE.
WHY WOULD THEY BUILD AN AMUSEMENT PARK ABOUT THE CALIFORNIA EXPERIENCE *IN* CALIFORNIA? THAT DOESN'T MAKE ANY SENSE!
IT MAKES *PERFECT* SENSE, LISA! YOU CAN PAN FOR GOLD, TAKE PART IN A FREEWAY SHOOTING, AND GET A SAME SEX MARRIAGE LICENSE ALL IN ONE DAY. LET'S SEE THE MAGIC KINGDOM TOP *THAT*!

EARL KRESS SCRIPT
JAMES LLOYD PENCILS
ANDREW PEPOY INKS
ART VILLANUEVA COLORS
KAREN BATES LETTERS
BILL MORRISON EDITOR

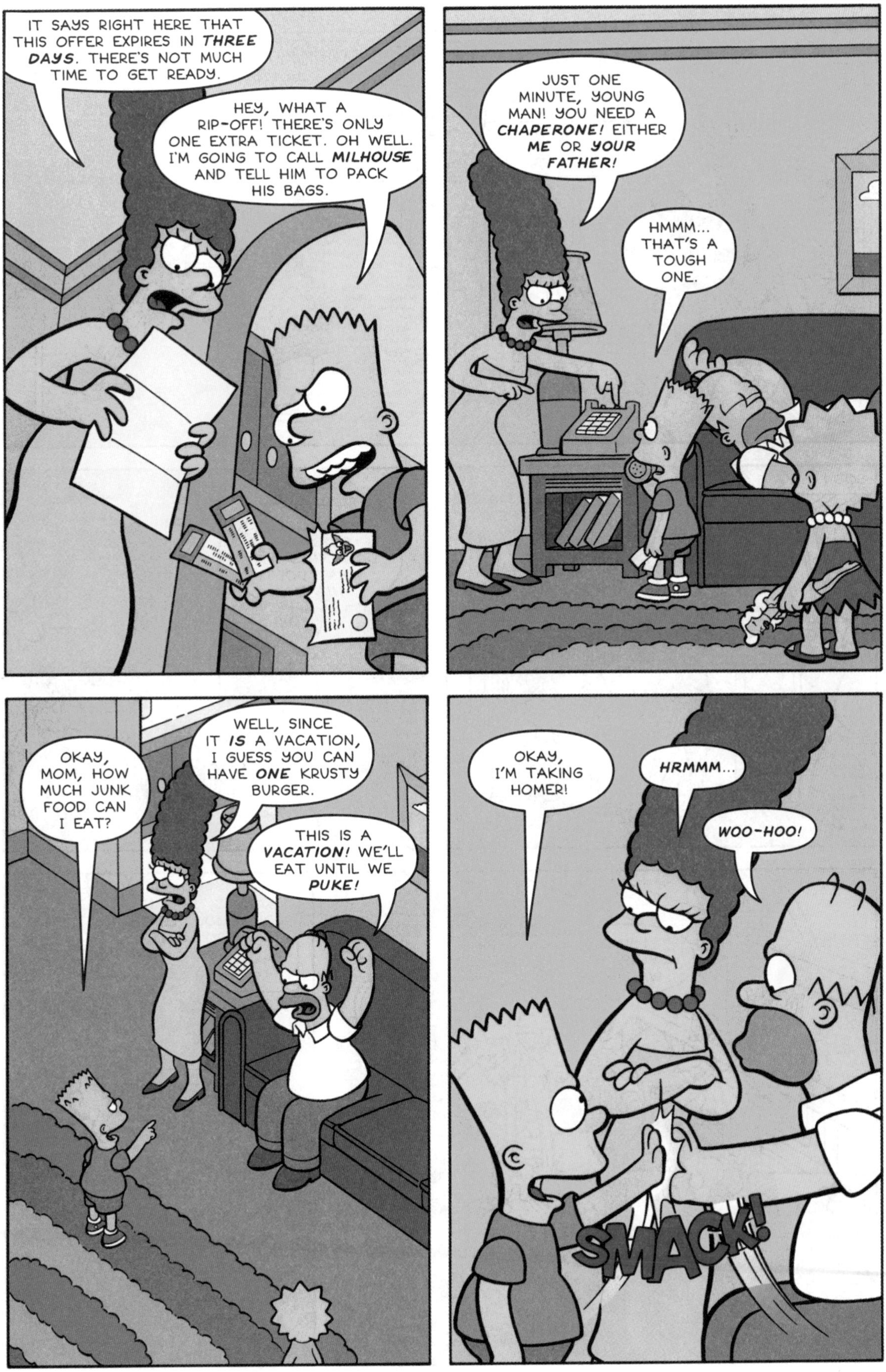
IT SAYS RIGHT HERE THAT THIS OFFER EXPIRES IN **THREE DAYS**. THERE'S NOT MUCH TIME TO GET READY.
HEY, WHAT A RIP-OFF! THERE'S ONLY ONE EXTRA TICKET. OH WELL. I'M GOING TO CALL **MILHOUSE** AND TELL HIM TO PACK HIS BAGS.
JUST ONE MINUTE, YOUNG MAN! YOU NEED A **CHAPERONE!** EITHER **ME** OR **YOUR FATHER!**
HMMM... THAT'S A TOUGH ONE.
OKAY, MOM, HOW MUCH JUNK FOOD CAN I EAT?
WELL, SINCE IT **IS** A VACATION, I GUESS YOU CAN HAVE **ONE** KRUSTY BURGER.
THIS IS A **VACATION!** WE'LL EAT UNTIL WE **PUKE!**
OKAY, I'M TAKING HOMER!
HRMMM...
WOO-HOO!
SMACK!

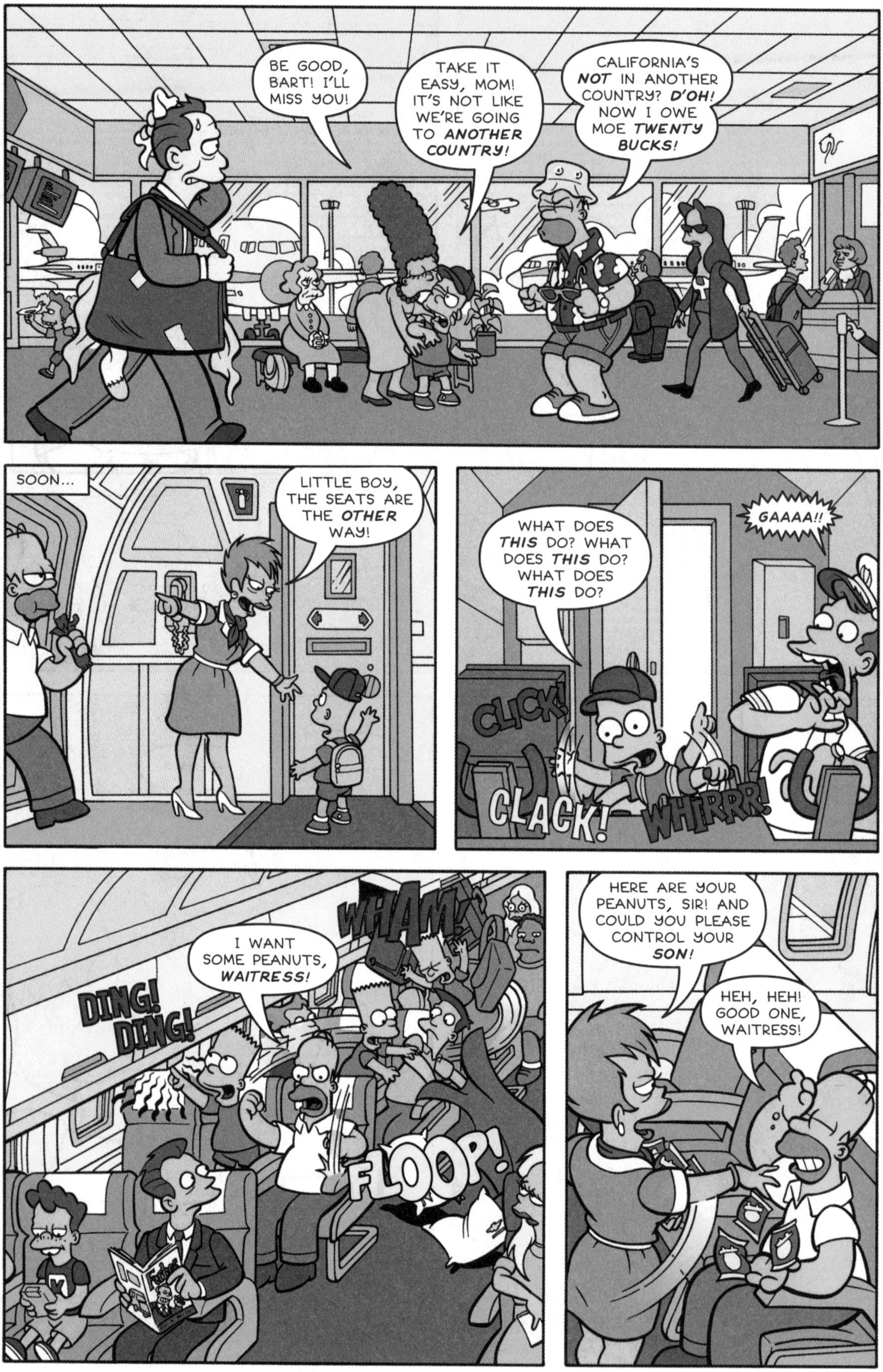
BE GOOD, BART! I'LL MISS YOU!
TAKE IT EASY, MOM! IT'S NOT LIKE WE'RE GOING TO ANOTHER COUNTRY!
CALIFORNIA'S NOT IN ANOTHER COUNTRY? D'OH! NOW I OWE MOE TWENTY BUCKS!
SOON...
LITTLE BOY, THE SEATS ARE THE OTHER WAY!
WHAT DOES THIS DO? WHAT DOES THIS DO? WHAT DOES THIS DO?
GAAAA!!
CLICK!
CLACK!
WHIRRR!
I WANT SOME PEANUTS, WAITRESS!
WHAM!
DING! DING!
FLOOP!
HERE ARE YOUR PEANUTS, SIR! AND COULD YOU PLEASE CONTROL YOUR SON!
HEH, HEH! GOOD ONE, WAITRESS!

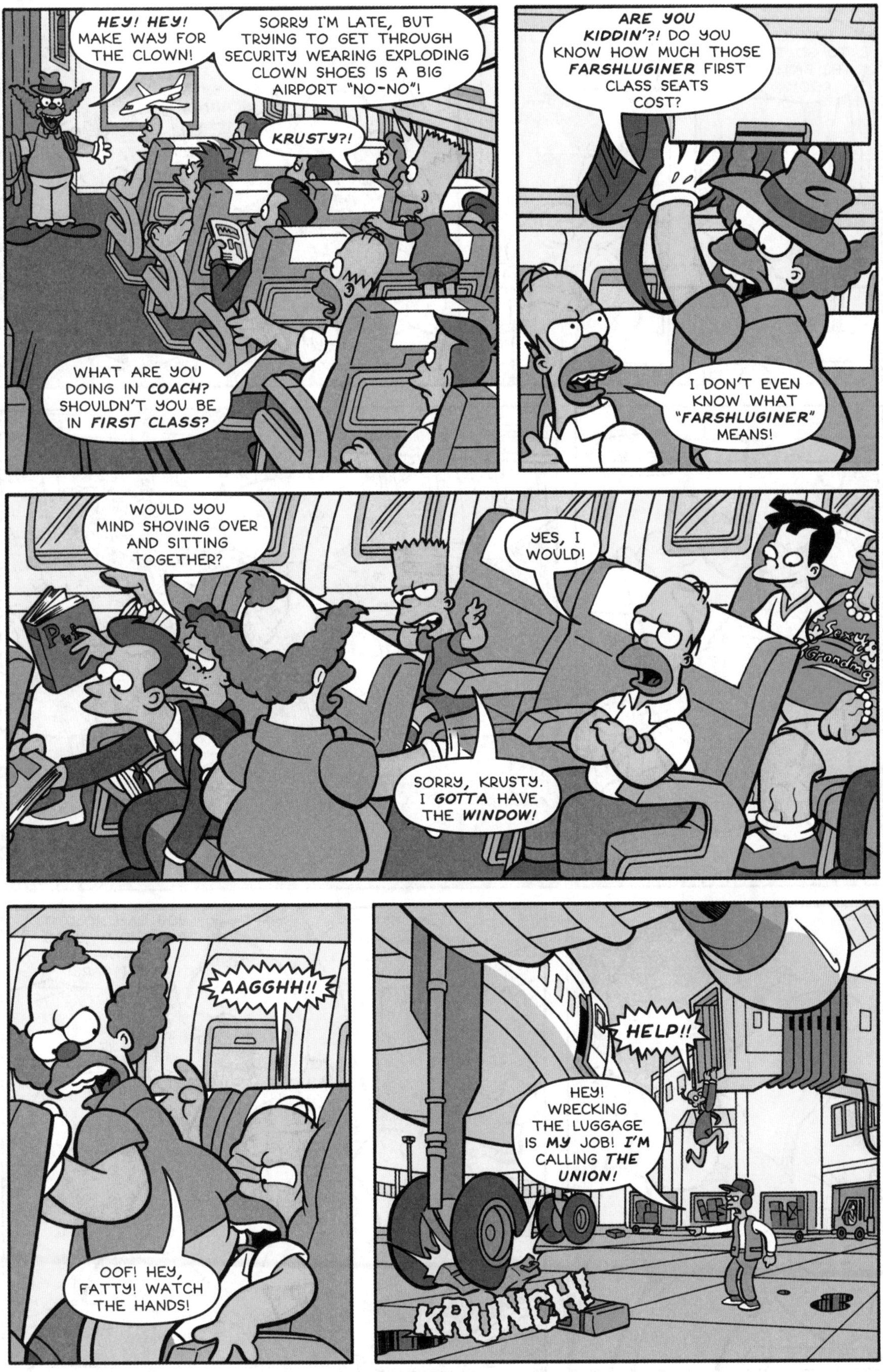
HEY! HEY! MAKE WAY FOR THE CLOWN!
SORRY I'M LATE, BUT TRYING TO GET THROUGH SECURITY WEARING EXPLODING CLOWN SHOES IS A BIG AIRPORT "NO-NO"!
KRUSTY?!
WHAT ARE YOU DOING IN COACH? SHOULDN'T YOU BE IN FIRST CLASS?
ARE YOU KIDDIN'?! DO YOU KNOW HOW MUCH THOSE FARSHLUGINER FIRST CLASS SEATS COST?
I DON'T EVEN KNOW WHAT "FARSHLUGINER" MEANS!
WOULD YOU MIND SHOVING OVER AND SITTING TOGETHER?
YES, I WOULD!
SORRY, KRUSTY. I GOTTA HAVE THE WINDOW!
AAGGHH!!
OOF! HEY, FATTY! WATCH THE HANDS!
HELP!!
HEY! WRECKING THE LUGGAGE IS MY JOB! I'M CALLING THE UNION!
KRUNCH!

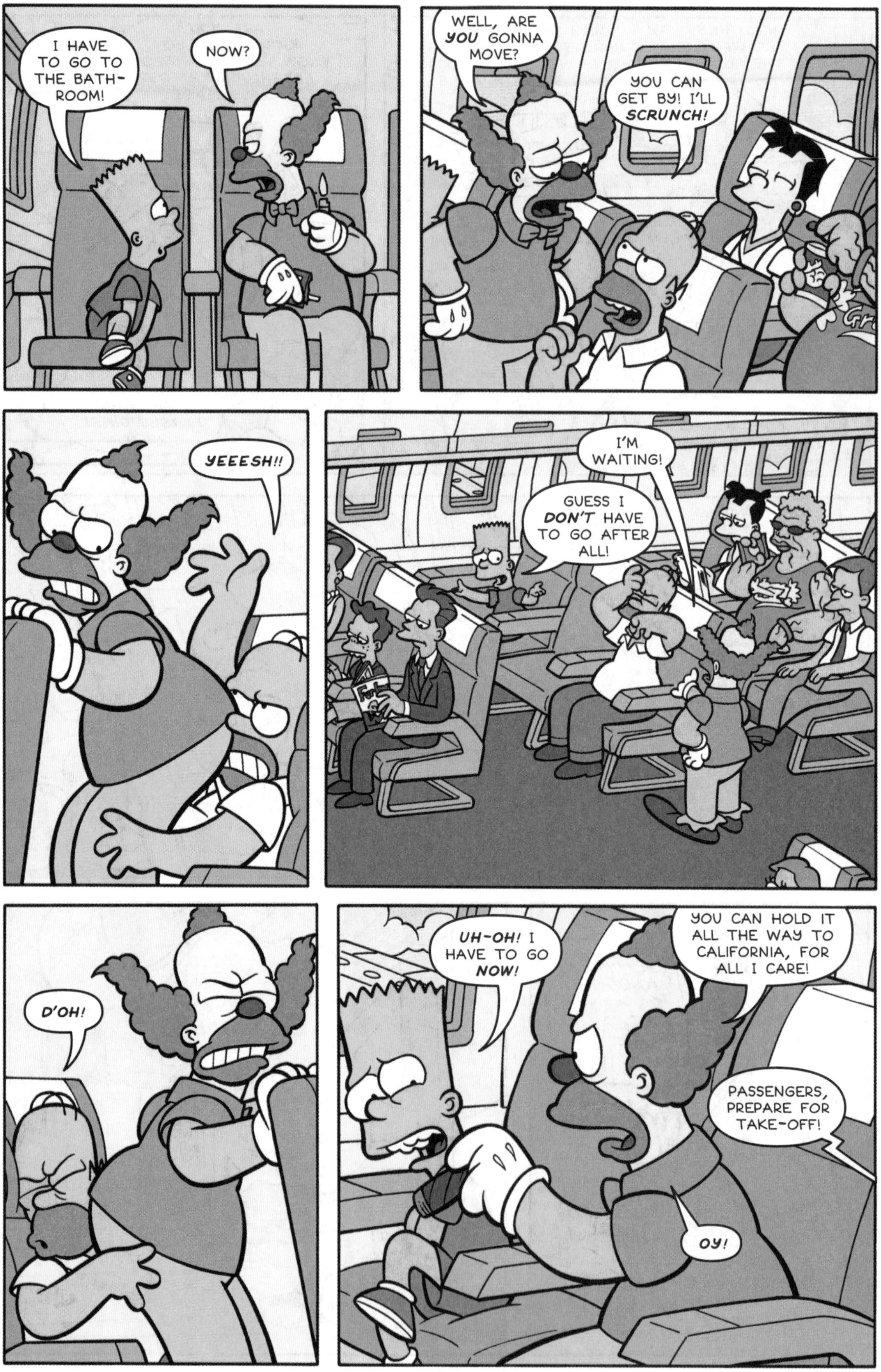
I HAVE TO GO TO THE BATH-ROOM!
NOW?
WELL, ARE *YOU* GONNA MOVE?
YOU CAN GET BY! I'LL *SCRUNCH!*
YEEESH!!
I'M WAITING!
GUESS I *DON'T* HAVE TO GO AFTER ALL!
D'OH!
UH-OH! I HAVE TO GO *NOW!*
YOU CAN HOLD IT ALL THE WAY TO CALIFORNIA, FOR ALL I CARE!
PASSENGERS, PREPARE FOR TAKE-OFF!
OY!

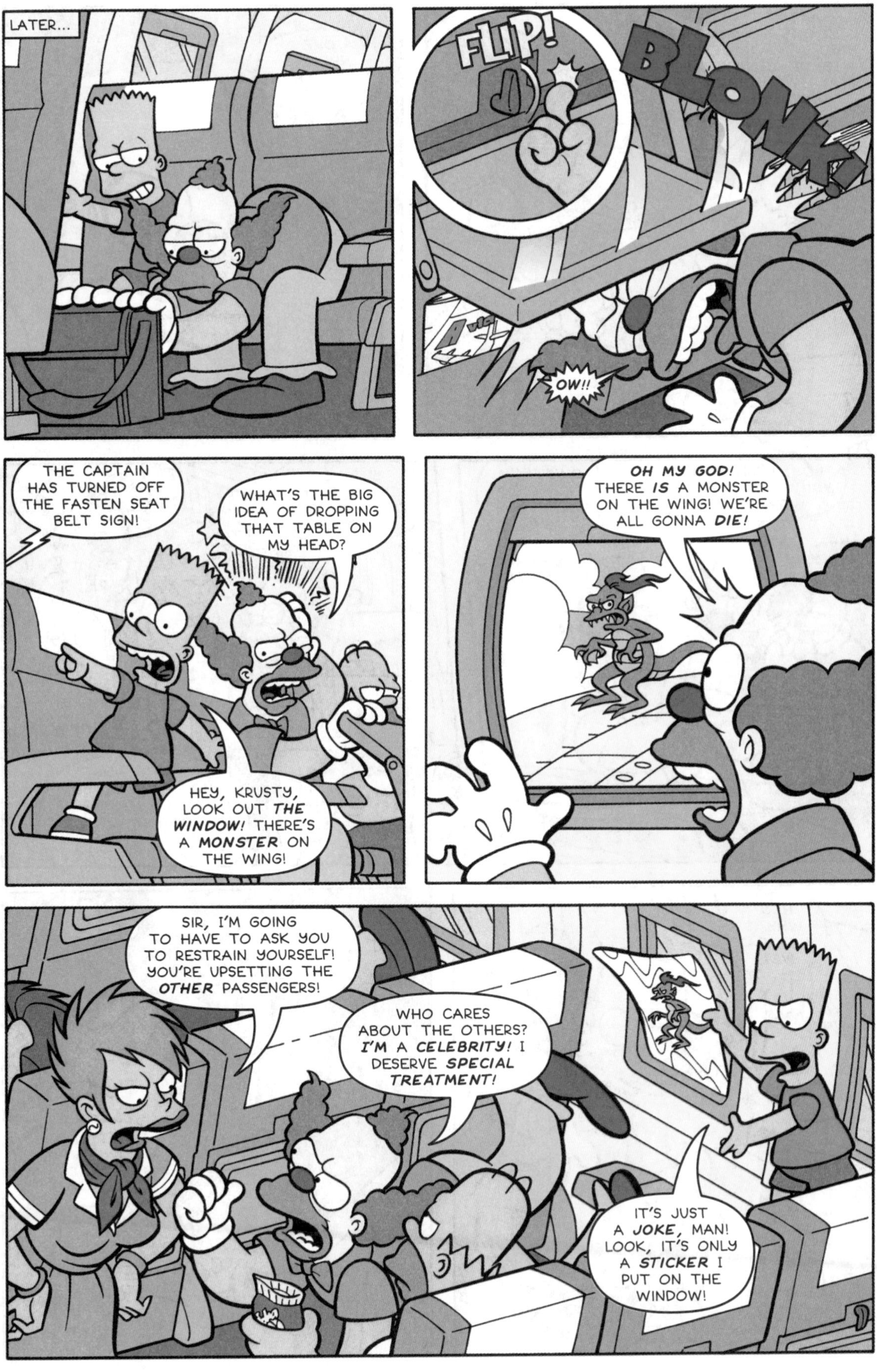
LATER...
FLIP!
BLONK!
OW!!
THE CAPTAIN HAS TURNED OFF THE FASTEN SEAT BELT SIGN!
WHAT'S THE BIG IDEA OF DROPPING THAT TABLE ON MY HEAD?
HEY, KRUSTY, LOOK OUT THE WINDOW! THERE'S A MONSTER ON THE WING!
OH MY GOD! THERE IS A MONSTER ON THE WING! WE'RE ALL GONNA DIE!
SIR, I'M GOING TO HAVE TO ASK YOU TO RESTRAIN YOURSELF! YOU'RE UPSETTING THE OTHER PASSENGERS!
WHO CARES ABOUT THE OTHERS? I'M A CELEBRITY! I DESERVE SPECIAL TREATMENT!
IT'S JUST A JOKE, MAN! LOOK, IT'S ONLY A STICKER I PUT ON THE WINDOW!

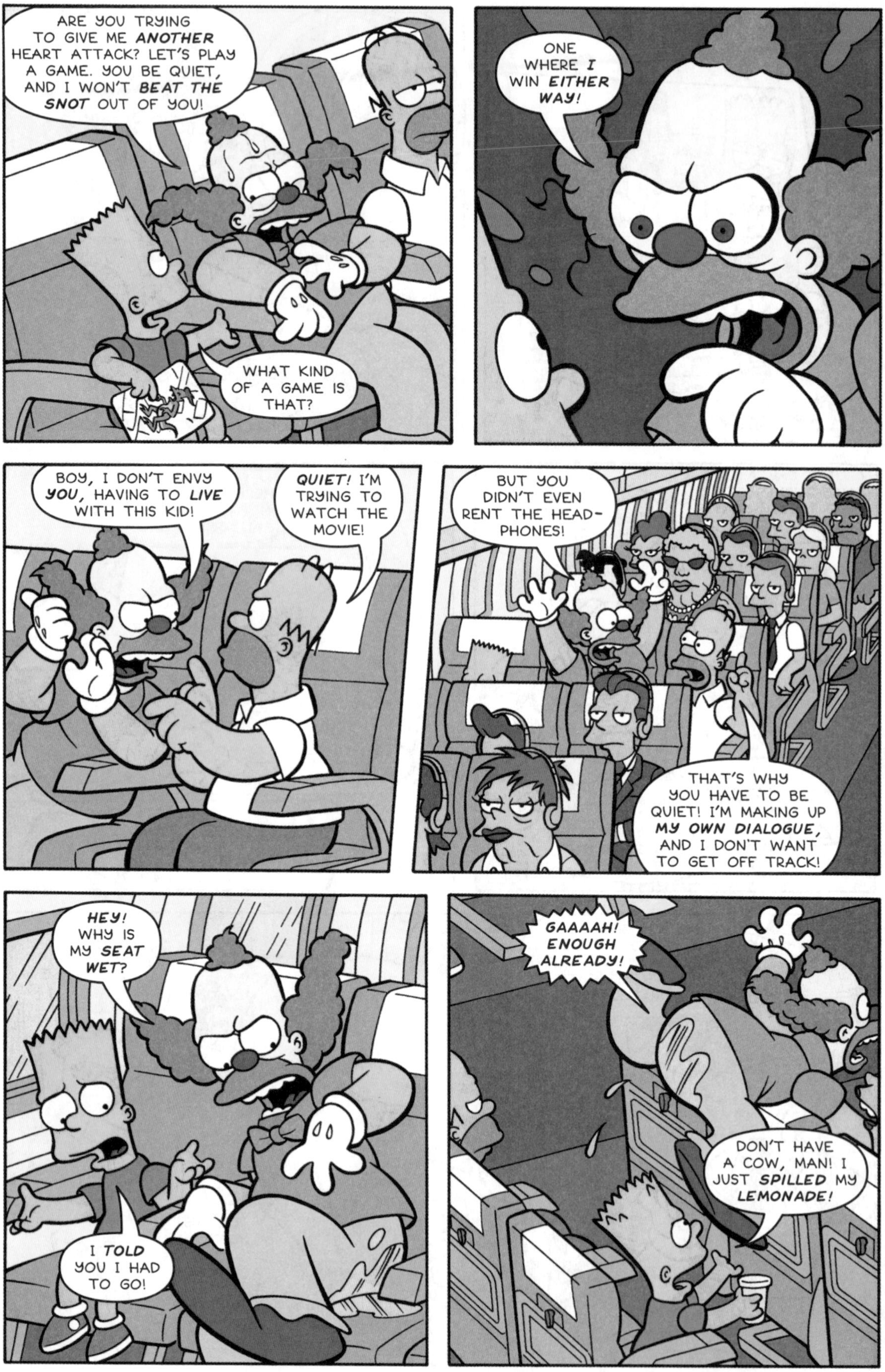
ARE YOU TRYING TO GIVE ME ANOTHER HEART ATTACK? LET'S PLAY A GAME. YOU BE QUIET, AND I WON'T BEAT THE SNOT OUT OF YOU!
WHAT KIND OF A GAME IS THAT?
ONE WHERE I WIN EITHER WAY!
BOY, I DON'T ENVY YOU, HAVING TO LIVE WITH THIS KID!
QUIET! I'M TRYING TO WATCH THE MOVIE!
BUT YOU DIDN'T EVEN RENT THE HEAD-PHONES!
THAT'S WHY YOU HAVE TO BE QUIET! I'M MAKING UP MY OWN DIALOGUE, AND I DON'T WANT TO GET OFF TRACK!
HEY! WHY IS MY SEAT WET?
I TOLD YOU I HAD TO GO!
GAAAAH! ENOUGH ALREADY!
DON'T HAVE A COW, MAN! I JUST SPILLED MY LEMONADE!

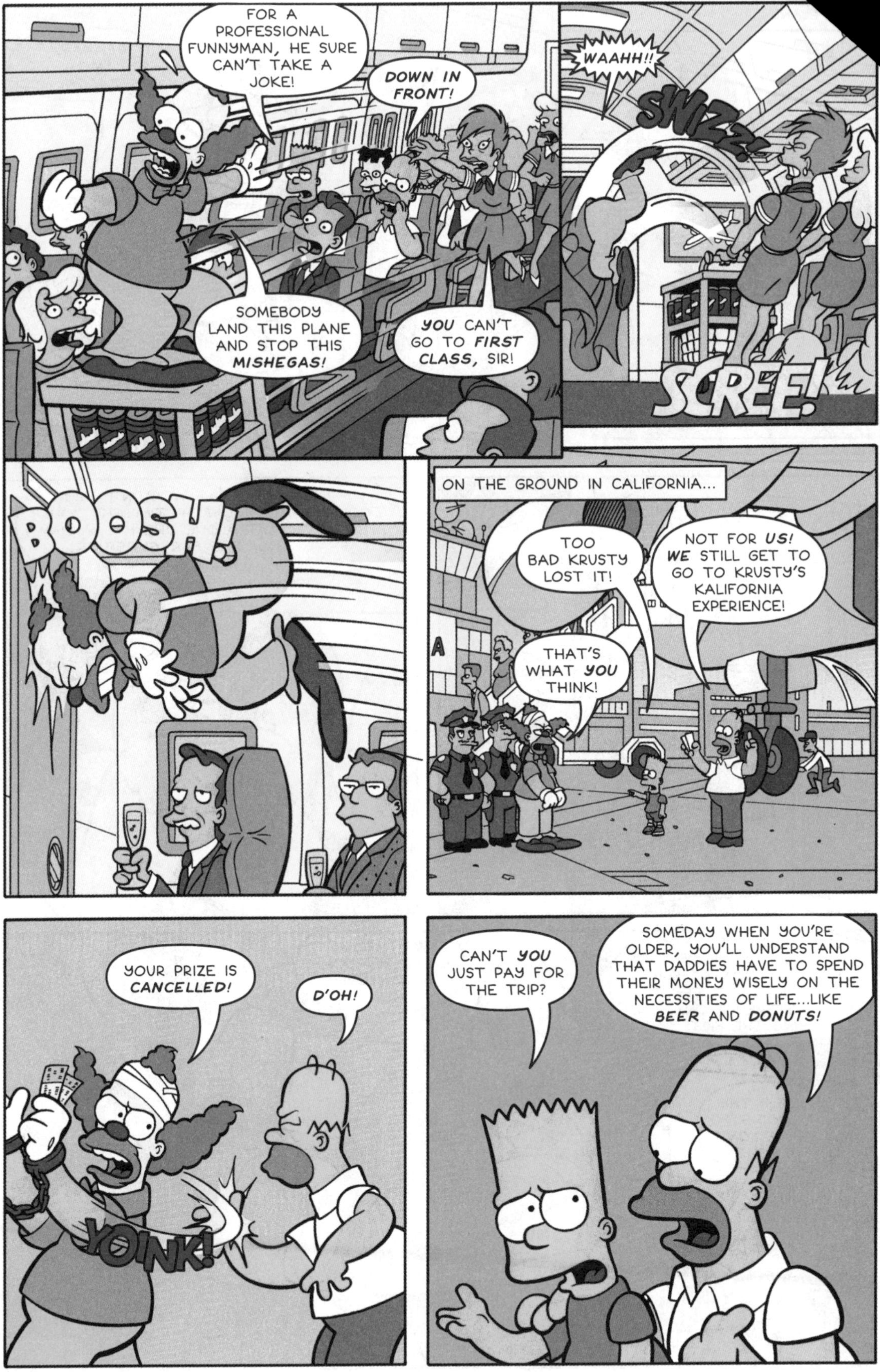

FOR A PROFESSIONAL FUNNYMAN, HE SURE CAN'T TAKE A JOKE!
DOWN IN FRONT!
SOMEBODY LAND THIS PLANE AND STOP THIS MISHEGAS!
YOU CAN'T GO TO FIRST CLASS, SIR!
WAAHH!!
SWIZZ!
SCREE!
BOOSH!
ON THE GROUND IN CALIFORNIA...
TOO BAD KRUSTY LOST IT!
NOT FOR US! WE STILL GET TO GO TO KRUSTY'S KALIFORNIA EXPERIENCE!
THAT'S WHAT YOU THINK!
YOUR PRIZE IS CANCELLED!
D'OH!
YOINK!
CAN'T YOU JUST PAY FOR THE TRIP?
SOMEDAY WHEN YOU'RE OLDER, YOU'LL UNDERSTAND THAT DADDIES HAVE TO SPEND THEIR MONEY WISELY ON THE NECESSITIES OF LIFE...LIKE BEER AND DONUTS!

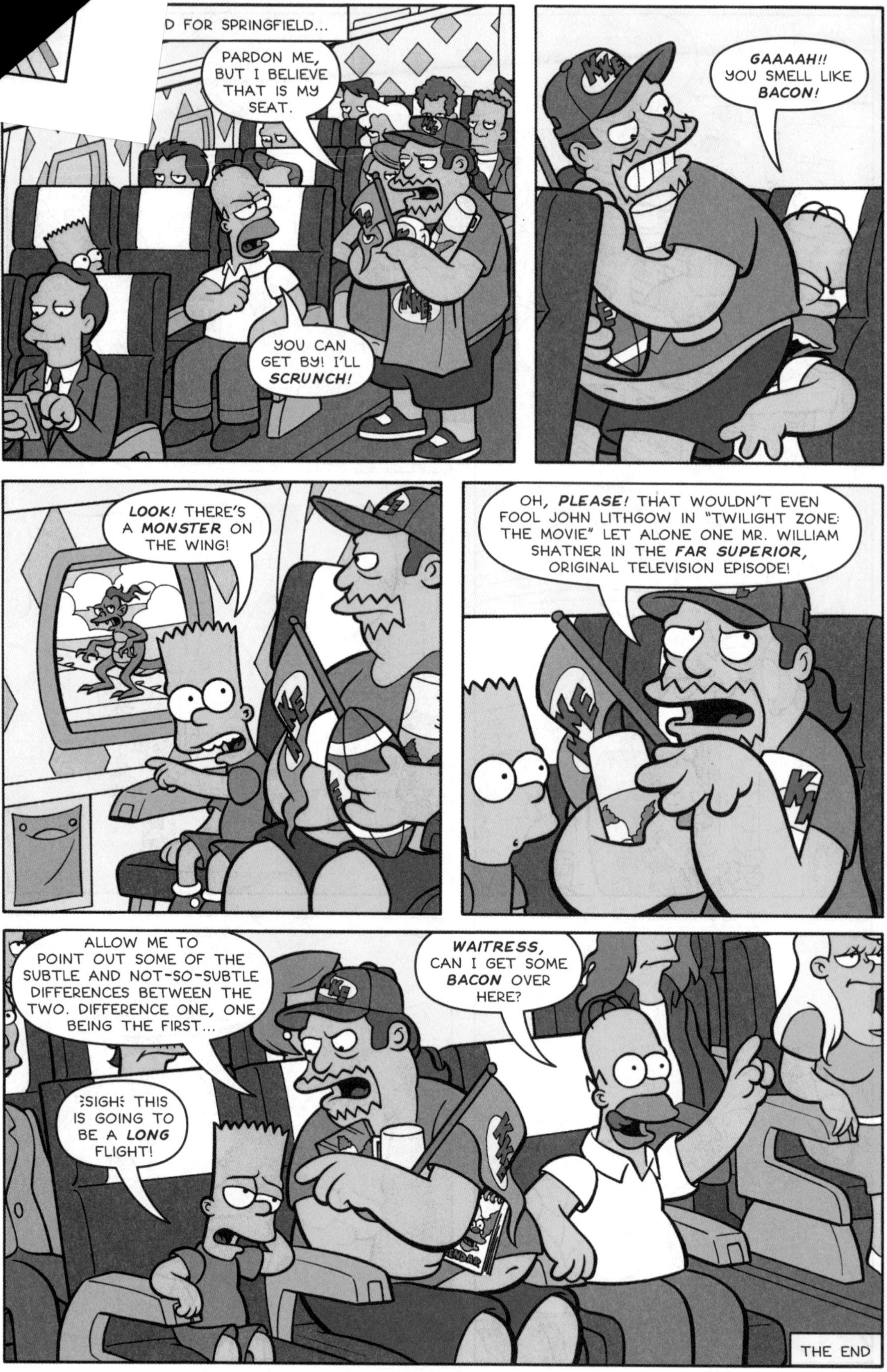

D FOR SPRINGFIELD...
PARDON ME, BUT I BELIEVE THAT IS MY SEAT.
YOU CAN GET BY! I'LL **SCRUNCH!**
GAAAAH!! YOU SMELL LIKE ***BACON!***
LOOK! THERE'S A ***MONSTER*** ON THE WING!
OH, ***PLEASE!*** THAT WOULDN'T EVEN FOOL JOHN LITHGOW IN "TWILIGHT ZONE: THE MOVIE" LET ALONE ONE MR. WILLIAM SHATNER IN THE ***FAR SUPERIOR,*** ORIGINAL TELEVISION EPISODE!
ALLOW ME TO POINT OUT SOME OF THE SUBTLE AND NOT-SO-SUBTLE DIFFERENCES BETWEEN THE TWO. DIFFERENCE ONE, ONE BEING THE FIRST...
WAITRESS, CAN I GET SOME ***BACON*** OVER HERE?
:SIGH: THIS IS GOING TO BE A ***LONG*** FLIGHT!
THE END

WHAT'S ON BART'S MIND?

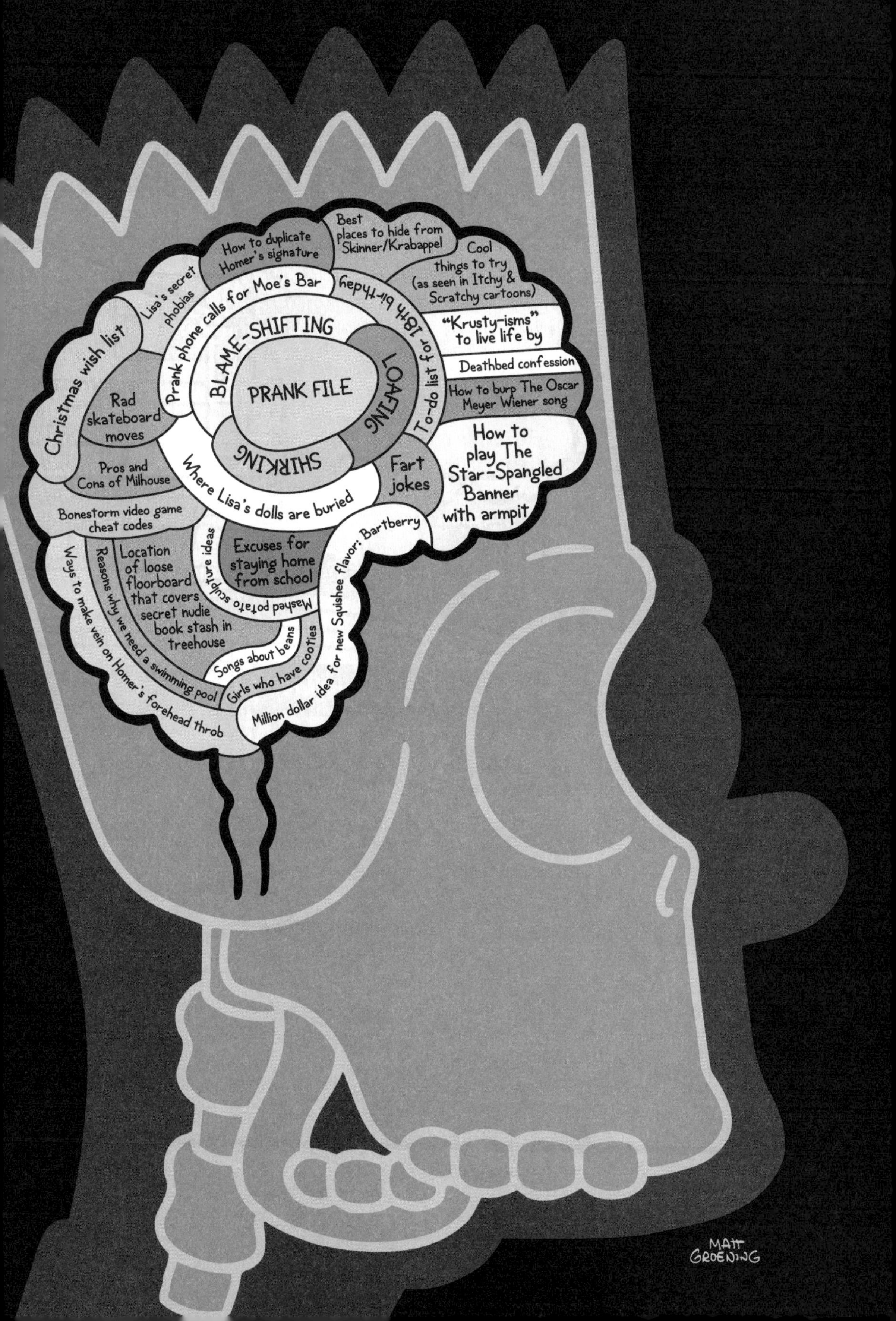
How to duplicate Homer's signature
Best places to hide from Skinner/Krabappel
Cool things to try (as seen in Itchy & Scratchy cartoons)
Lisa's secret phobias
Prank phone calls for Moe's Bar
To-do list for 18th birthday
"Krusty-isms" to live life by
Deathbed confession
How to burp The Oscar Meyer Wiener song
Christmas wish list
BLAME-SHIFTING
PRANK FILE
LOAFING
SHIRKING
Rad skateboard moves
How to play The Star-Spangled Banner with armpit
Fart jokes
Pros and Cons of Milhouse
Where Lisa's dolls are buried
Bonestorm video game cheat codes
Excuses for staying home from school
Idea for new Squishee flavor: Bartberry
Ways to make vein on Homer's forehead throb
Reasons why we need a swimming pool
Location of loose floorboard that covers secret nudie book stash in treehouse
Mashed potato sculpture ideas
Songs about beans
Girls who have cooties
Million dollar idea for new Squishee flavor: Bartberry
MATT GROENING

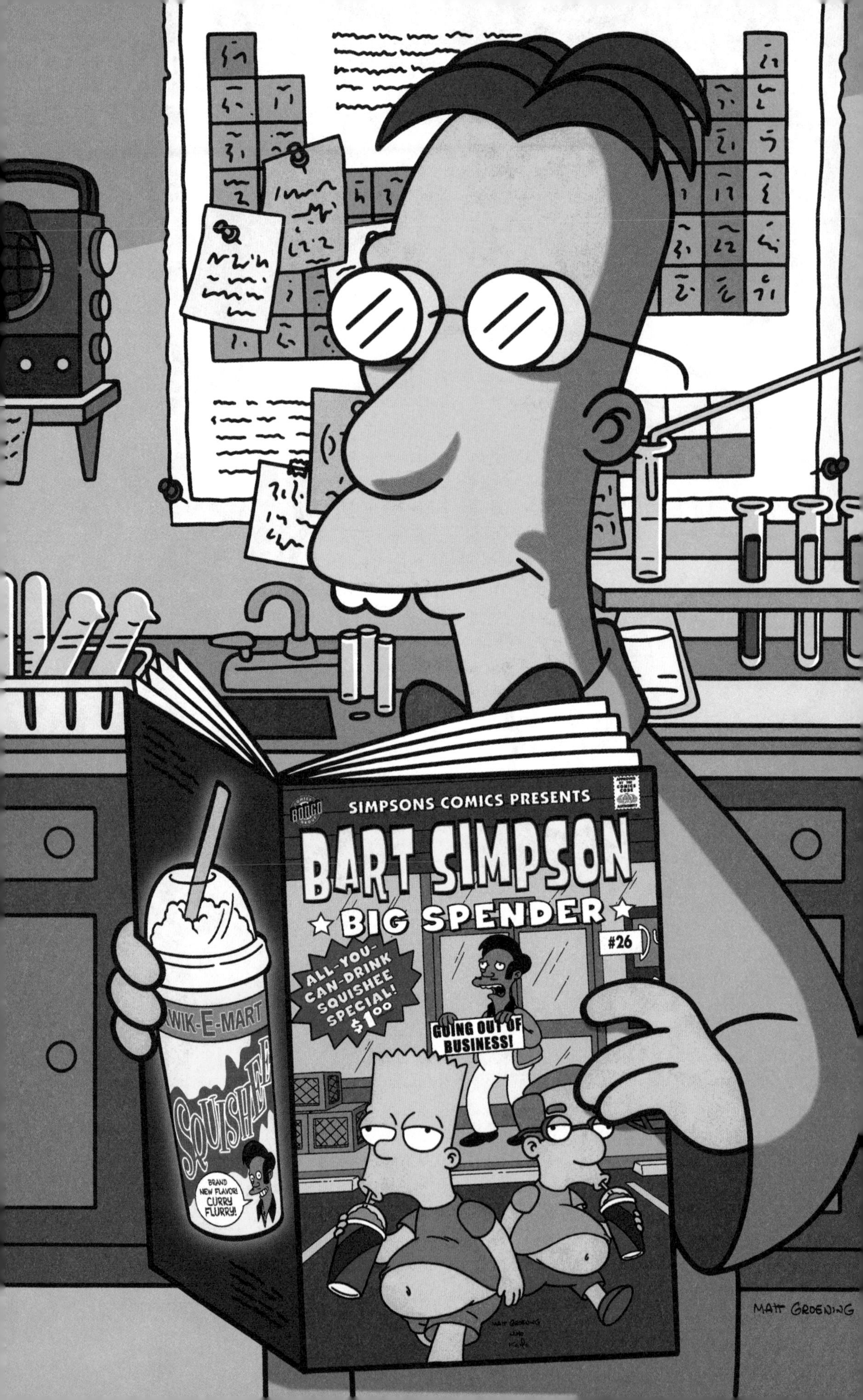
SIMPSONS COMICS PRESENTS
BART SIMPSON
BIG SPENDER
#26
ALL-YOU-CAN-DRINK SQUISHEE SPECIAL! $1.00
GOING OUT OF BUSINESS!
KWIK-E-MART
SQUISHEE
BRAND NEW FLAVOR! CURRY FLURRY!
MATT GROENING

MATT GROENING presents

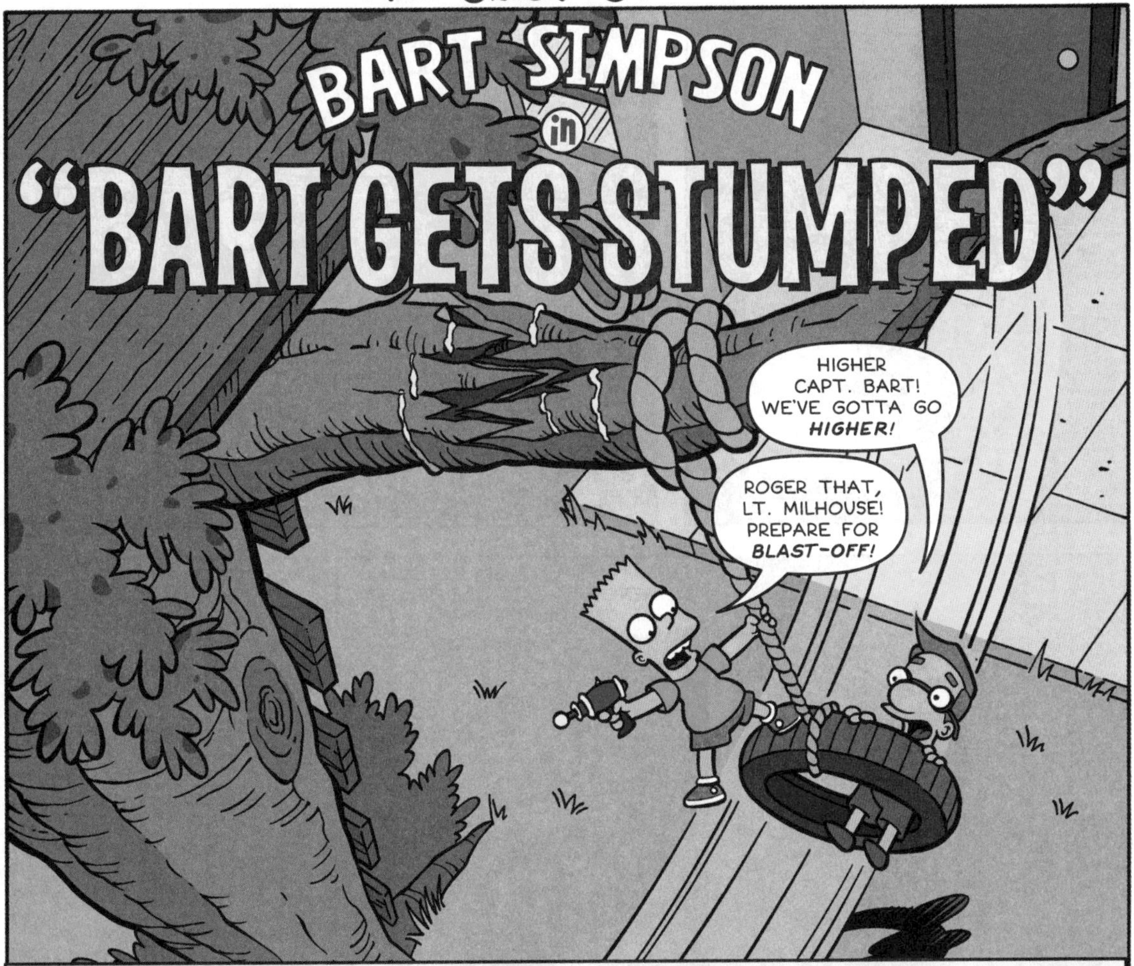
BART SIMPSON
in
"BART GETS STUMPED"
HIGHER CAPT. BART! WE'VE GOTTA GO *HIGHER!*
ROGER THAT, LT. MILHOUSE! PREPARE FOR *BLAST-OFF!*

CLAY & SUSAN GRIFFITH	JAMES LLOYD	ANDREW PEPOY	NATHAN HAMILL	KAREN BATES	BILL MORRISON
SCRIPT	PENCILS	INKS	COLORS	LETTERS	EDITOR

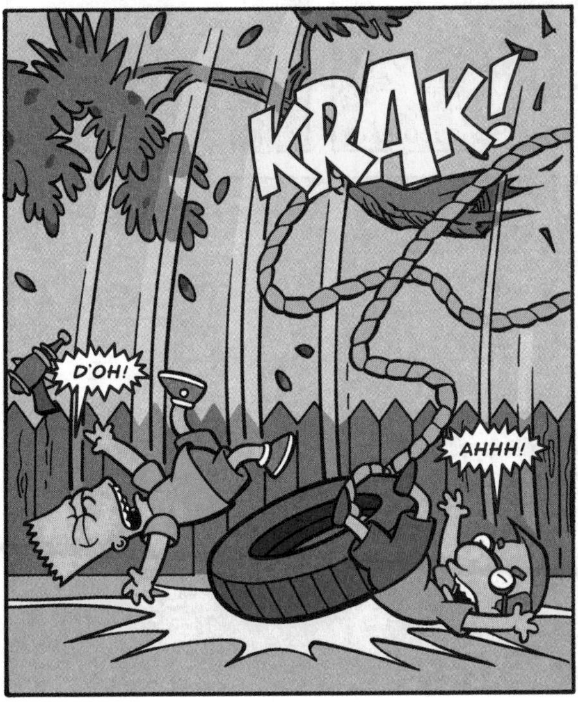
KRAK!
D'OH!
AHHH!

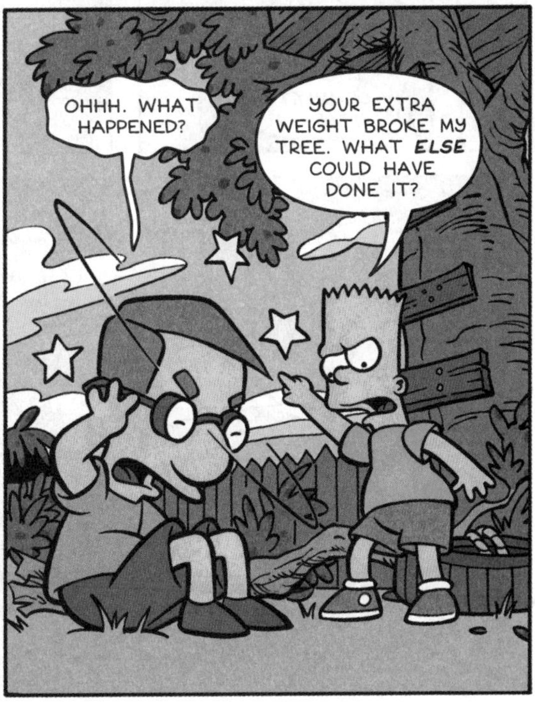
OHHH. WHAT HAPPENED?
YOUR EXTRA WEIGHT BROKE MY TREE. WHAT *ELSE* COULD HAVE DONE IT?

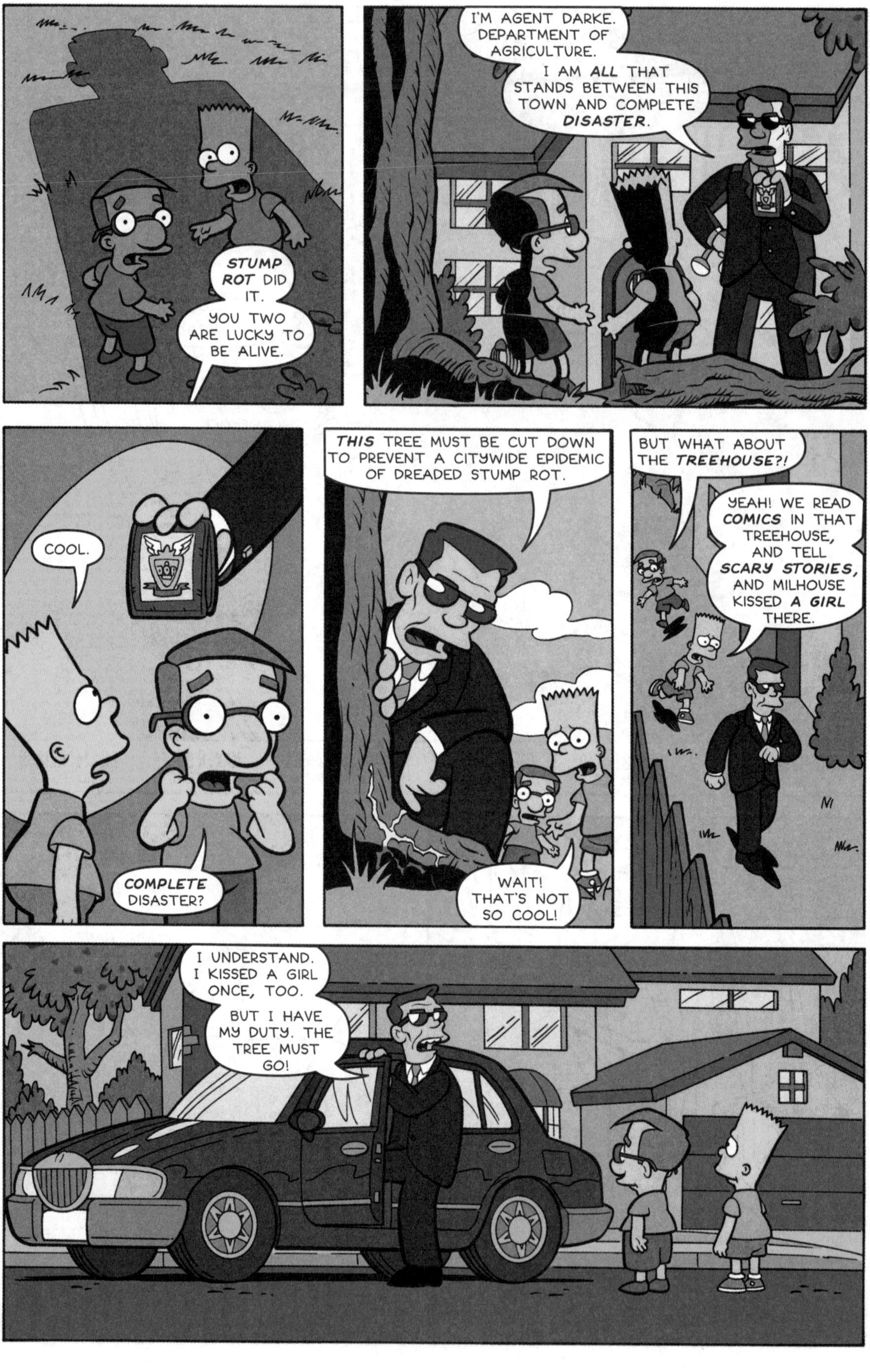
STUMP ROT DID IT.
YOU TWO ARE LUCKY TO BE ALIVE.
I'M AGENT DARKE. DEPARTMENT OF AGRICULTURE.
I AM ALL THAT STANDS BETWEEN THIS TOWN AND COMPLETE DISASTER.
COOL.
COMPLETE DISASTER?
THIS TREE MUST BE CUT DOWN TO PREVENT A CITYWIDE EPIDEMIC OF DREADED STUMP ROT.
WAIT! THAT'S NOT SO COOL!
BUT WHAT ABOUT THE TREEHOUSE?!
YEAH! WE READ COMICS IN THAT TREEHOUSE, AND TELL SCARY STORIES, AND MILHOUSE KISSED A GIRL THERE.
I UNDERSTAND. I KISSED A GIRL ONCE, TOO.
BUT I HAVE MY DUTY. THE TREE MUST GO!

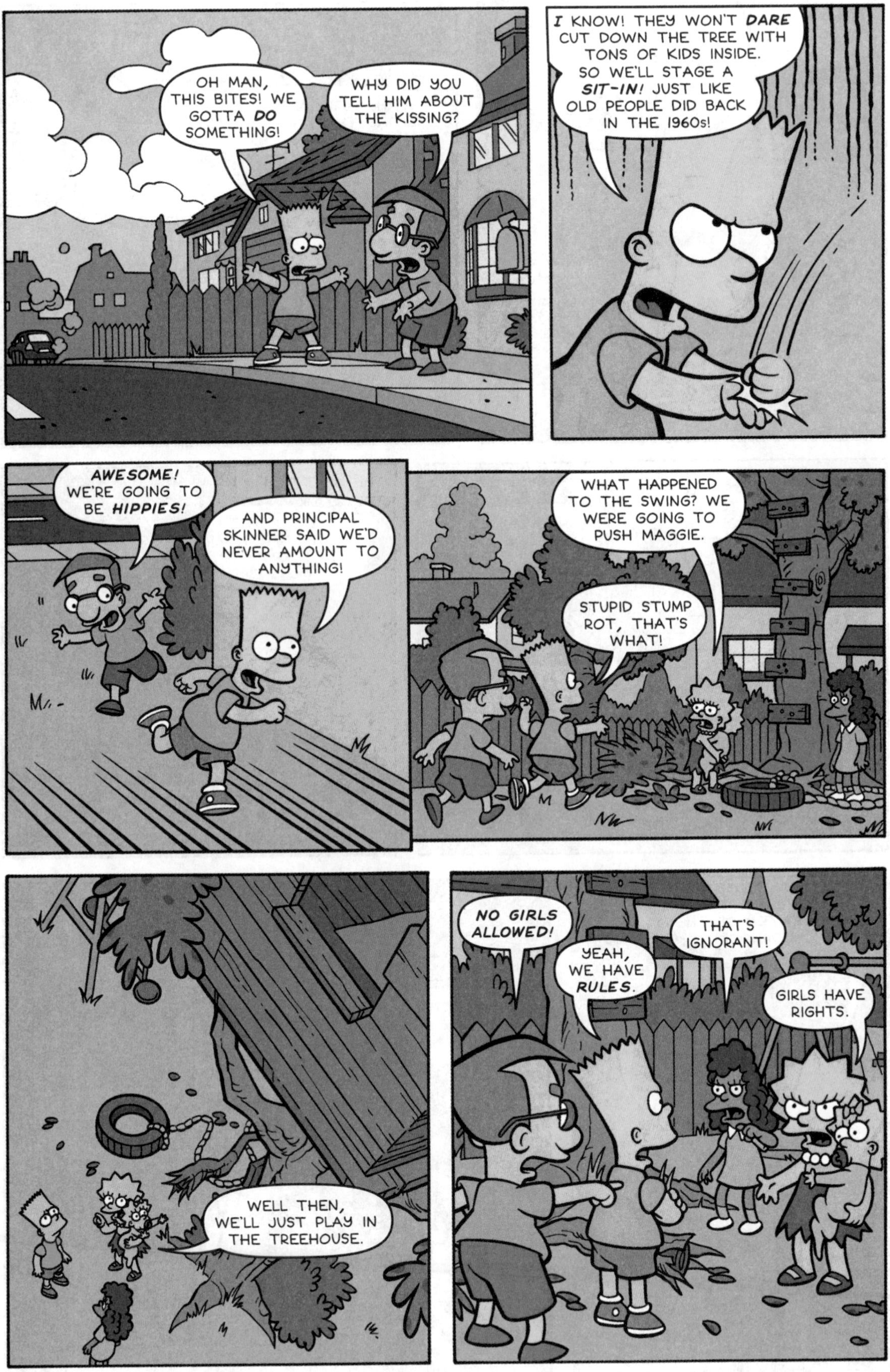
OH MAN, THIS BITES! WE GOTTA *DO* SOMETHING!
WHY DID YOU TELL HIM ABOUT THE KISSING?
I KNOW! THEY WON'T *DARE* CUT DOWN THE TREE WITH TONS OF KIDS INSIDE. SO WE'LL STAGE A *SIT-IN!* JUST LIKE OLD PEOPLE DID BACK IN THE 1960s!
AWESOME! WE'RE GOING TO BE *HIPPIES!*
AND PRINCIPAL SKINNER SAID WE'D NEVER AMOUNT TO ANYTHING!
WHAT HAPPENED TO THE SWING? WE WERE GOING TO PUSH MAGGIE.
STUPID STUMP ROT, THAT'S WHAT!
WELL THEN, WE'LL JUST PLAY IN THE TREEHOUSE.
NO GIRLS ALLOWED!
YEAH, WE HAVE *RULES*.
THAT'S IGNORANT!
GIRLS HAVE RIGHTS.

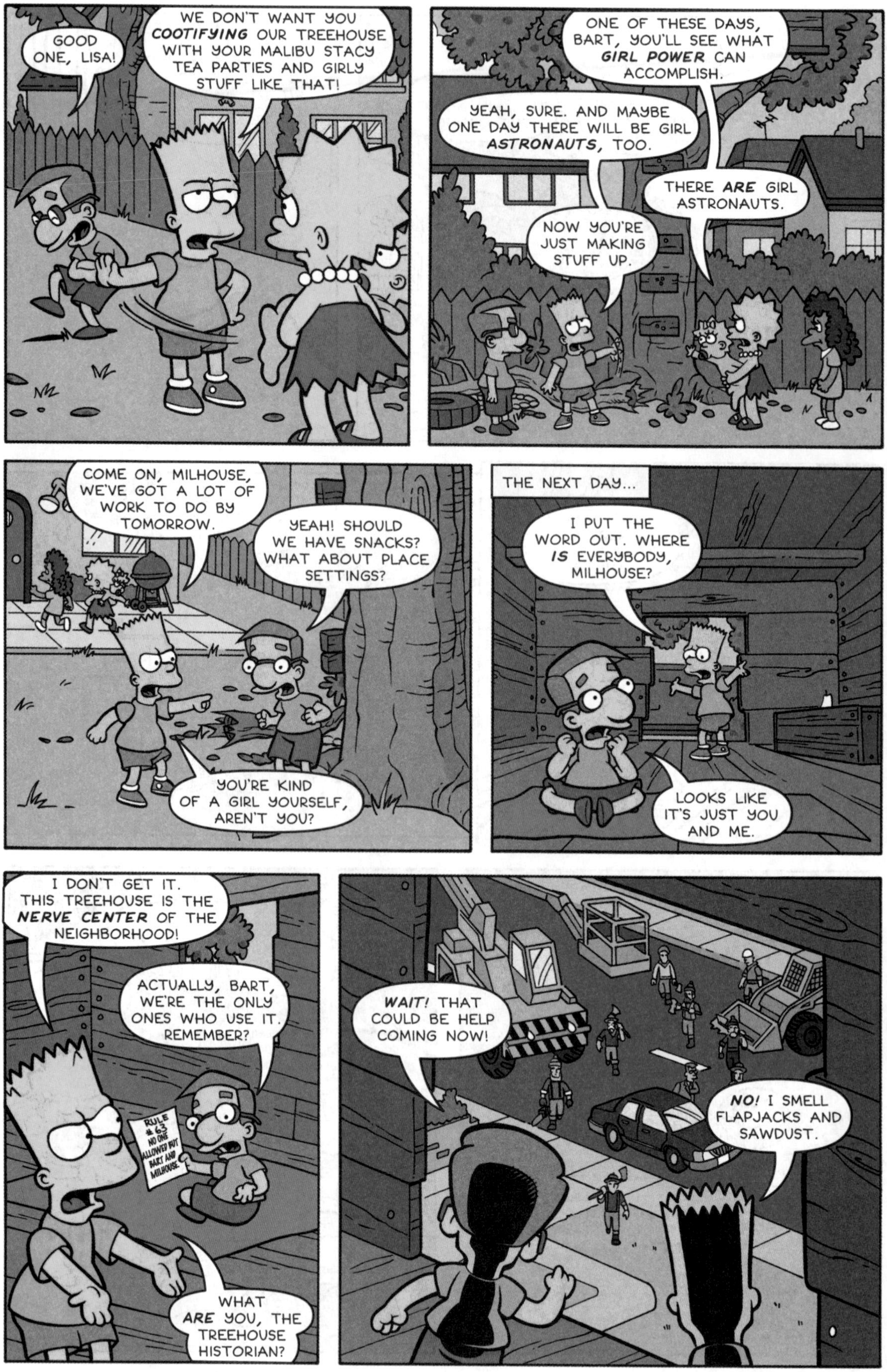
GOOD ONE, LISA!
WE DON'T WANT YOU COOTIFYING OUR TREEHOUSE WITH YOUR MALIBU STACY TEA PARTIES AND GIRLY STUFF LIKE THAT!
ONE OF THESE DAYS, BART, YOU'LL SEE WHAT GIRL POWER CAN ACCOMPLISH.
YEAH, SURE. AND MAYBE ONE DAY THERE WILL BE GIRL ASTRONAUTS, TOO.
THERE ARE GIRL ASTRONAUTS.
NOW YOU'RE JUST MAKING STUFF UP.
COME ON, MILHOUSE, WE'VE GOT A LOT OF WORK TO DO BY TOMORROW.
YEAH! SHOULD WE HAVE SNACKS? WHAT ABOUT PLACE SETTINGS?
YOU'RE KIND OF A GIRL YOURSELF, AREN'T YOU?
THE NEXT DAY...
I PUT THE WORD OUT. WHERE IS EVERYBODY, MILHOUSE?
LOOKS LIKE IT'S JUST YOU AND ME.
I DON'T GET IT. THIS TREEHOUSE IS THE NERVE CENTER OF THE NEIGHBORHOOD!
ACTUALLY, BART, WE'RE THE ONLY ONES WHO USE IT. REMEMBER?
RULE #63 NO ONE ALLOWED BUT BART AND MILHOUSE.
WHAT ARE YOU, THE TREEHOUSE HISTORIAN?
WAIT! THAT COULD BE HELP COMING NOW!
NO! I SMELL FLAPJACKS AND SAWDUST.

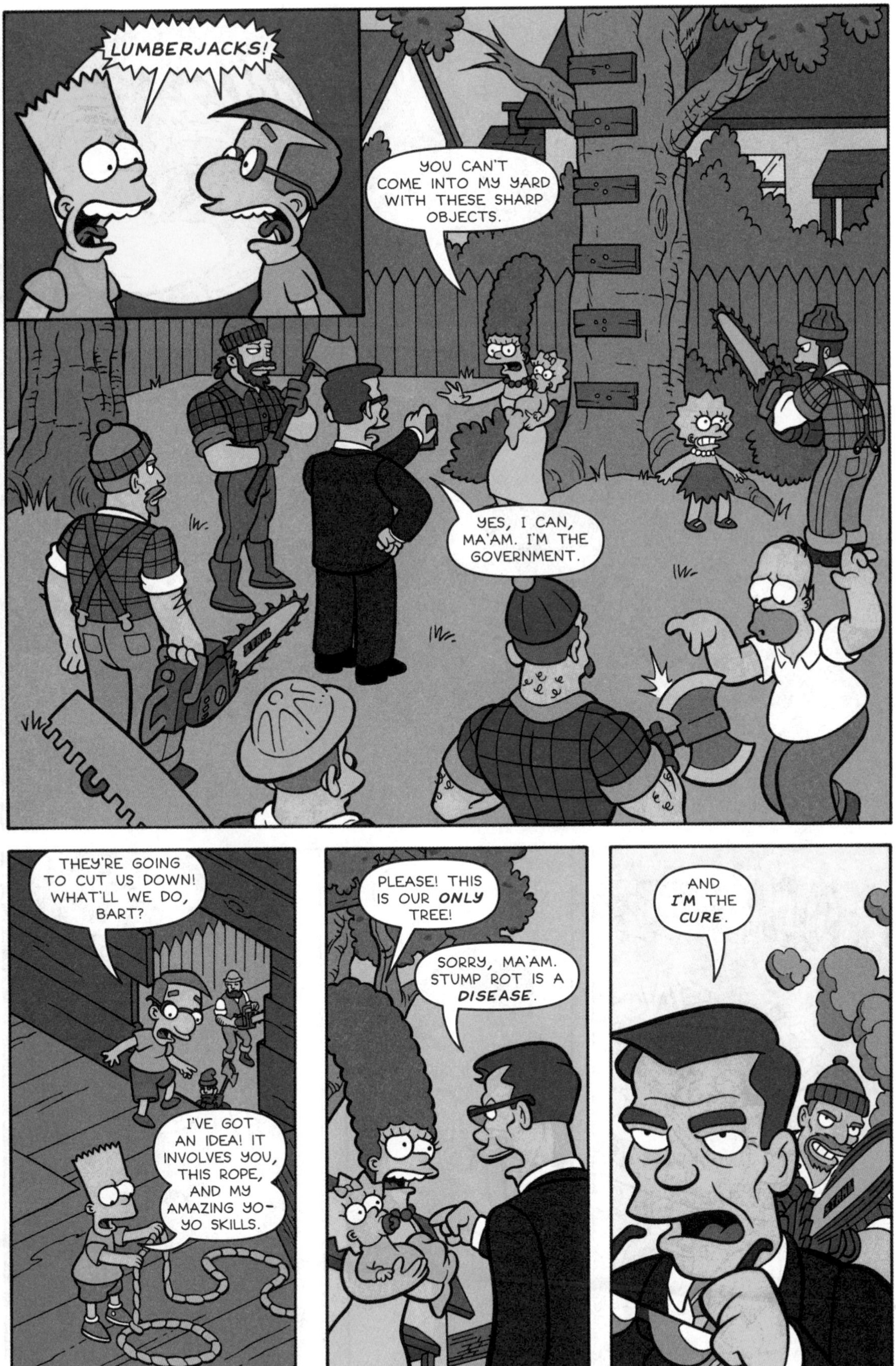
LUMBERJACKS!
YOU CAN'T COME INTO MY YARD WITH THESE SHARP OBJECTS.
YES, I CAN, MA'AM. I'M THE GOVERNMENT.
THEY'RE GOING TO CUT US DOWN! WHAT'LL WE DO, BART?
I'VE GOT AN IDEA! IT INVOLVES YOU, THIS ROPE, AND MY AMAZING YO-YO SKILLS.
PLEASE! THIS IS OUR *ONLY* TREE!
SORRY, MA'AM. STUMP ROT IS A *DISEASE*.
AND *I'M* THE *CURE*.

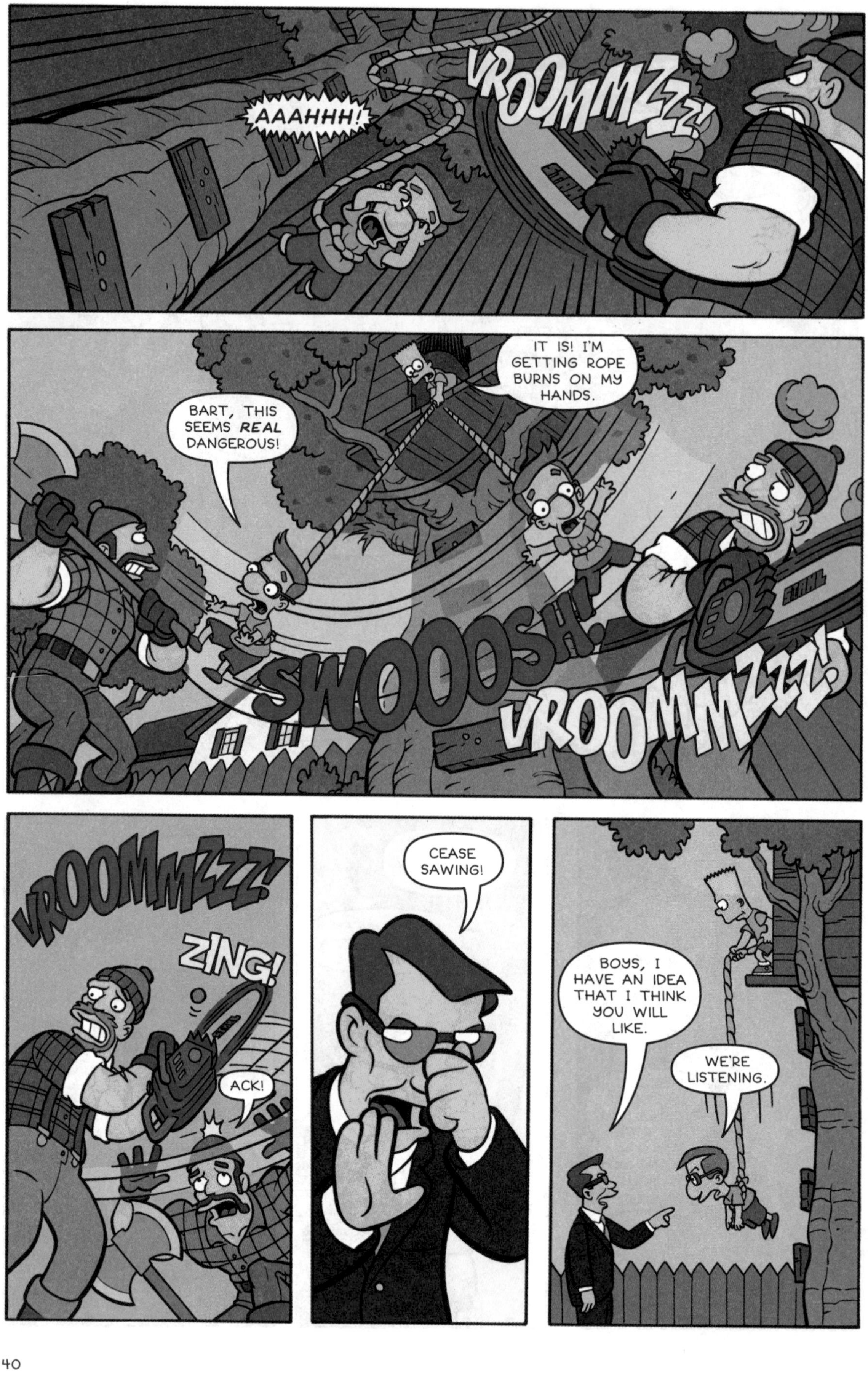
AAAHHH!
VROOMMZZZ!
BART, THIS SEEMS REAL DANGEROUS!
IT IS! I'M GETTING ROPE BURNS ON MY HANDS.
SWOOOSH!
VROOMMZZZ!
VROOMMZZZ!
ZING!
ACK!
CEASE SAWING!
BOYS, I HAVE AN IDEA THAT I THINK YOU WILL LIKE.
WE'RE LISTENING.

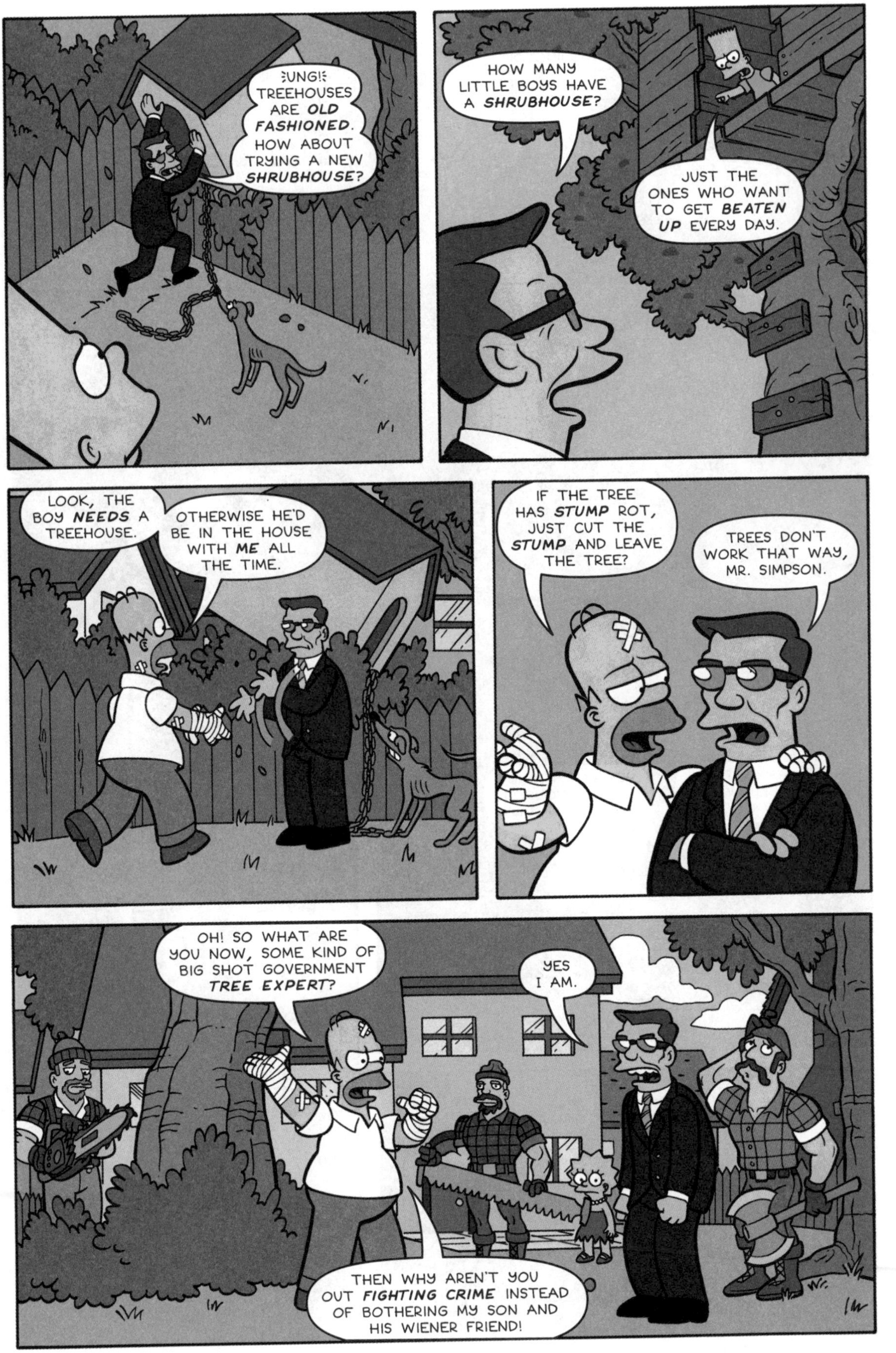
UNG!
TREEHOUSES ARE OLD FASHIONED. HOW ABOUT TRYING A NEW SHRUBHOUSE?
HOW MANY LITTLE BOYS HAVE A SHRUBHOUSE?
JUST THE ONES WHO WANT TO GET BEATEN UP EVERY DAY.
LOOK, THE BOY NEEDS A TREEHOUSE.
OTHERWISE HE'D BE IN THE HOUSE WITH ME ALL THE TIME.
IF THE TREE HAS STUMP ROT, JUST CUT THE STUMP AND LEAVE THE TREE?
TREES DON'T WORK THAT WAY, MR. SIMPSON.
OH! SO WHAT ARE YOU NOW, SOME KIND OF BIG SHOT GOVERNMENT TREE EXPERT?
YES I AM.
THEN WHY AREN'T YOU OUT FIGHTING CRIME INSTEAD OF BOTHERING MY SON AND HIS WIENER FRIEND!

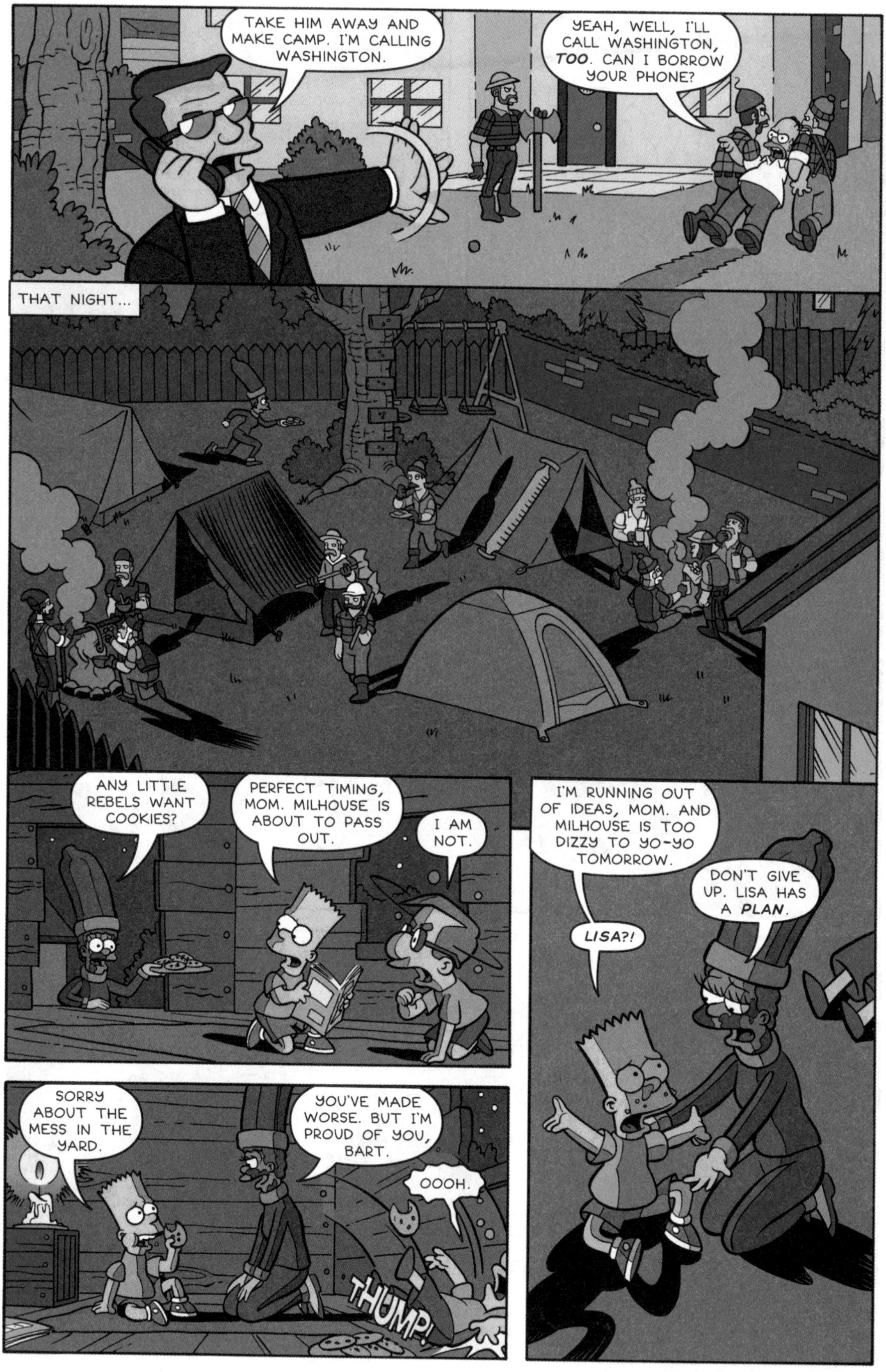
TAKE HIM AWAY AND MAKE CAMP. I'M CALLING WASHINGTON.
YEAH, WELL, I'LL CALL WASHINGTON, *TOO*. CAN I BORROW YOUR PHONE?
THAT NIGHT...
ANY LITTLE REBELS WANT COOKIES?
PERFECT TIMING, MOM. MILHOUSE IS ABOUT TO PASS OUT.
I AM NOT.
SORRY ABOUT THE MESS IN THE YARD.
YOU'VE MADE WORSE. BUT I'M PROUD OF YOU, BART.
OOOH.
THUMP!
I'M RUNNING OUT OF IDEAS, MOM. AND MILHOUSE IS TOO DIZZY TO YO-YO TOMORROW.
DON'T GIVE UP. LISA HAS A *PLAN*.
LISA?!

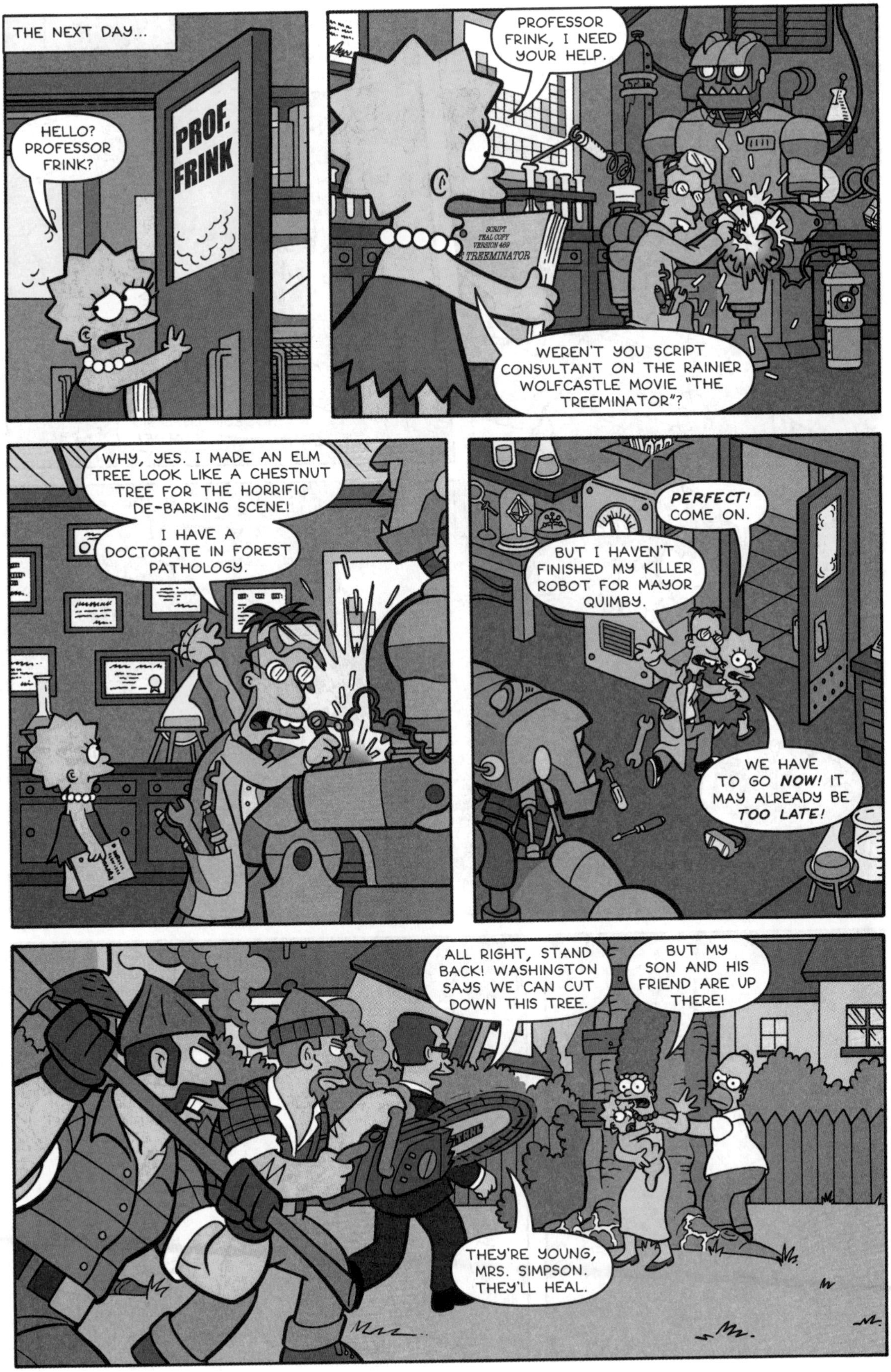
THE NEXT DAY...
HELLO? PROFESSOR FRINK?
PROF. FRINK
PROFESSOR FRINK, I NEED YOUR HELP.
SCRIPT TEAL COPY VERSION 469 TREEMINATOR
WEREN'T YOU SCRIPT CONSULTANT ON THE RAINIER WOLFCASTLE MOVIE "THE TREEMINATOR"?
WHY, YES. I MADE AN ELM TREE LOOK LIKE A CHESTNUT TREE FOR THE HORRIFIC DE-BARKING SCENE!
I HAVE A DOCTORATE IN FOREST PATHOLOGY.
PERFECT! COME ON.
BUT I HAVEN'T FINISHED MY KILLER ROBOT FOR MAYOR QUIMBY.
WE HAVE TO GO NOW! IT MAY ALREADY BE TOO LATE!
ALL RIGHT, STAND BACK! WASHINGTON SAYS WE CAN CUT DOWN THIS TREE.
BUT MY SON AND HIS FRIEND ARE UP THERE!
THEY'RE YOUNG, MRS. SIMPSON. THEY'LL HEAL.

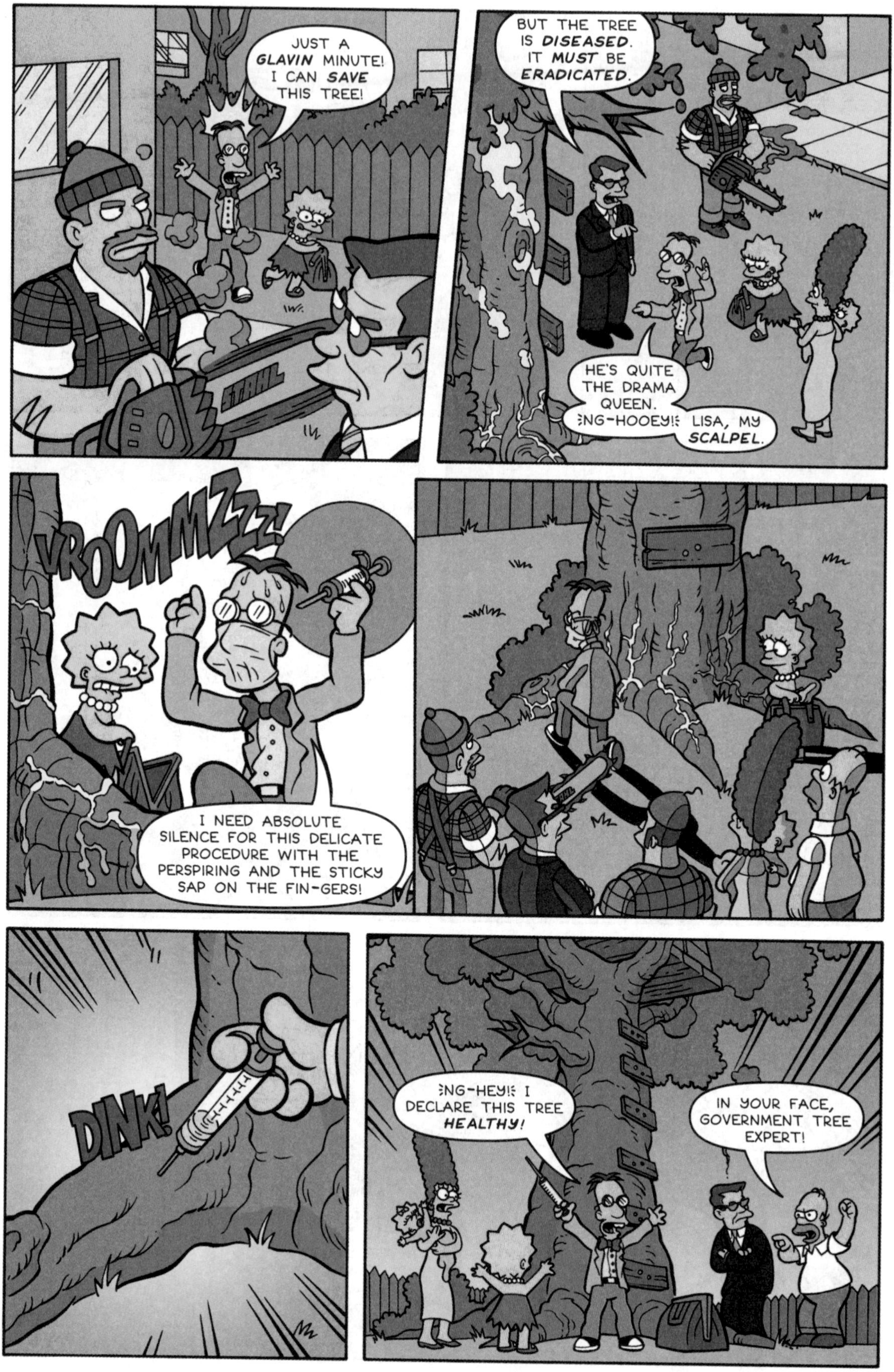
JUST A GLAVIN MINUTE! I CAN SAVE THIS TREE!
BUT THE TREE IS DISEASED. IT MUST BE ERADICATED.
HE'S QUITE THE DRAMA QUEEN.
NG-HOOEY! LISA, MY SCALPEL.
VROOMMZZZ!
I NEED ABSOLUTE SILENCE FOR THIS DELICATE PROCEDURE WITH THE PERSPIRING AND THE STICKY SAP ON THE FIN-GERS!
DINK!
NG-HEY! I DECLARE THIS TREE HEALTHY!
IN YOUR FACE, GOVERNMENT TREE EXPERT!

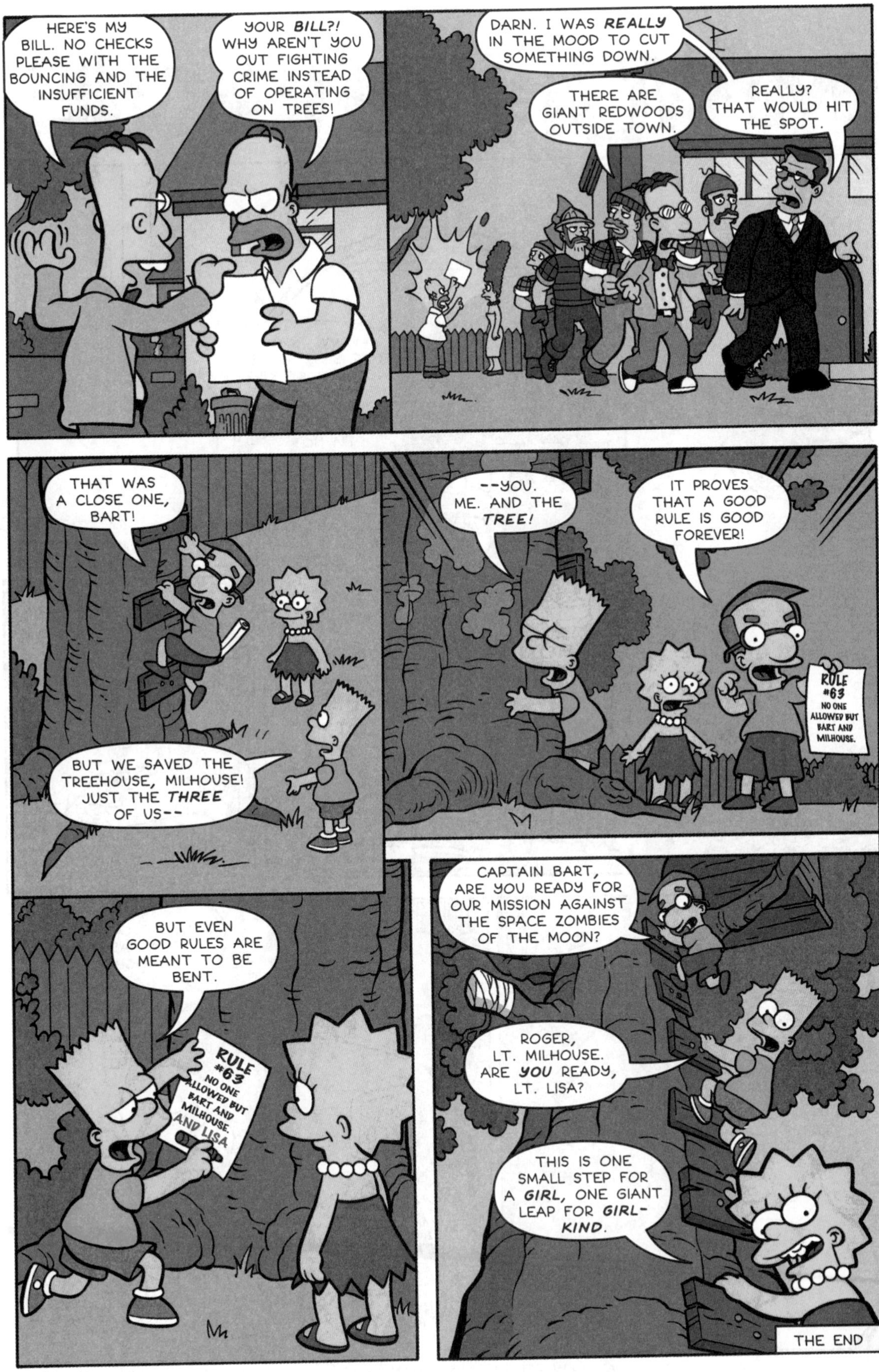
HERE'S MY BILL. NO CHECKS PLEASE WITH THE BOUNCING AND THE INSUFFICIENT FUNDS.
YOUR *BILL*?! WHY AREN'T YOU OUT FIGHTING CRIME INSTEAD OF OPERATING ON TREES!
DARN. I WAS *REALLY* IN THE MOOD TO CUT SOMETHING DOWN.
THERE ARE GIANT REDWOODS OUTSIDE TOWN.
REALLY? THAT WOULD HIT THE SPOT.
THAT WAS A CLOSE ONE, BART!
BUT WE SAVED THE TREEHOUSE, MILHOUSE! JUST THE *THREE* OF US--
--YOU. ME. AND THE *TREE!*
IT PROVES THAT A GOOD RULE IS GOOD FOREVER!
RULE #63 NO ONE ALLOWED BUT BART AND MILHOUSE.
BUT EVEN GOOD RULES ARE MEANT TO BE BENT.
RULE #63 NO ONE ALLOWED BUT BART AND MILHOUSE. AND LISA
CAPTAIN BART, ARE YOU READY FOR OUR MISSION AGAINST THE SPACE ZOMBIES OF THE MOON?
ROGER, LT. MILHOUSE. ARE *YOU* READY, LT. LISA?
THIS IS ONE SMALL STEP FOR A *GIRL*, ONE GIANT LEAP FOR *GIRL-KIND*.
THE END

MAYOR MAGGIE

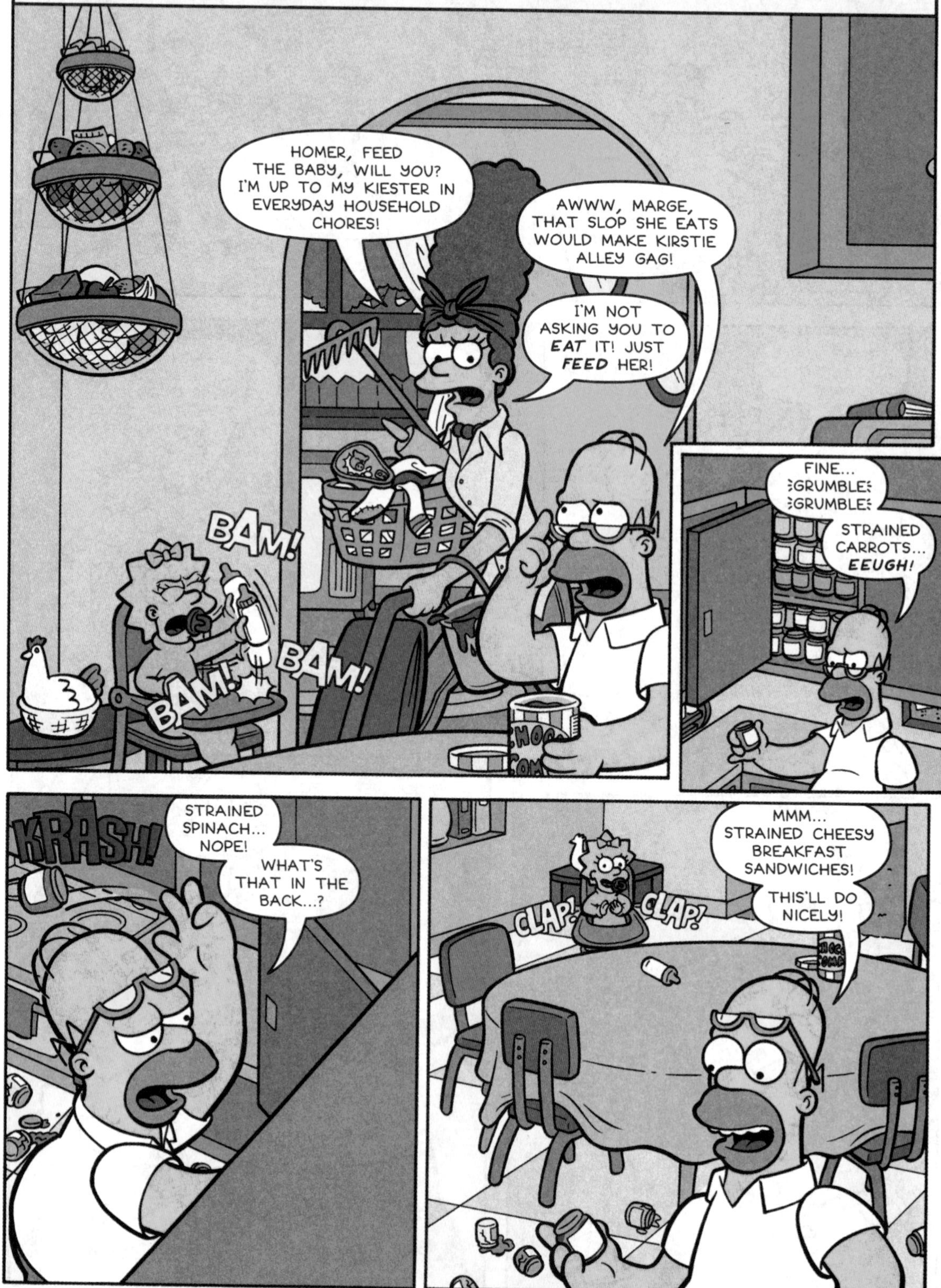
HOMER, FEED THE BABY, WILL YOU? I'M UP TO MY KIESTER IN EVERYDAY HOUSEHOLD CHORES!
AWWW, MARGE, THAT SLOP SHE EATS WOULD MAKE KIRSTIE ALLEY GAG!
I'M NOT ASKING YOU TO EAT IT! JUST FEED HER!
BAM!
BAM!
BAM!
FINE... GRUMBLE GRUMBLE
STRAINED CARROTS... EEUGH!
KRASH!
STRAINED SPINACH... NOPE!
WHAT'S THAT IN THE BACK...?
CLAP!
CLAP!
MMM... STRAINED CHEESY BREAKFAST SANDWICHES!
THIS'LL DO NICELY!

TOM PEYER SCRIPT | JASON HO PENCILS | ANDREW PEPOY INKS | NATHAN HAMILL COLORS | KAREN BATES LETTERS | BILL MORRISON EDITOR

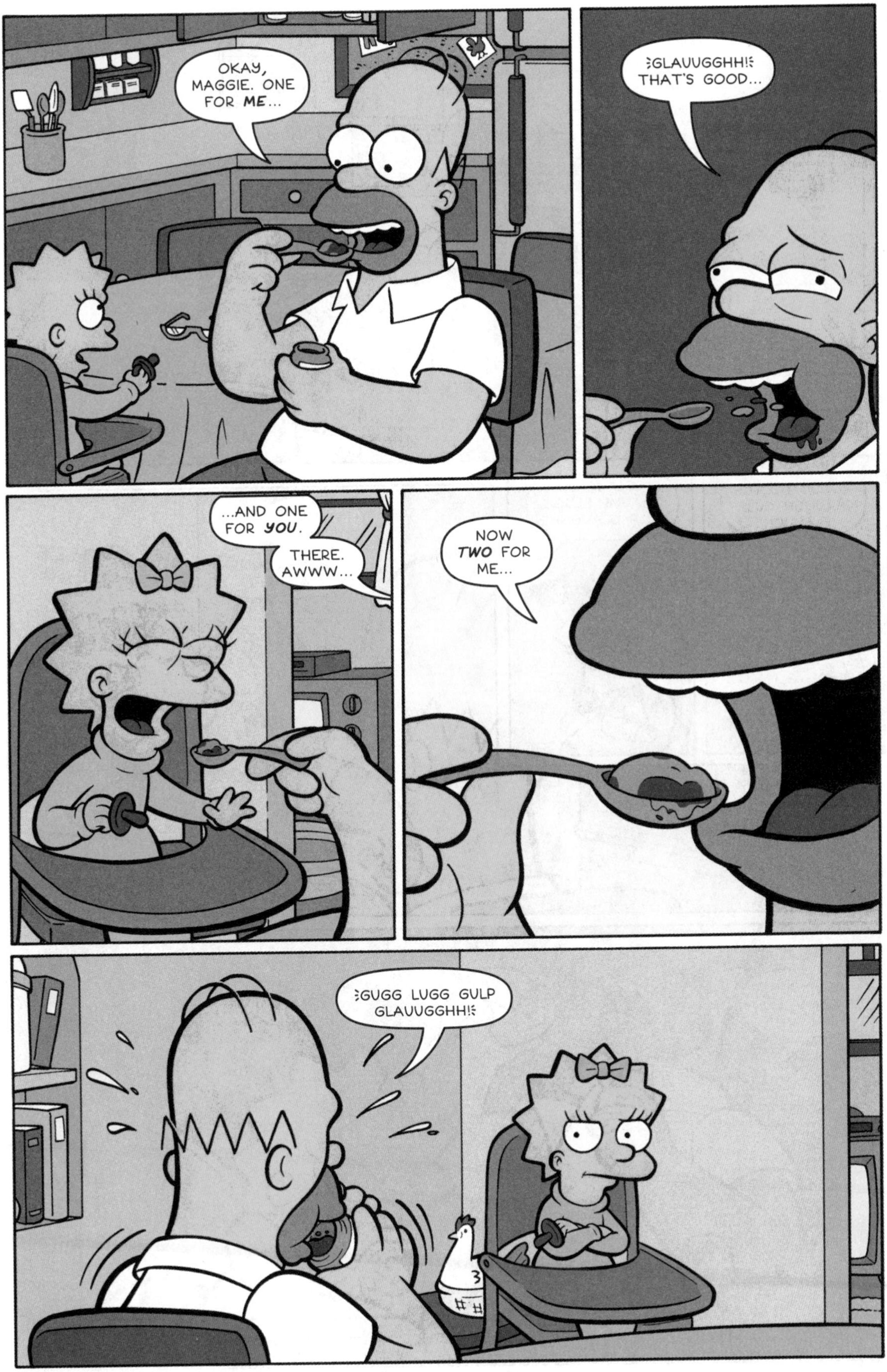
OKAY, MAGGIE. ONE FOR **ME**...
GLAUUGGHH! THAT'S GOOD...
...AND ONE FOR **YOU**.
THERE. AWWW...
NOW **TWO** FOR ME...
GUGG LUGG GULP GLAUUGGHH!

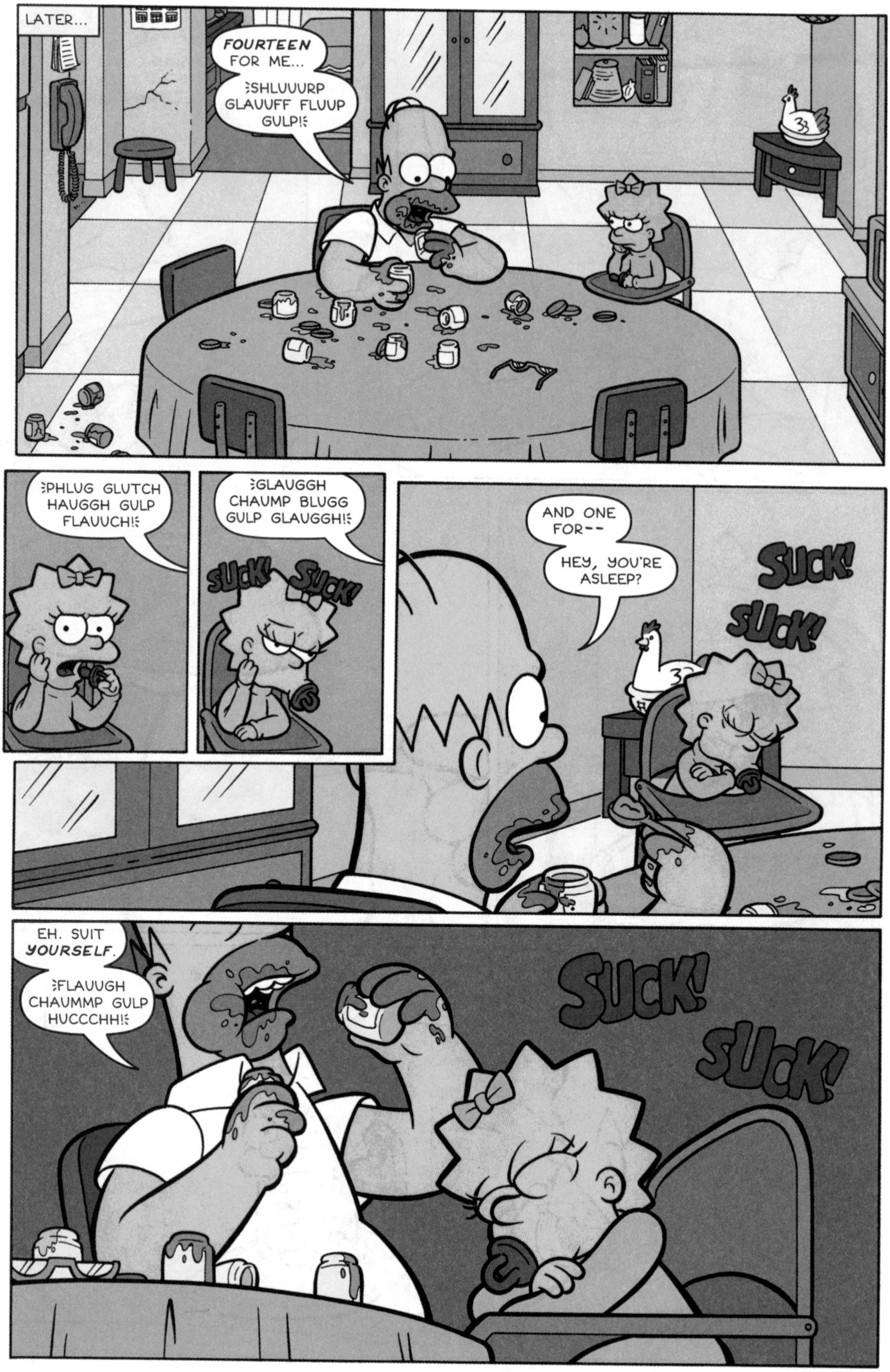

LATER...
FOURTEEN FOR ME...
SHLUUURP GLAUUFF FLUUP GULP!
PHLUG GLUTCH HAUGGH GULP FLAUUCH!
GLAUGGH CHAUMP BLUGG GULP GLAUGGH!
SUCK! SUCK!
AND ONE FOR--
HEY, YOU'RE ASLEEP?
SUCK! SUCK!
EH. SUIT YOURSELF.
FLAUUGH CHAUMMP GULP HUCCCHH!
SUCK! SUCK!

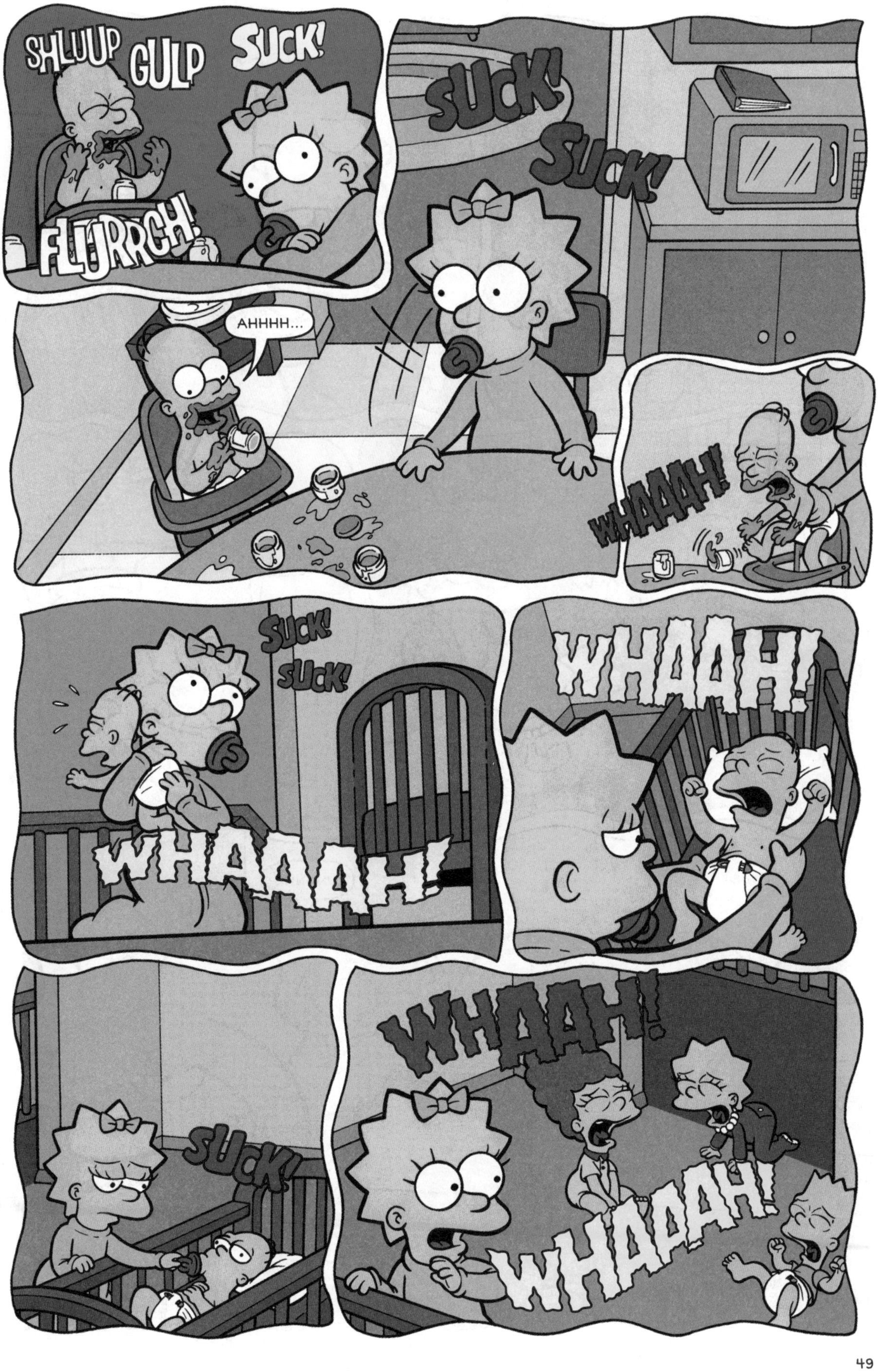
SHLUUP
GULP
SUCK!
FLURRCH!
SUCK!
SUCK!
AHHHH...
WHAAAH!
SUCK!
SUCK!
WHAAAH!
WHAAH!
SUCK!
WHAAH!
WHAAAH!

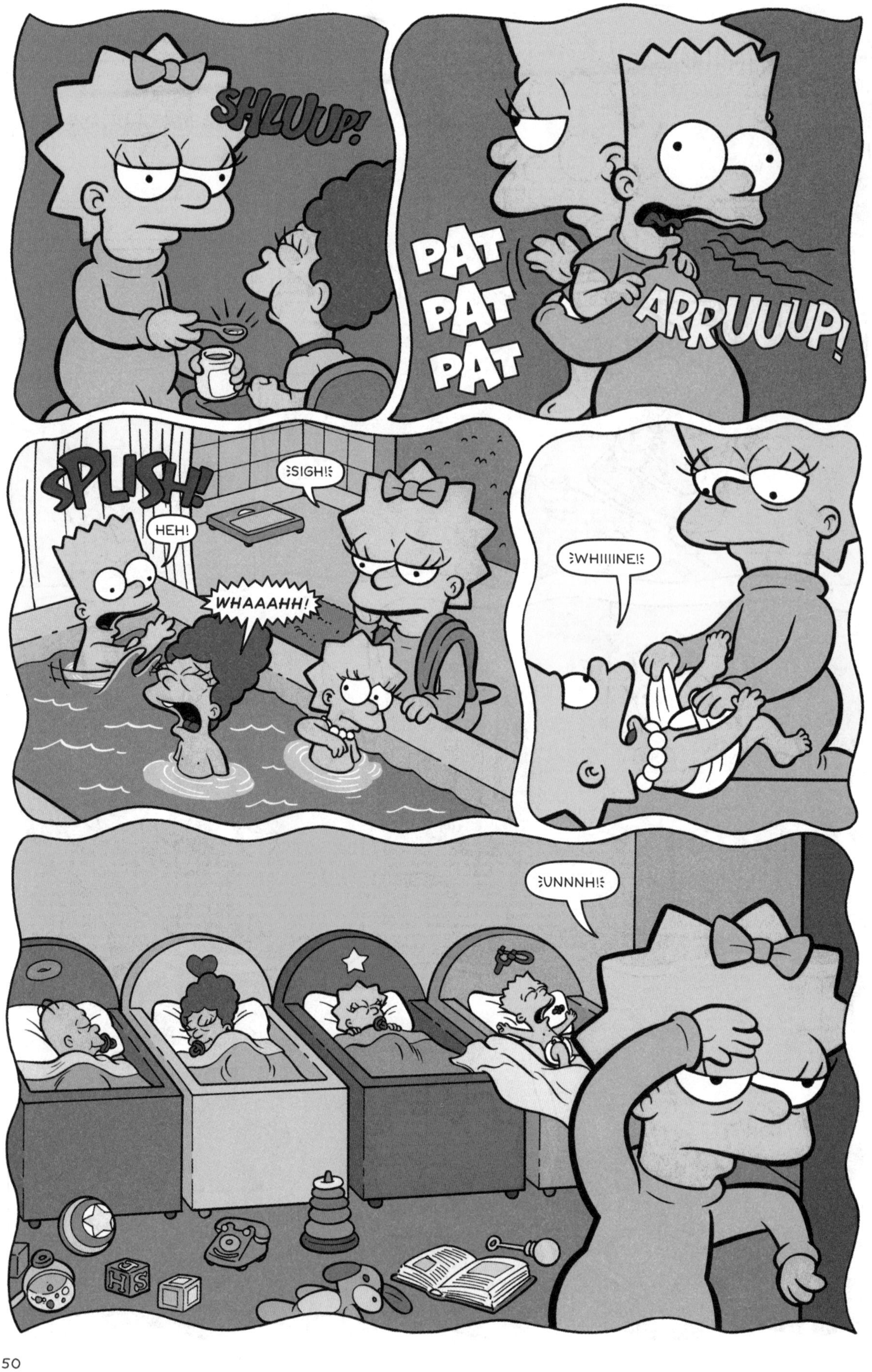
SHLUUUP!
PAT
PAT
PAT
ARRUUUP!
SPLISH!
SIGH!
HEH!
WHAAAHH!
WHIIIINE!
UNNNH!

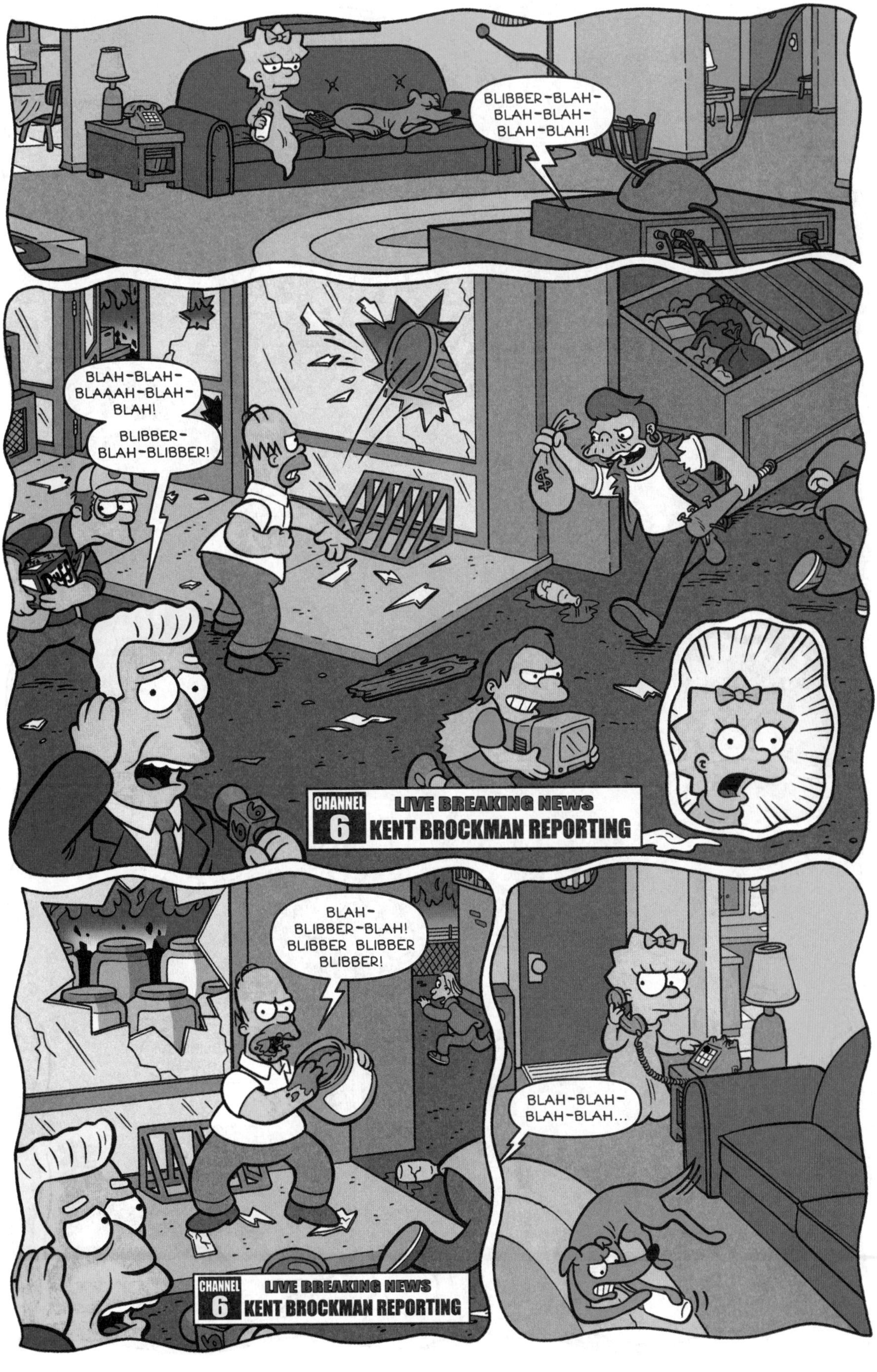

BLIBBER-BLAH-BLAH-BLAH-BLAH-BLAH!
BLAH-BLAH-BLAAAH-BLAH-BLAH!
BLIBBER-BLAH-BLIBBER!
CHANNEL 6 LIVE BREAKING NEWS KENT BROCKMAN REPORTING
BLAH-BLIBBER-BLAH! BLIBBER BLIBBER BLIBBER!
CHANNEL 6 LIVE BREAKING NEWS KENT BROCKMAN REPORTING
BLAH-BLAH-BLAH-BLAH...

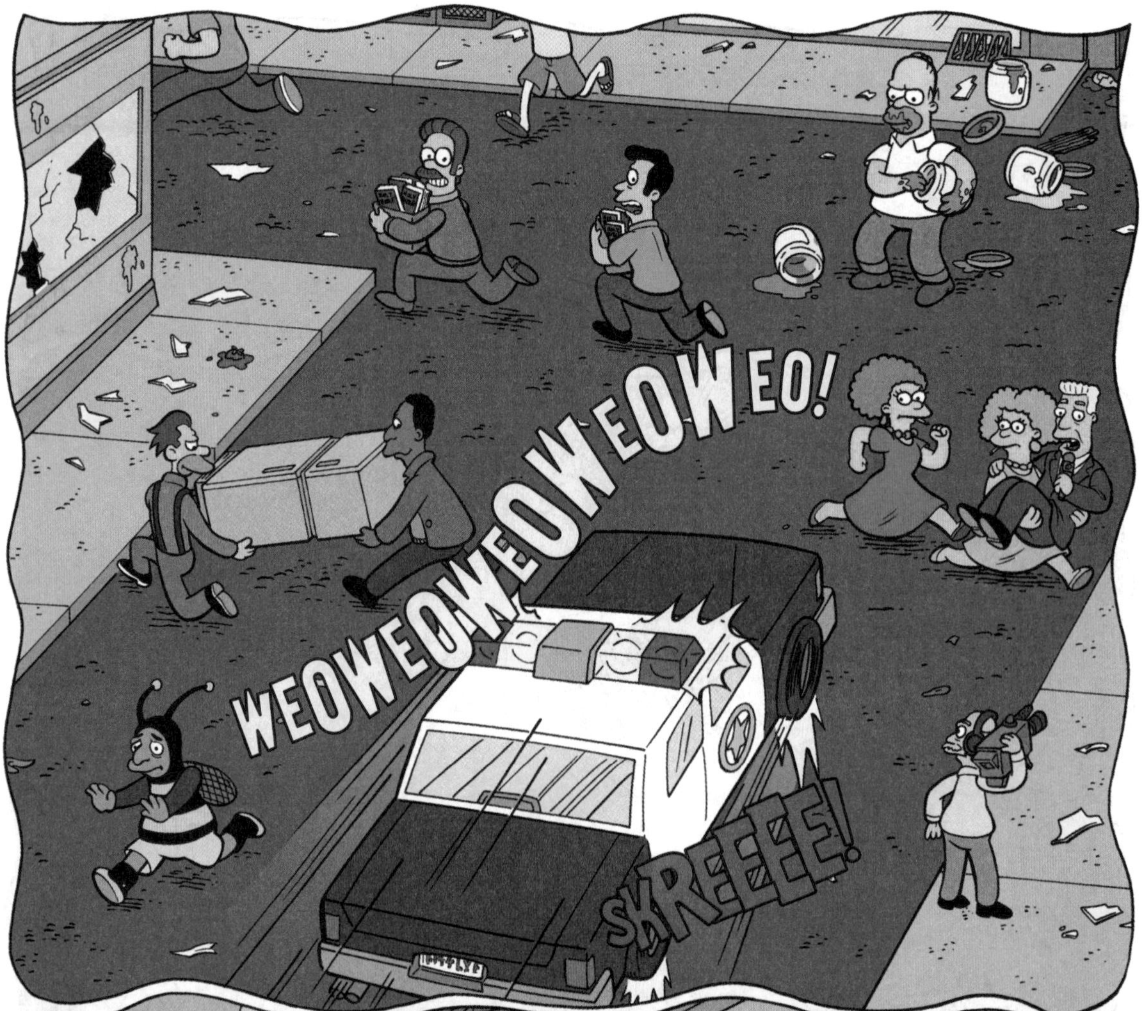
WEOWEOWEOWEOWEO!
SKREEEE!

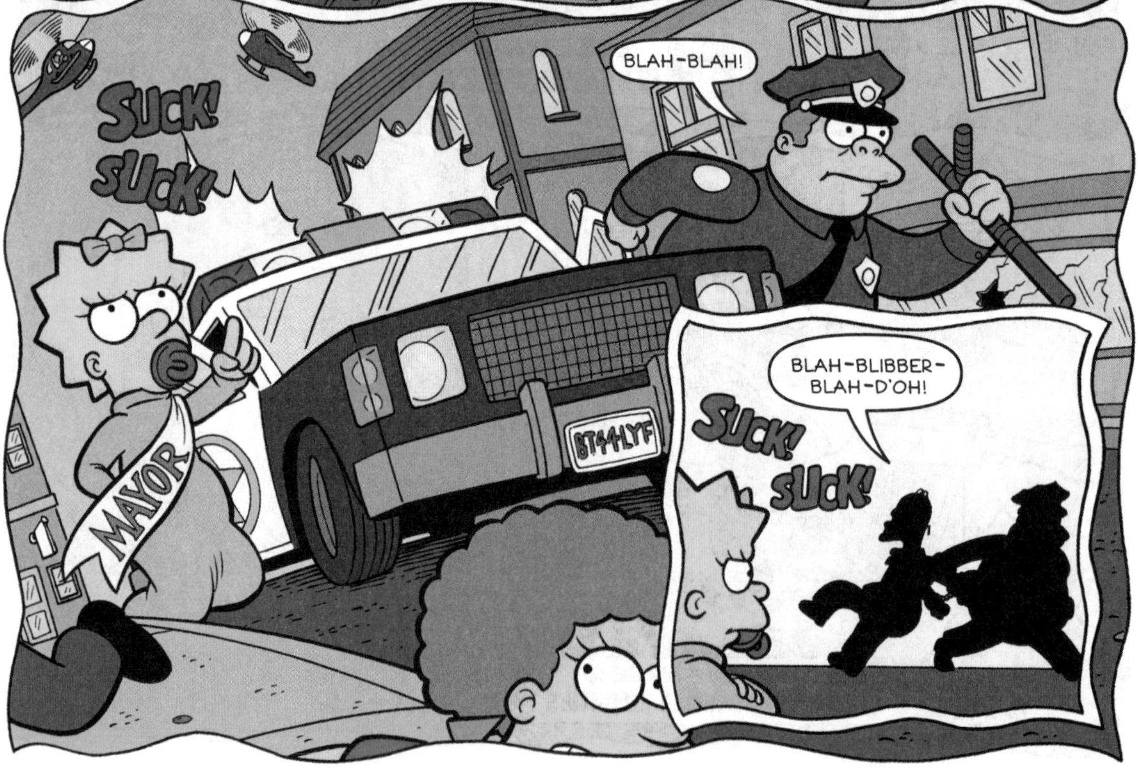
SUCK!
SUCK!
BLAH-BLAH!
BT44LYF
MAYOR
BLAH-BLIBBER-
BLAH-D'OH!
SUCK!
SUCK!

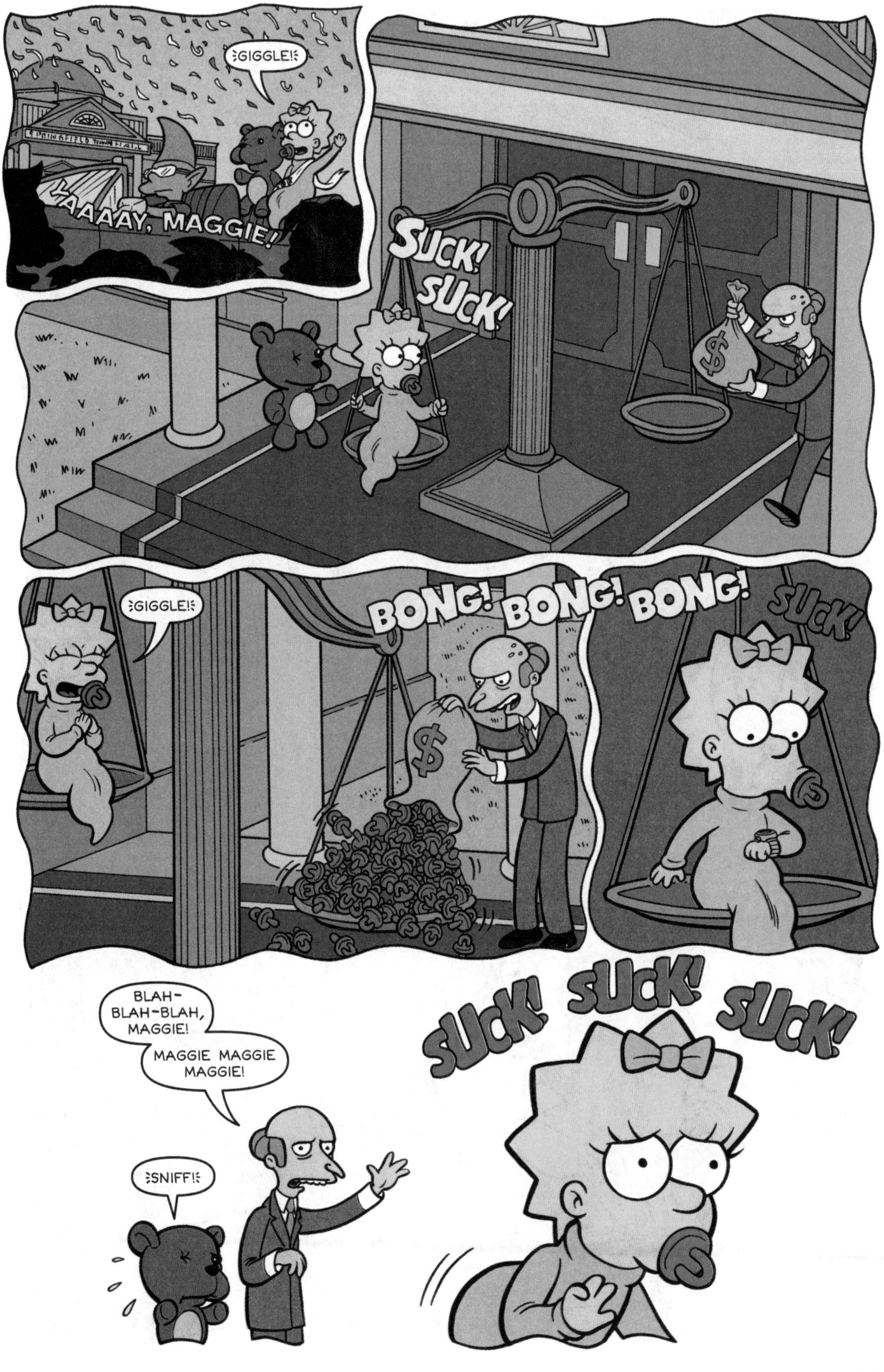
GIGGLE!
YAAAAY, MAGGIE!
SUCK!
SUCK!
GIGGLE!
BONG! BONG! BONG!
SUCK!
BLAH-BLAH-BLAH, MAGGIE!
MAGGIE MAGGIE MAGGIE!
SNIFF!
SUCK! SUCK! SUCK!

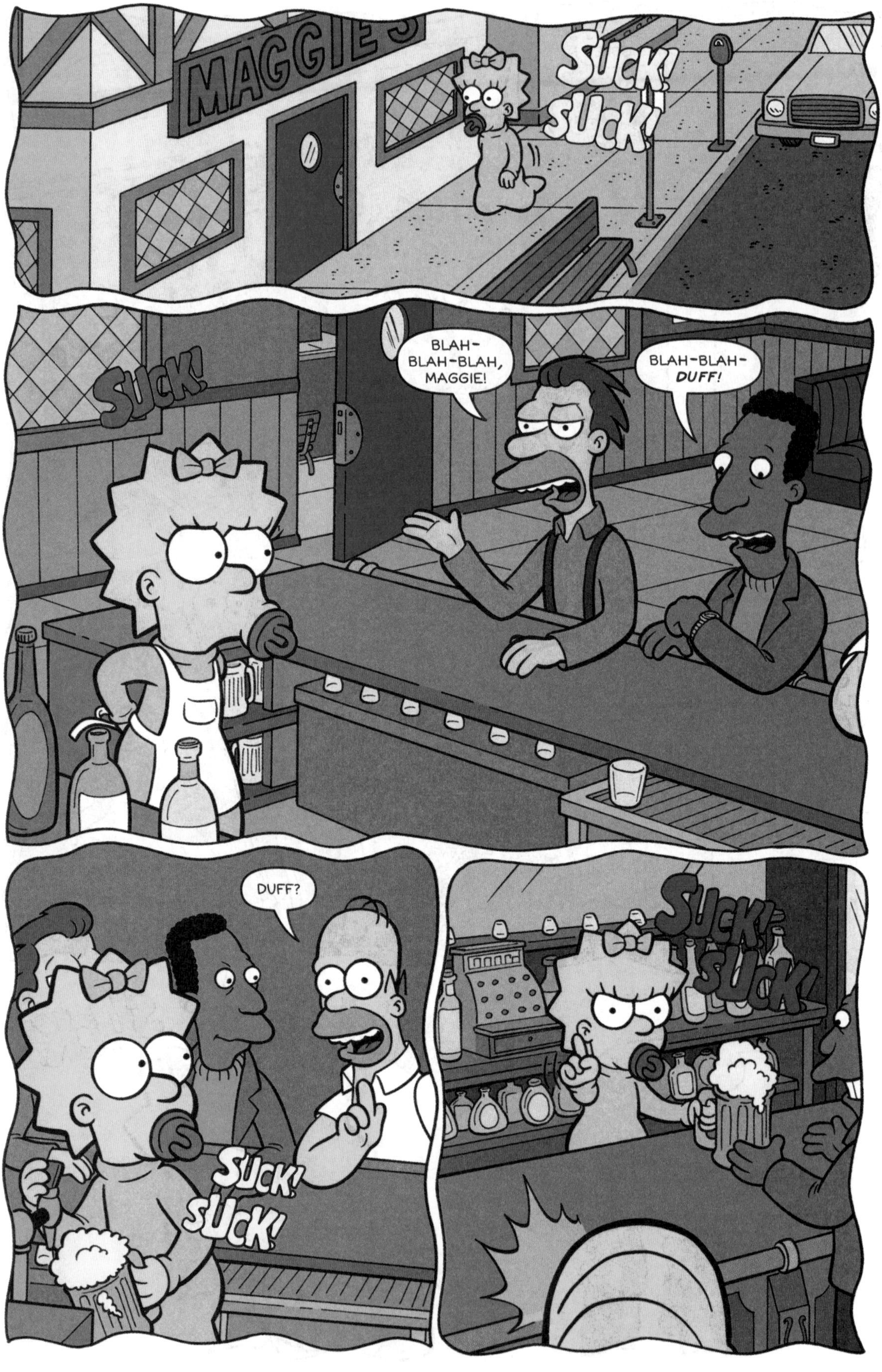
MAGGIE'S
SUCK!
SUCK!
SUCK!
BLAH-BLAH-BLAH, MAGGIE!
BLAH-BLAH-DUFF!
DUFF?
SUCK!
SUCK!
SUCK!
SUCK!

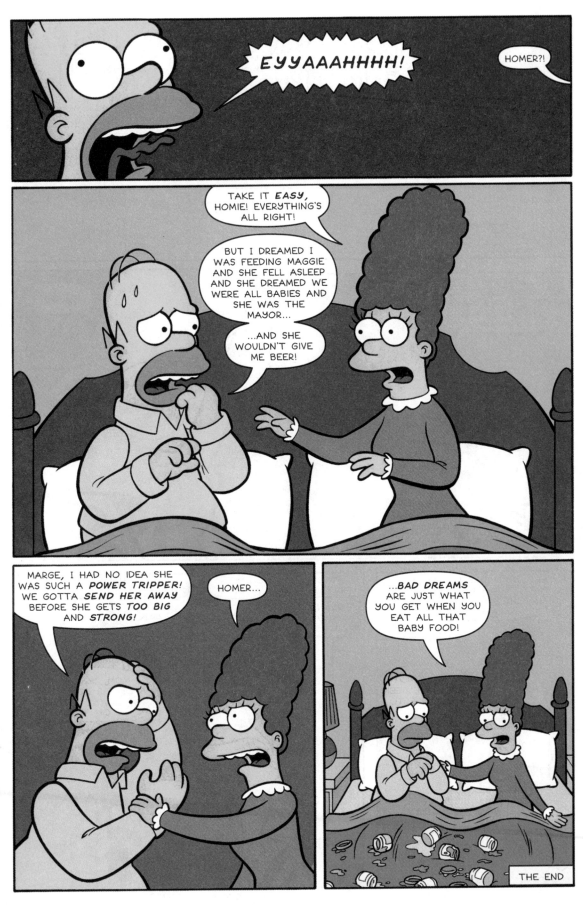

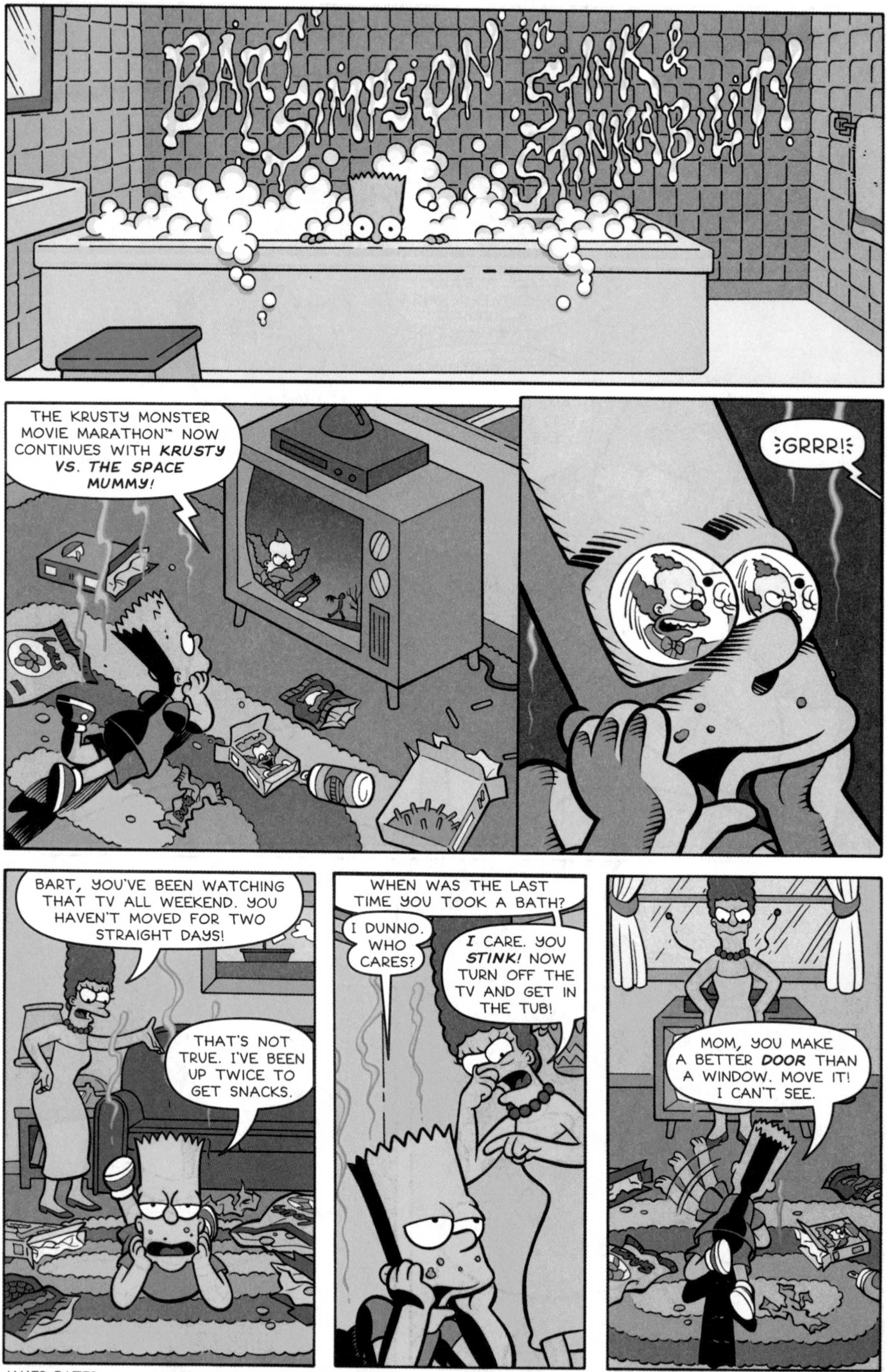
BART SIMPSON in STINK & STINKABILITY!
THE KRUSTY MONSTER MOVIE MARATHON™ NOW CONTINUES WITH *KRUSTY VS. THE SPACE MUMMY!*
GRRR!
BART, YOU'VE BEEN WATCHING THAT TV ALL WEEKEND. YOU HAVEN'T MOVED FOR TWO STRAIGHT DAYS!
THAT'S NOT TRUE. I'VE BEEN UP TWICE TO GET SNACKS.
WHEN WAS THE LAST TIME YOU TOOK A BATH?
I DUNNO. WHO CARES?
I CARE. YOU *STINK!* NOW TURN OFF THE TV AND GET IN THE TUB!
MOM, YOU MAKE A BETTER **DOOR** THAN A WINDOW. MOVE IT! I CAN'T SEE.

JAMES BATES
SCRIPT

JAMES LLOYD
PENCILS

ANDREW PEPOY
INKS

ART VILLANUEVA
COLORS

KAREN BATES
LETTERS

BILL MORRISON
EDITOR

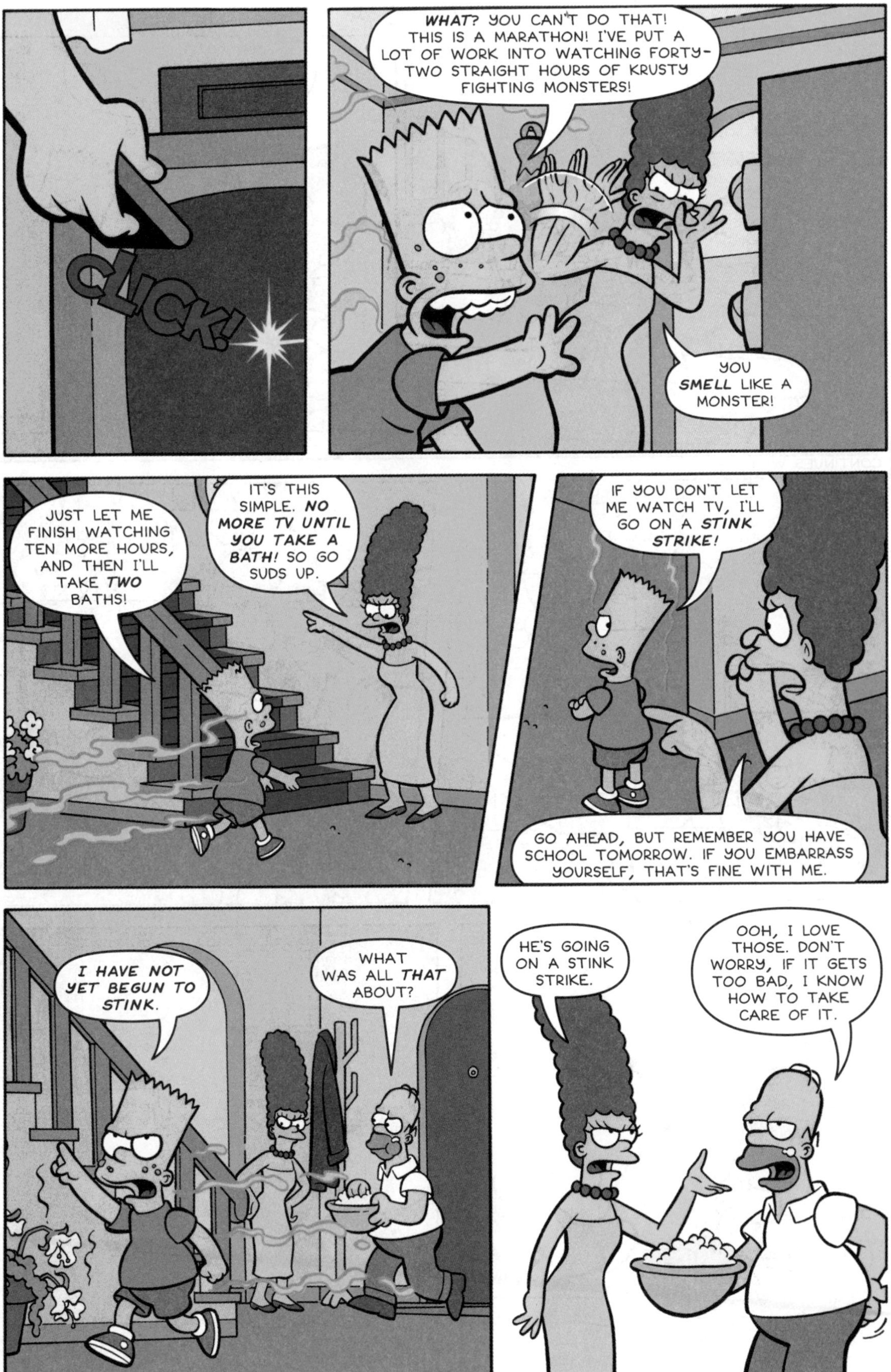
CLICK!
WHAT? YOU CAN'T DO THAT! THIS IS A MARATHON! I'VE PUT A LOT OF WORK INTO WATCHING FORTY-TWO STRAIGHT HOURS OF KRUSTY FIGHTING MONSTERS!
YOU SMELL LIKE A MONSTER!
JUST LET ME FINISH WATCHING TEN MORE HOURS, AND THEN I'LL TAKE TWO BATHS!
IT'S THIS SIMPLE. NO MORE TV UNTIL YOU TAKE A BATH! SO GO SUDS UP.
IF YOU DON'T LET ME WATCH TV, I'LL GO ON A STINK STRIKE!
GO AHEAD, BUT REMEMBER YOU HAVE SCHOOL TOMORROW. IF YOU EMBARRASS YOURSELF, THAT'S FINE WITH ME.
I HAVE NOT YET BEGUN TO STINK.
WHAT WAS ALL THAT ABOUT?
HE'S GOING ON A STINK STRIKE.
OOH, I LOVE THOSE. DON'T WORRY, IF IT GETS TOO BAD, I KNOW HOW TO TAKE CARE OF IT.

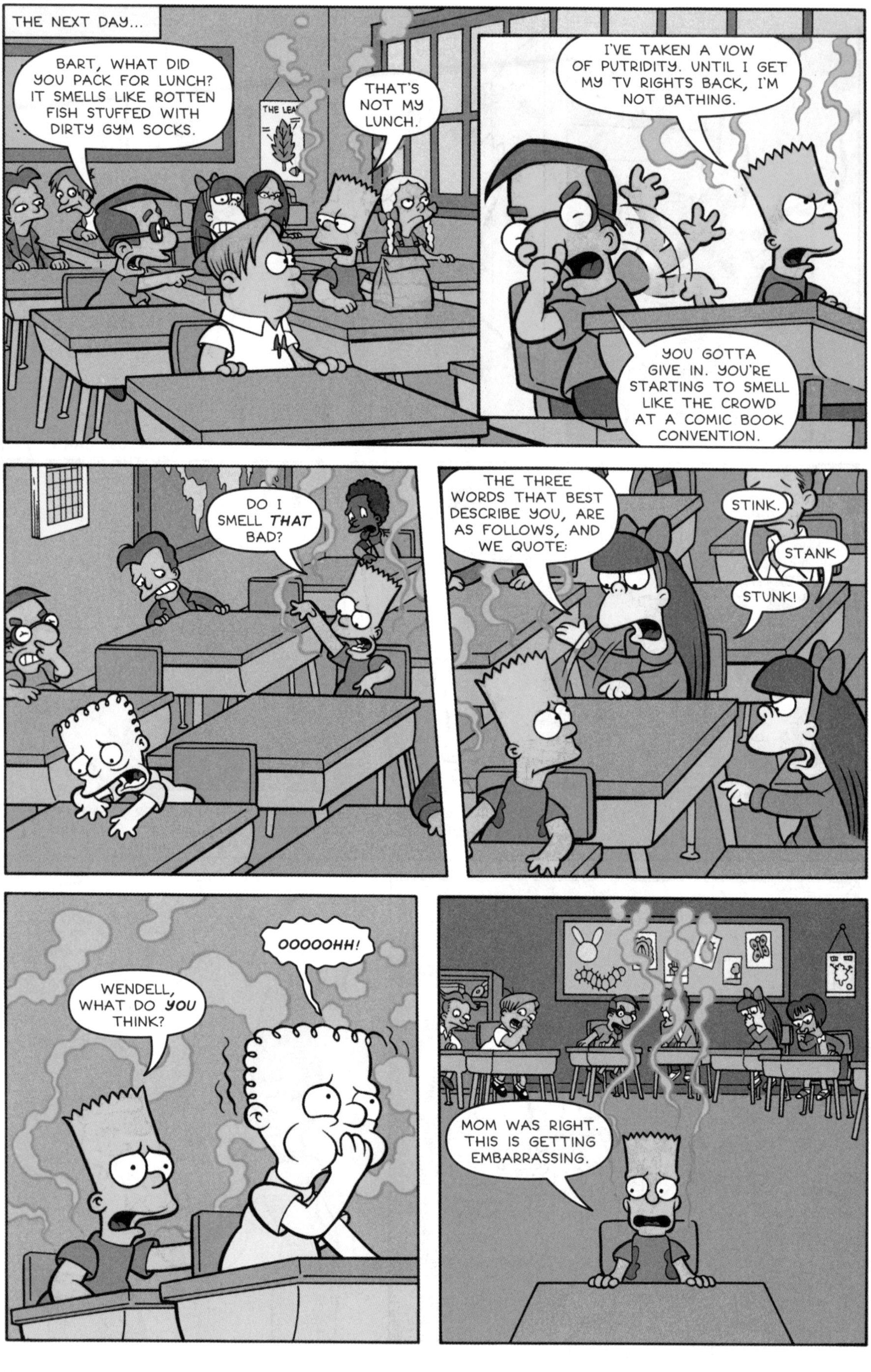
THE NEXT DAY...
BART, WHAT DID YOU PACK FOR LUNCH? IT SMELLS LIKE ROTTEN FISH STUFFED WITH DIRTY GYM SOCKS.
THAT'S NOT MY LUNCH.
I'VE TAKEN A VOW OF PUTRIDITY. UNTIL I GET MY TV RIGHTS BACK, I'M NOT BATHING.
YOU GOTTA GIVE IN. YOU'RE STARTING TO SMELL LIKE THE CROWD AT A COMIC BOOK CONVENTION.
DO I SMELL THAT BAD?
THE THREE WORDS THAT BEST DESCRIBE YOU, ARE AS FOLLOWS, AND WE QUOTE:
STINK.
STANK
STUNK!
OOOOOHH!
WENDELL, WHAT DO YOU THINK?
MOM WAS RIGHT. THIS IS GETTING EMBARRASSING.

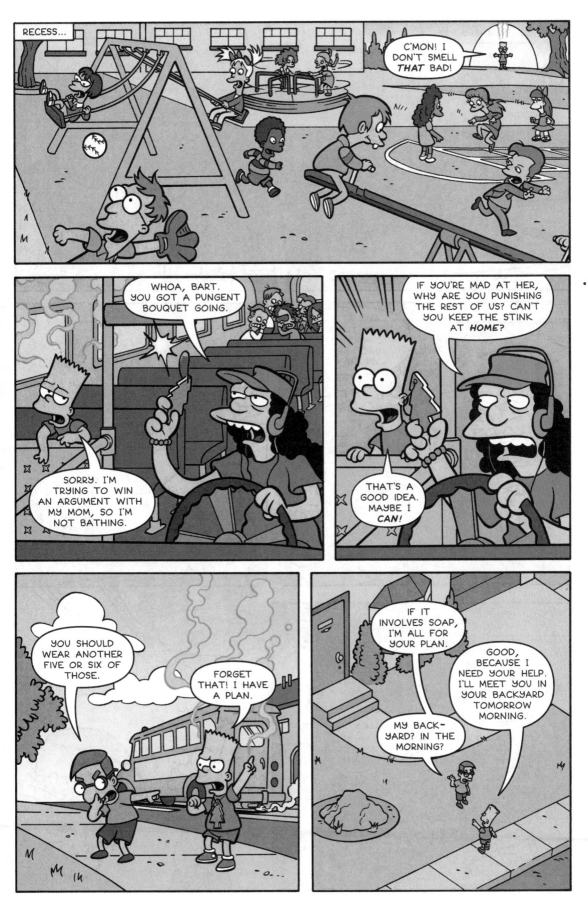

RECESS...

C'MON! I DON'T SMELL *THAT* BAD!

WHOA, BART. YOU GOT A PUNGENT BOUQUET GOING.

SORRY. I'M TRYING TO WIN AN ARGUMENT WITH MY MOM, SO I'M NOT BATHING.

IF YOU'RE MAD AT HER, WHY ARE YOU PUNISHING THE REST OF US? CAN'T YOU KEEP THE STINK AT *HOME*?

THAT'S A GOOD IDEA. MAYBE I *CAN!*

YOU SHOULD WEAR ANOTHER FIVE OR SIX OF THOSE.

FORGET THAT! I HAVE A PLAN.

IF IT INVOLVES SOAP, I'M ALL FOR YOUR PLAN.

GOOD, BECAUSE I NEED YOUR HELP. I'LL MEET YOU IN YOUR BACKYARD TOMORROW MORNING.

MY BACK-YARD? IN THE MORNING?

59

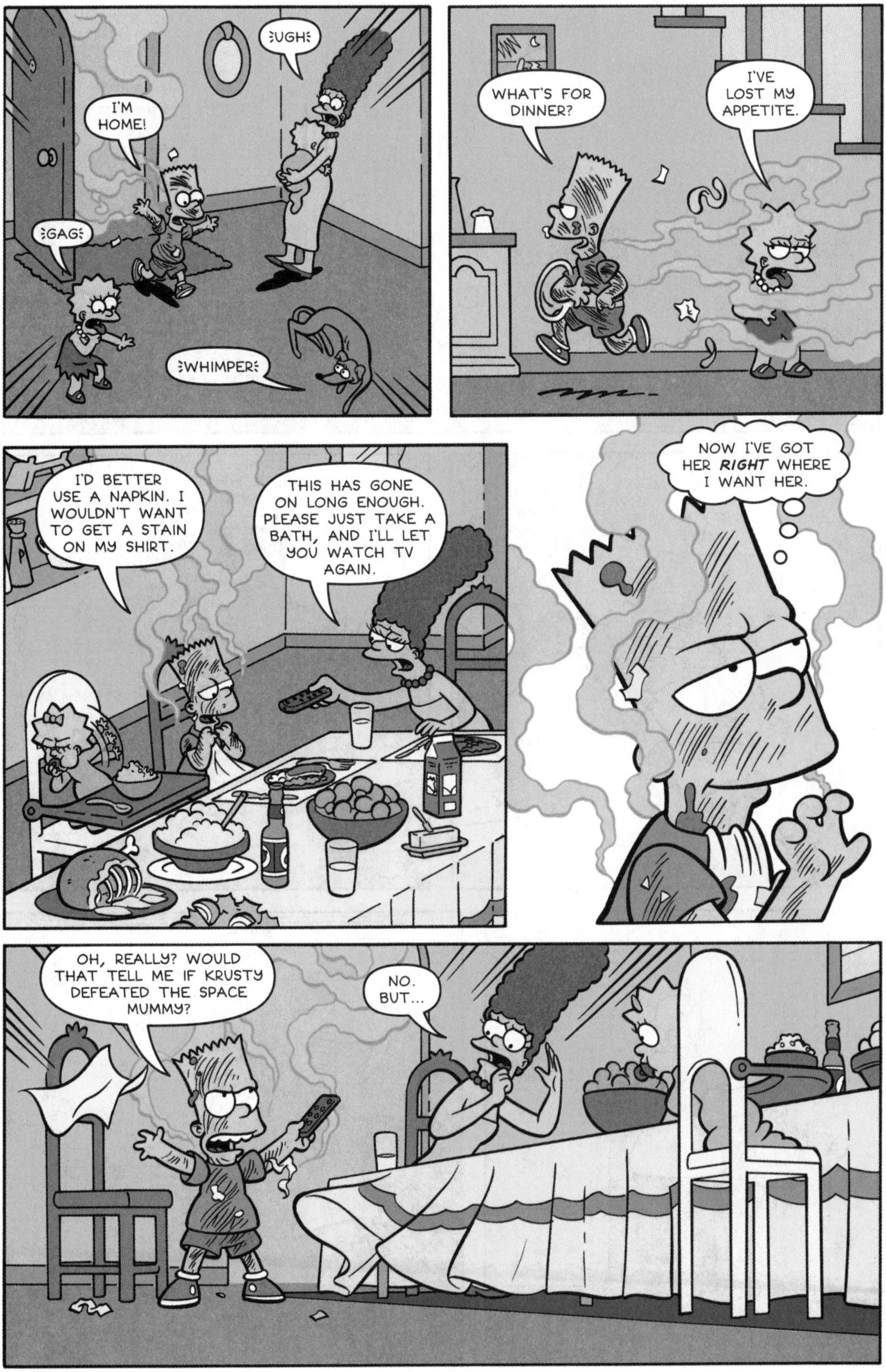

I'M HOME!
UGH
GAG
WHIMPER
WHAT'S FOR DINNER?
I'VE LOST MY APPETITE.
I'D BETTER USE A NAPKIN. I WOULDN'T WANT TO GET A STAIN ON MY SHIRT.
THIS HAS GONE ON LONG ENOUGH. PLEASE JUST TAKE A BATH, AND I'LL LET YOU WATCH TV AGAIN.
NOW I'VE GOT HER RIGHT WHERE I WANT HER.
OH, REALLY? WOULD THAT TELL ME IF KRUSTY DEFEATED THE SPACE MUMMY?
NO. BUT...

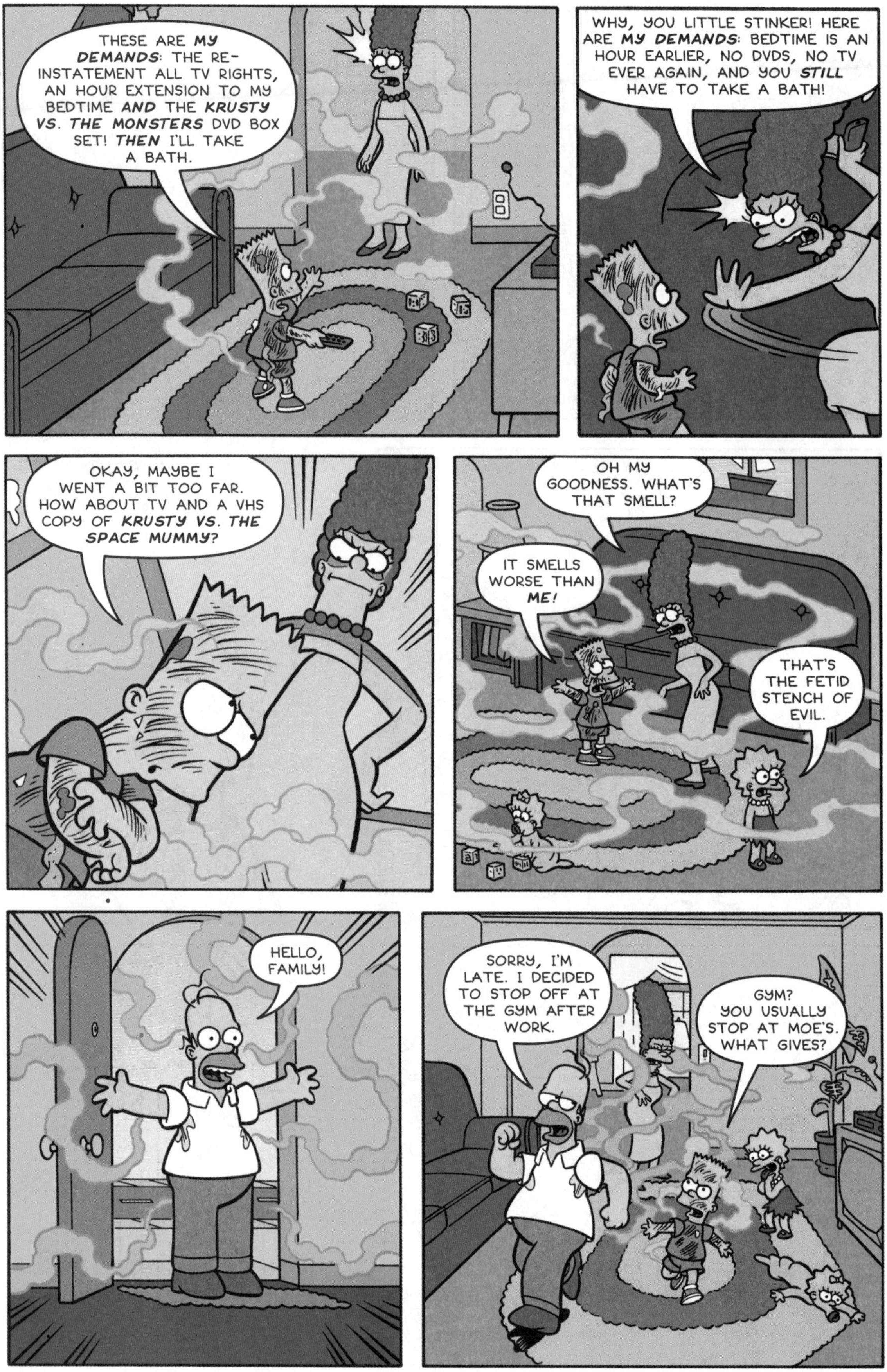

THESE ARE MY DEMANDS: THE RE-INSTATEMENT ALL TV RIGHTS, AN HOUR EXTENSION TO MY BEDTIME AND THE KRUSTY VS. THE MONSTERS DVD BOX SET! THEN I'LL TAKE A BATH.
WHY, YOU LITTLE STINKER! HERE ARE MY DEMANDS: BEDTIME IS AN HOUR EARLIER, NO DVDS, NO TV EVER AGAIN, AND YOU STILL HAVE TO TAKE A BATH!
OKAY, MAYBE I WENT A BIT TOO FAR. HOW ABOUT TV AND A VHS COPY OF KRUSTY VS. THE SPACE MUMMY?
OH MY GOODNESS. WHAT'S THAT SMELL?
IT SMELLS WORSE THAN ME!
THAT'S THE FETID STENCH OF EVIL.
HELLO, FAMILY!
SORRY, I'M LATE. I DECIDED TO STOP OFF AT THE GYM AFTER WORK.
GYM? YOU USUALLY STOP AT MOE'S. WHAT GIVES?

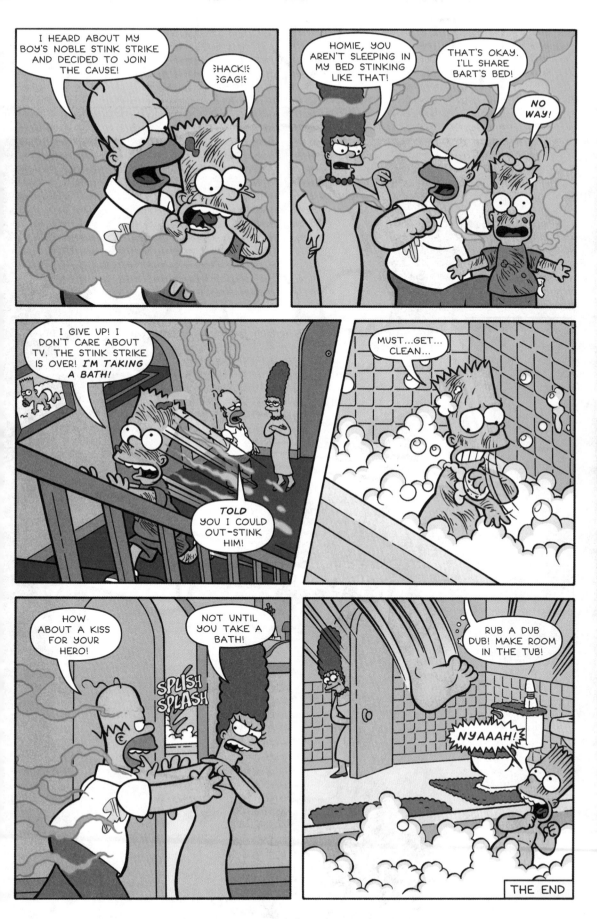

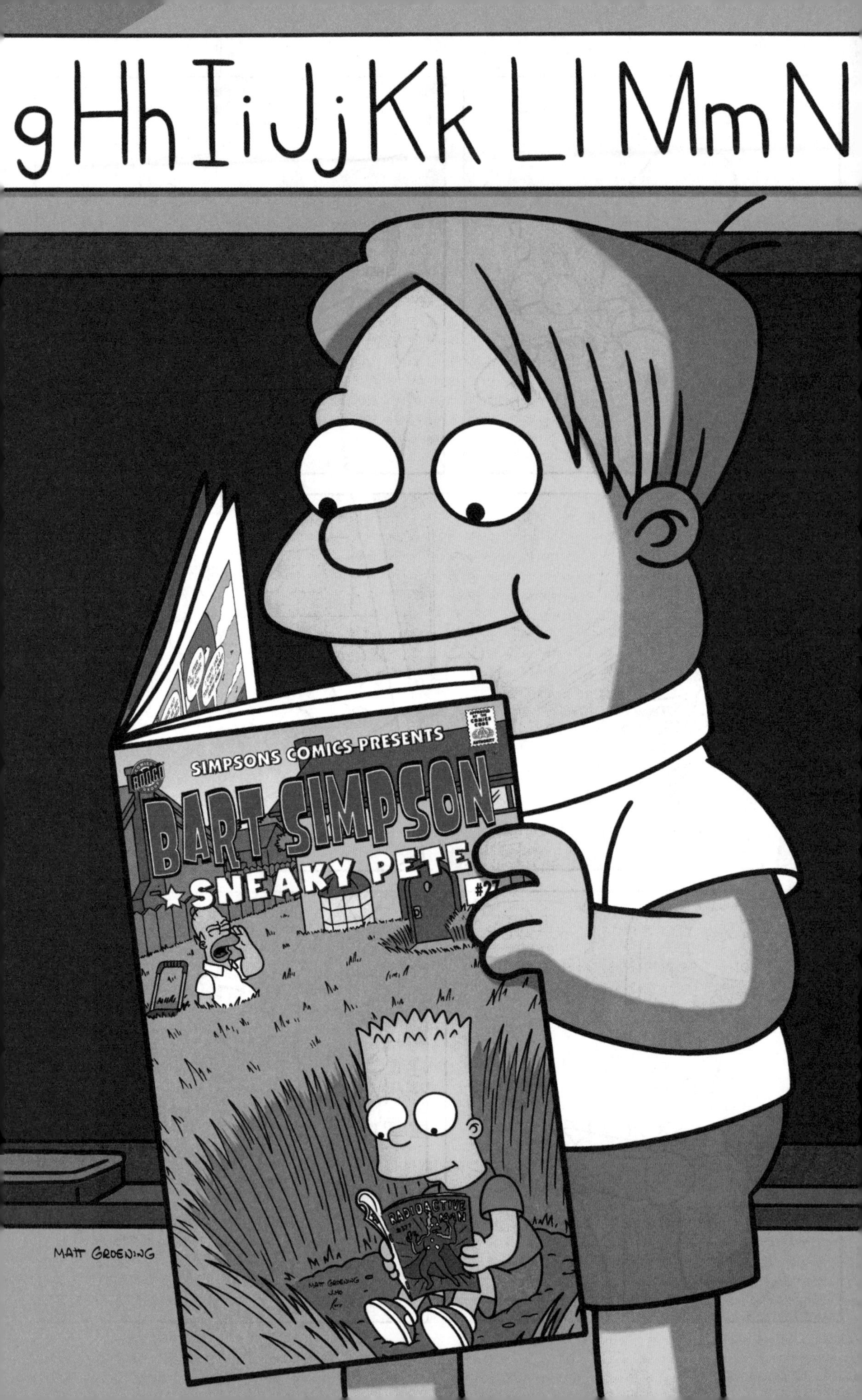
gHhIiJjKkLlMmN
SIMPSONS COMICS PRESENTS
BART SIMPSON
SNEAKY PETE
RADIOACTIVE MAN
MATT GROENING

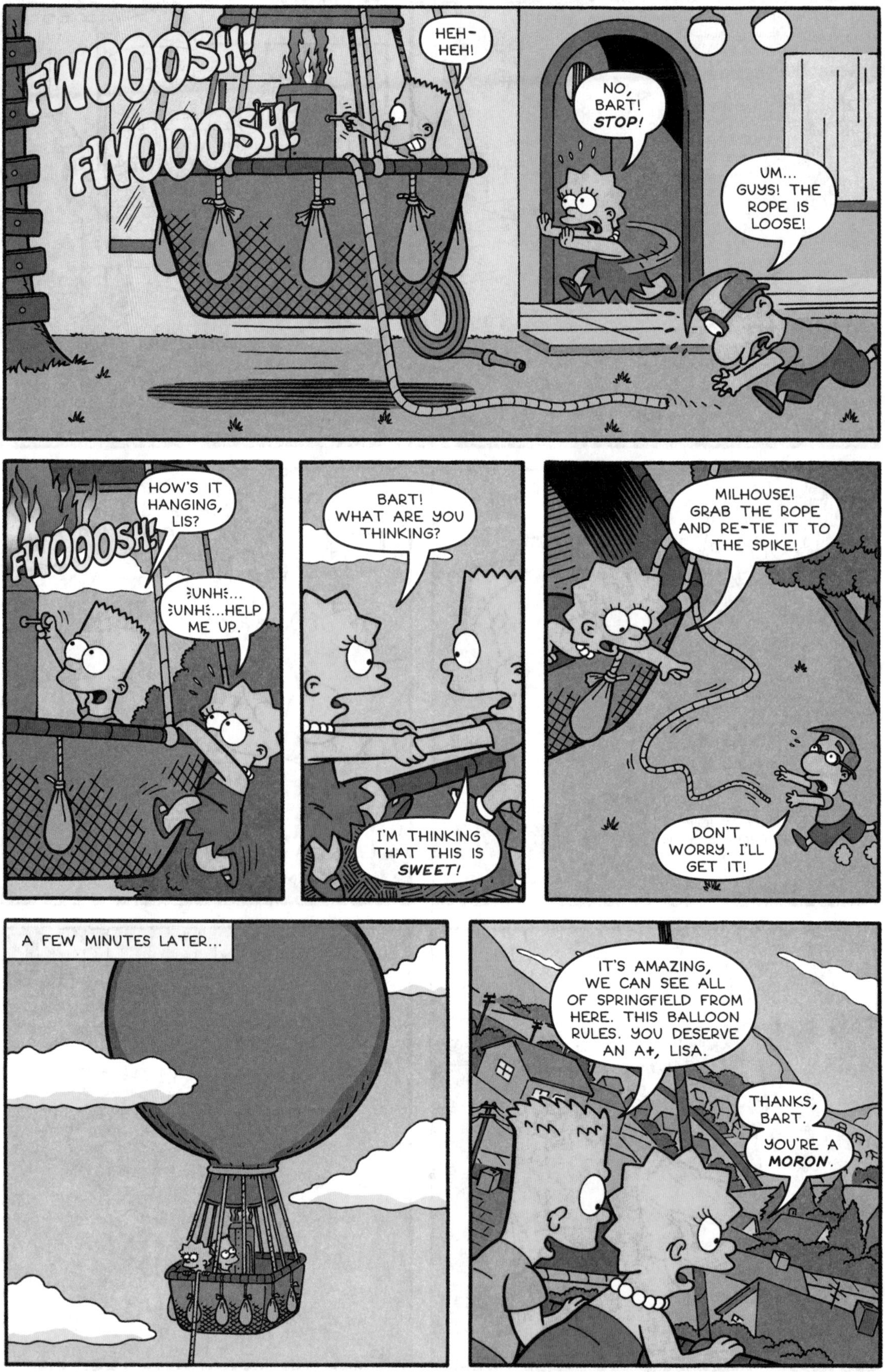
FWOOOSH!
FWOOOSH!
HEH-HEH!
NO, BART! STOP!
UM... GUYS! THE ROPE IS LOOSE!
FWOOOSH!
HOW'S IT HANGING, LIS?
UNH... UNH...HELP ME UP.
BART! WHAT ARE YOU THINKING?
I'M THINKING THAT THIS IS SWEET!
MILHOUSE! GRAB THE ROPE AND RE-TIE IT TO THE SPIKE!
DON'T WORRY. I'LL GET IT!
A FEW MINUTES LATER...
IT'S AMAZING, WE CAN SEE ALL OF SPRINGFIELD FROM HERE. THIS BALLOON RULES. YOU DESERVE AN A+, LISA.
THANKS, BART.
YOU'RE A MORON.

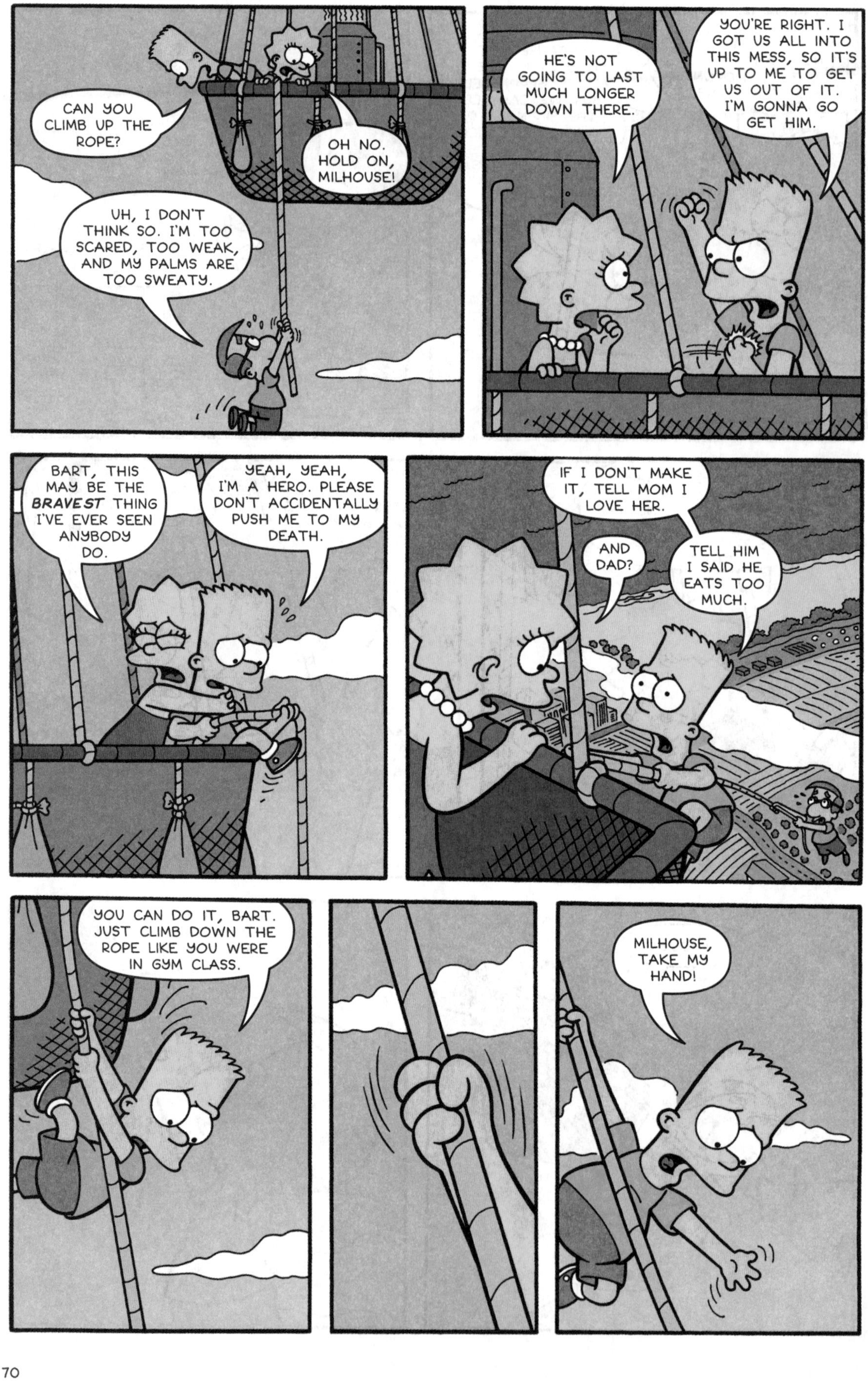
CAN YOU CLIMB UP THE ROPE?
OH NO. HOLD ON, MILHOUSE!
UH, I DON'T THINK SO. I'M TOO SCARED, TOO WEAK, AND MY PALMS ARE TOO SWEATY.
HE'S NOT GOING TO LAST MUCH LONGER DOWN THERE.
YOU'RE RIGHT. I GOT US ALL INTO THIS MESS, SO IT'S UP TO ME TO GET US OUT OF IT. I'M GONNA GO GET HIM.
BART, THIS MAY BE THE ***BRAVEST*** THING I'VE EVER SEEN ANYBODY DO.
YEAH, YEAH, I'M A HERO. PLEASE DON'T ACCIDENTALLY PUSH ME TO MY DEATH.
IF I DON'T MAKE IT, TELL MOM I LOVE HER.
AND DAD?
TELL HIM I SAID HE EATS TOO MUCH.
YOU CAN DO IT, BART. JUST CLIMB DOWN THE ROPE LIKE YOU WERE IN GYM CLASS.
MILHOUSE, TAKE MY HAND!

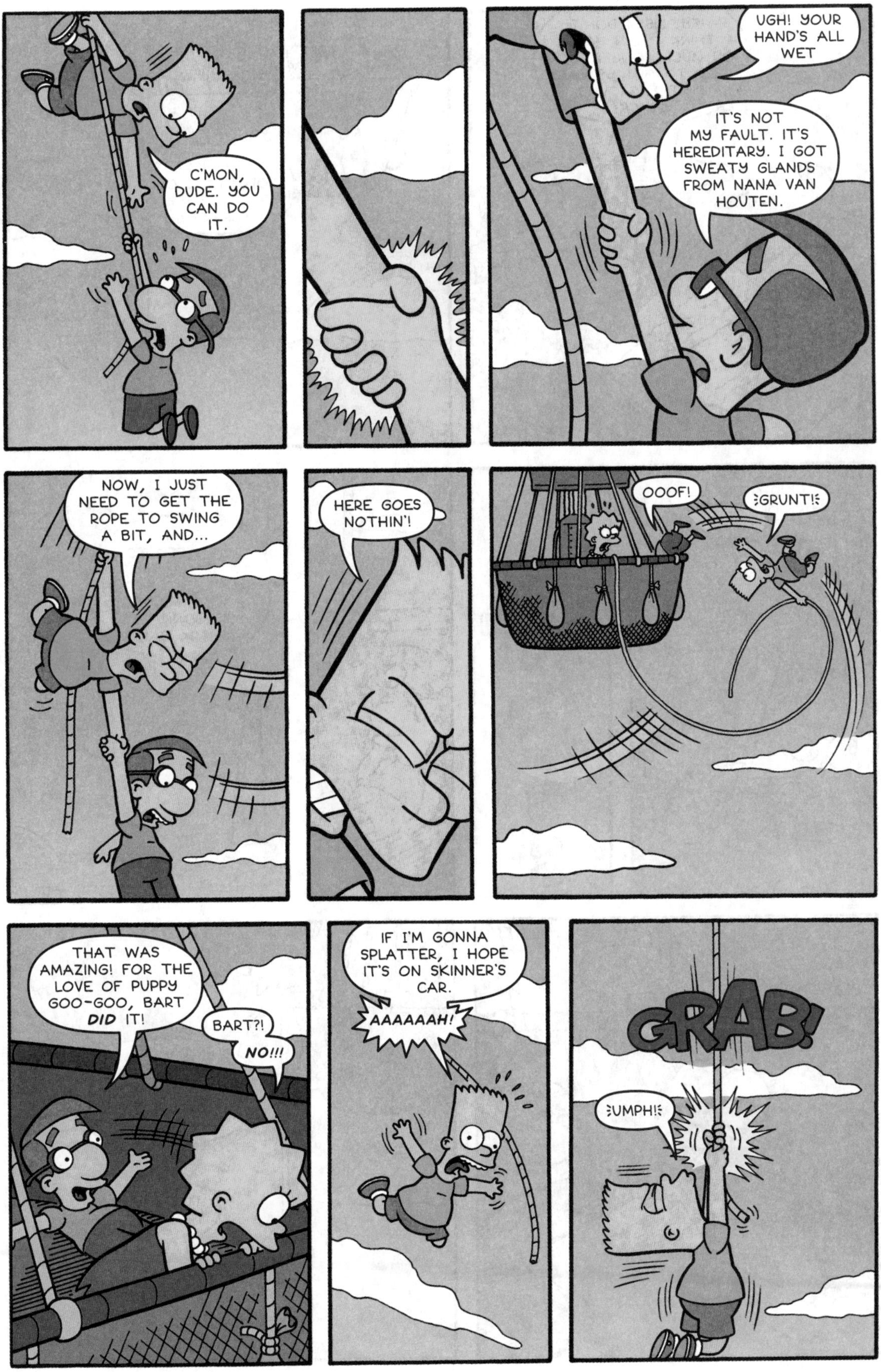
C'MON, DUDE. YOU CAN DO IT.
UGH! YOUR HAND'S ALL WET
IT'S NOT MY FAULT. IT'S HEREDITARY. I GOT SWEATY GLANDS FROM NANA VAN HOUTEN.
NOW, I JUST NEED TO GET THE ROPE TO SWING A BIT, AND...
HERE GOES NOTHIN'!
OOOF!
GRUNT!
THAT WAS AMAZING! FOR THE LOVE OF PUPPY GOO-GOO, BART DID IT!
BART?!
NO!!!
IF I'M GONNA SPLATTER, I HOPE IT'S ON SKINNER'S CAR.
AAAAAAH!
GRAB!
UMPH!

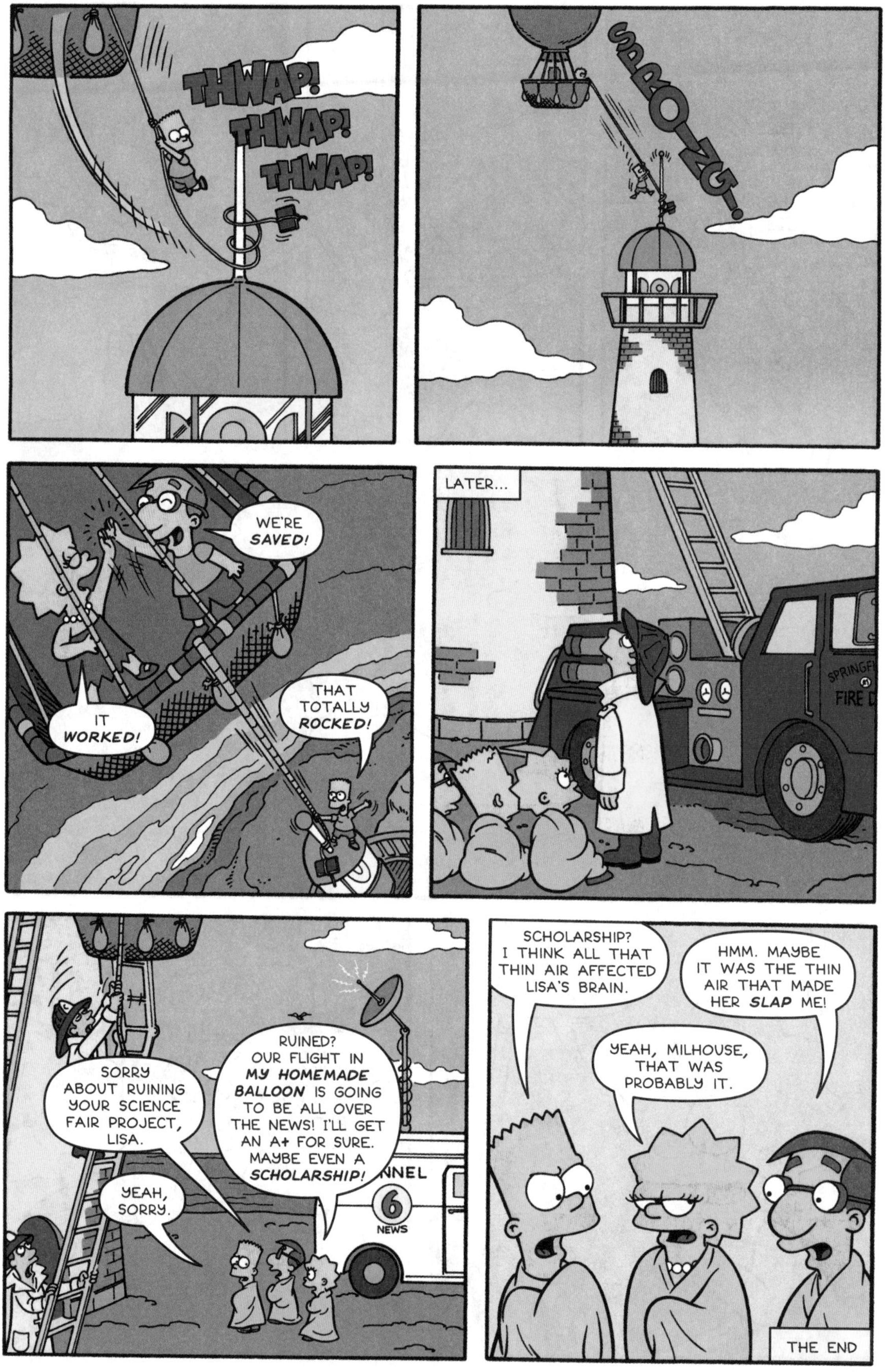
THWAP! THWAP! THWAP!
SPROING!
WE'RE SAVED!
IT WORKED!
THAT TOTALLY ROCKED!
LATER...
SPRINGFI
FIRE D
SORRY ABOUT RUINING YOUR SCIENCE FAIR PROJECT, LISA.
YEAH, SORRY.
RUINED? OUR FLIGHT IN MY HOMEMADE BALLOON IS GOING TO BE ALL OVER THE NEWS! I'LL GET AN A+ FOR SURE. MAYBE EVEN A SCHOLARSHIP!
NNEL
6
NEWS
SCHOLARSHIP? I THINK ALL THAT THIN AIR AFFECTED LISA'S BRAIN.
HMM. MAYBE IT WAS THE THIN AIR THAT MADE HER SLAP ME!
YEAH, MILHOUSE, THAT WAS PROBABLY IT.
THE END

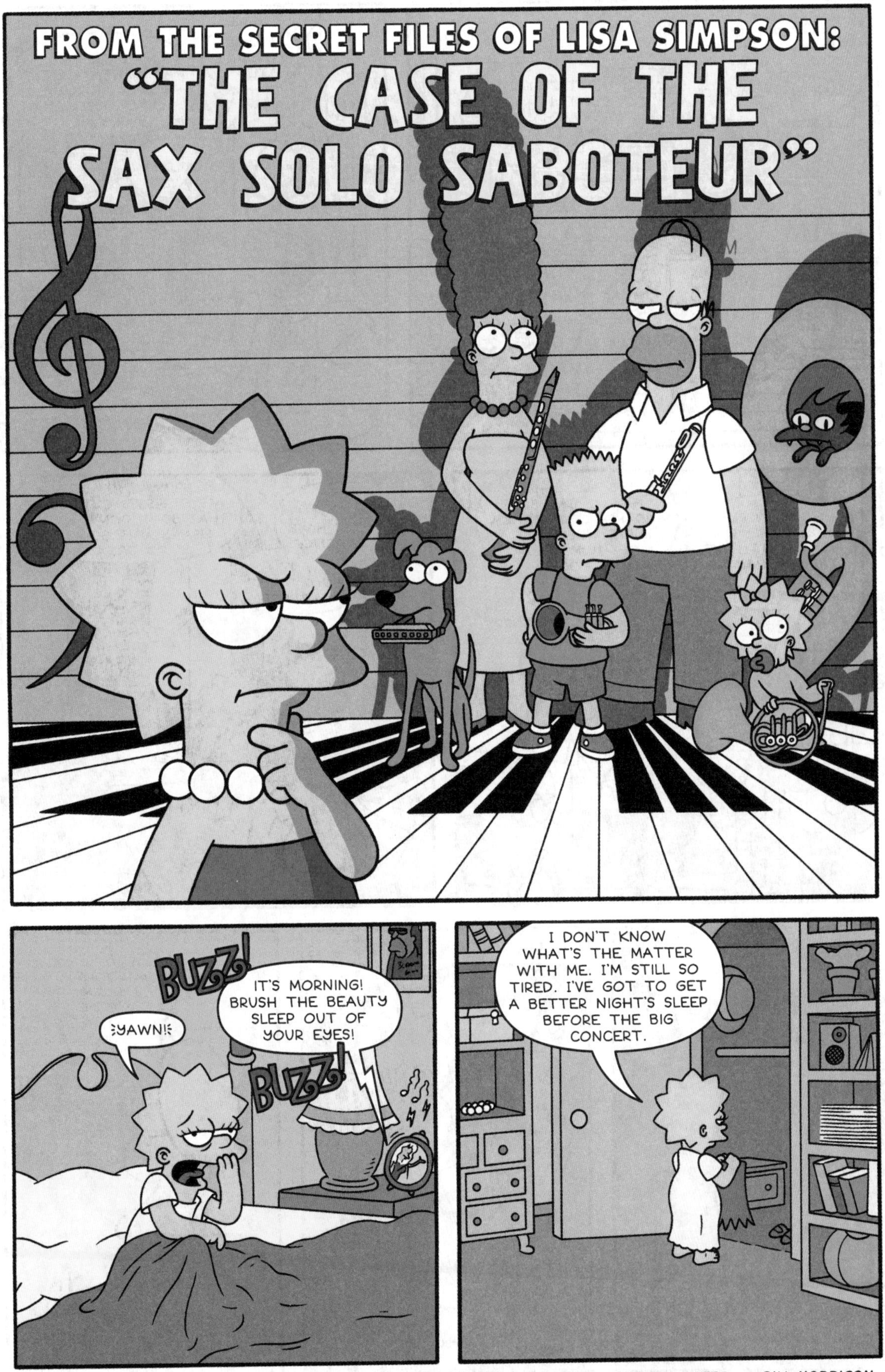
FROM THE SECRET FILES OF LISA SIMPSON:
"THE CASE OF THE SAX SOLO SABOTEUR"
BUZZ!
IT'S MORNING! BRUSH THE BEAUTY SLEEP OUT OF YOUR EYES!
YAWN!
BUZZ!
I DON'T KNOW WHAT'S THE MATTER WITH ME. I'M STILL SO TIRED. I'VE GOT TO GET A BETTER NIGHT'S SLEEP BEFORE THE BIG CONCERT.

JAMES W. BATES SCRIPT | *MIKE WORLEY* PENCILS | *MIKE ROTE* INKS | *ART VILLANUEVA* COLORS | *KAREN BATES* LETTERS | *BILL MORRISON* EDITOR

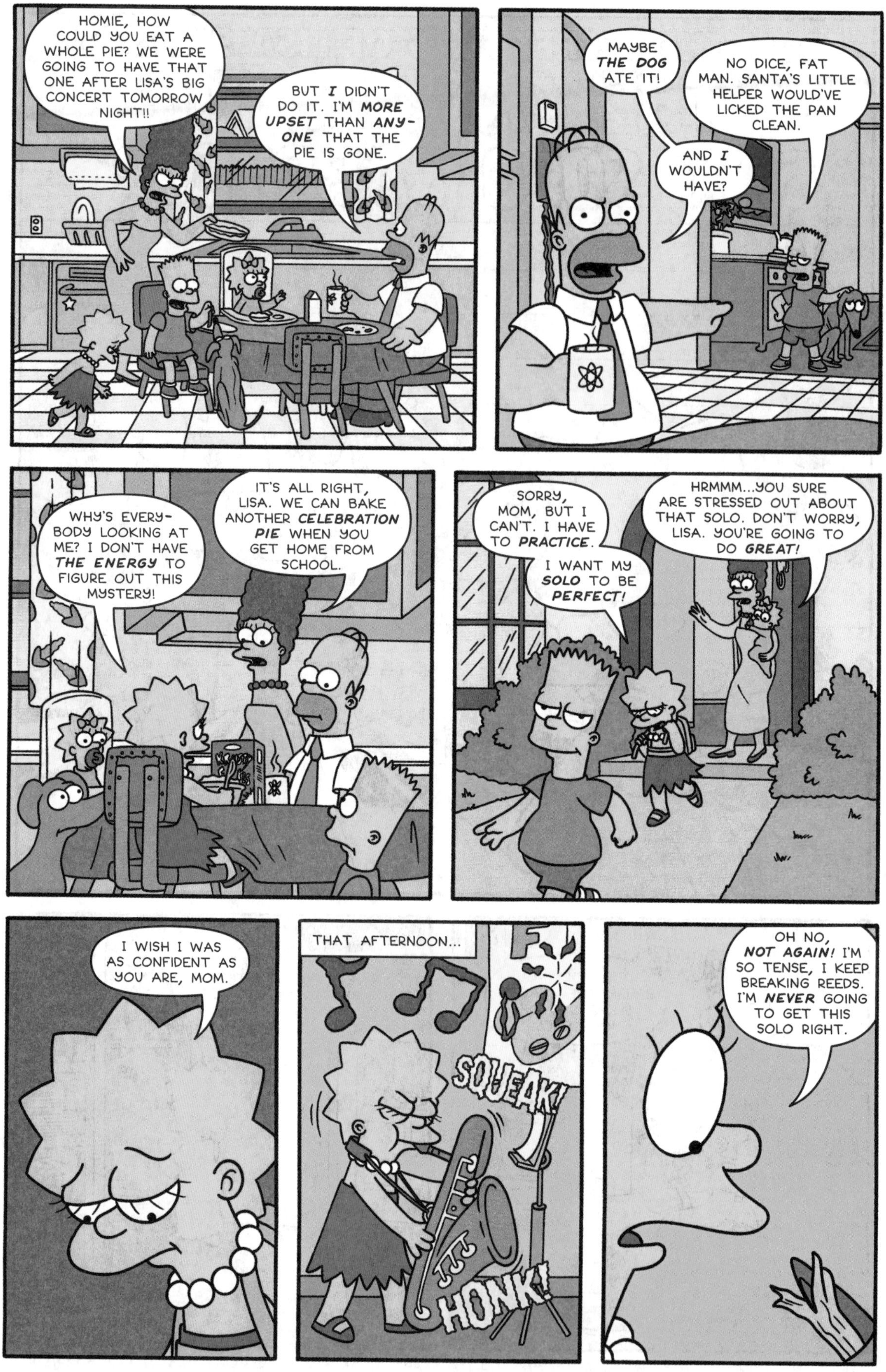
HOMIE, HOW COULD YOU EAT A WHOLE PIE? WE WERE GOING TO HAVE THAT ONE AFTER LISA'S BIG CONCERT TOMORROW NIGHT!!
BUT I DIDN'T DO IT. I'M MORE UPSET THAN ANYONE THAT THE PIE IS GONE.
MAYBE THE DOG ATE IT!
AND I WOULDN'T HAVE?
NO DICE, FAT MAN. SANTA'S LITTLE HELPER WOULD'VE LICKED THE PAN CLEAN.
WHY'S EVERYBODY LOOKING AT ME? I DON'T HAVE THE ENERGY TO FIGURE OUT THIS MYSTERY!
IT'S ALL RIGHT, LISA. WE CAN BAKE ANOTHER CELEBRATION PIE WHEN YOU GET HOME FROM SCHOOL.
SORRY, MOM, BUT I CAN'T. I HAVE TO PRACTICE.
I WANT MY SOLO TO BE PERFECT!
HRMMM...YOU SURE ARE STRESSED OUT ABOUT THAT SOLO. DON'T WORRY, LISA. YOU'RE GOING TO DO GREAT!
I WISH I WAS AS CONFIDENT AS YOU ARE, MOM.
THAT AFTERNOON...
SQUEAK!
HONK!
OH NO, NOT AGAIN! I'M SO TENSE, I KEEP BREAKING REEDS. I'M NEVER GOING TO GET THIS SOLO RIGHT.

77

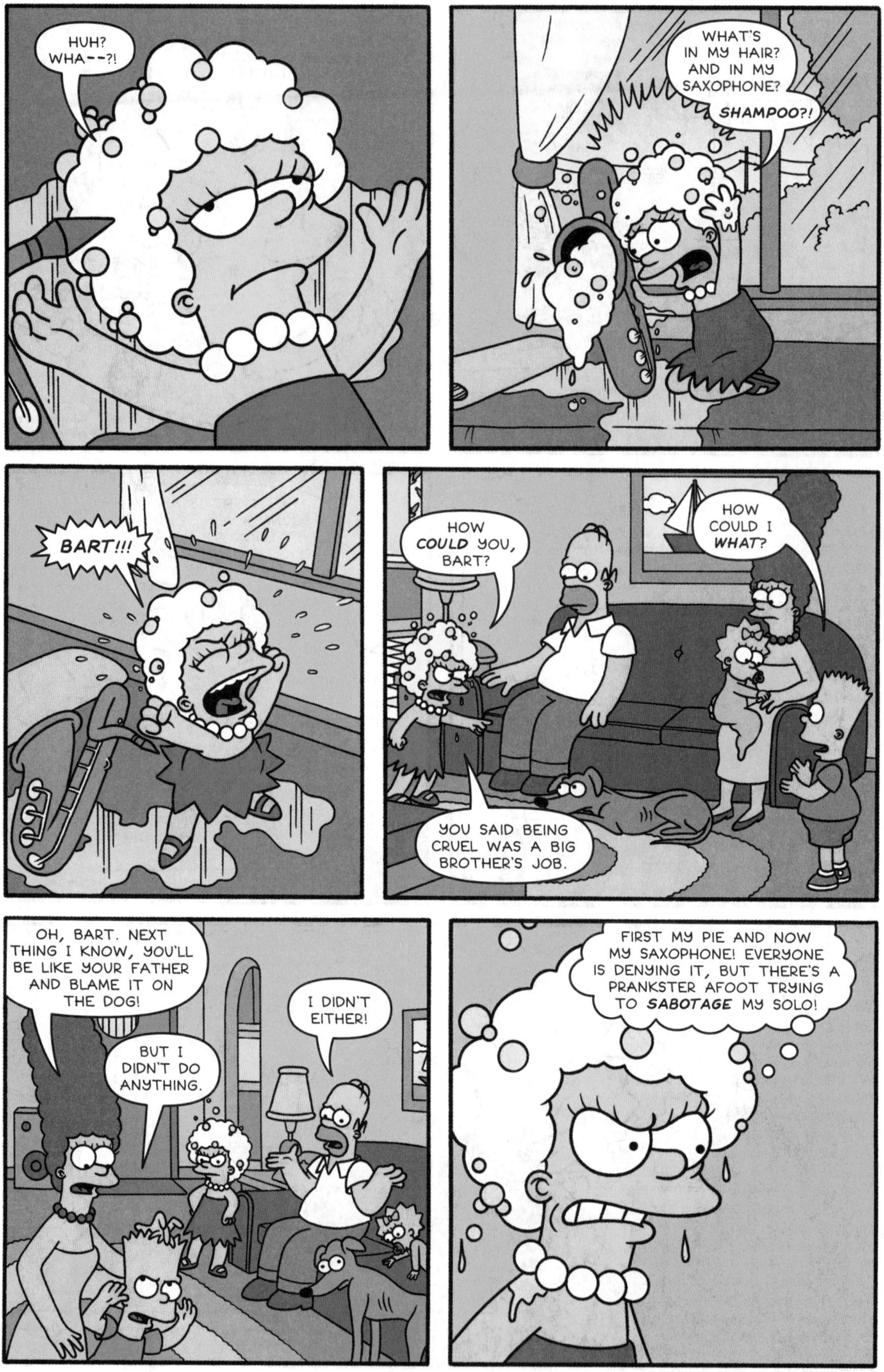
HUH? WHA--?!
WHAT'S IN MY HAIR? AND IN MY SAXOPHONE? *SHAMPOO?!*
BART!!!
HOW *COULD* YOU, BART?
HOW COULD I *WHAT*?
YOU SAID BEING CRUEL WAS A BIG BROTHER'S JOB.
OH, BART. NEXT THING I KNOW, YOU'LL BE LIKE YOUR FATHER AND BLAME IT ON THE DOG!
BUT I DIDN'T DO ANYTHING.
I DIDN'T EITHER!
FIRST MY PIE AND NOW MY SAXOPHONE! EVERYONE IS DENYING IT, BUT THERE'S A PRANKSTER AFOOT TRYING TO *SABOTAGE* MY SOLO!

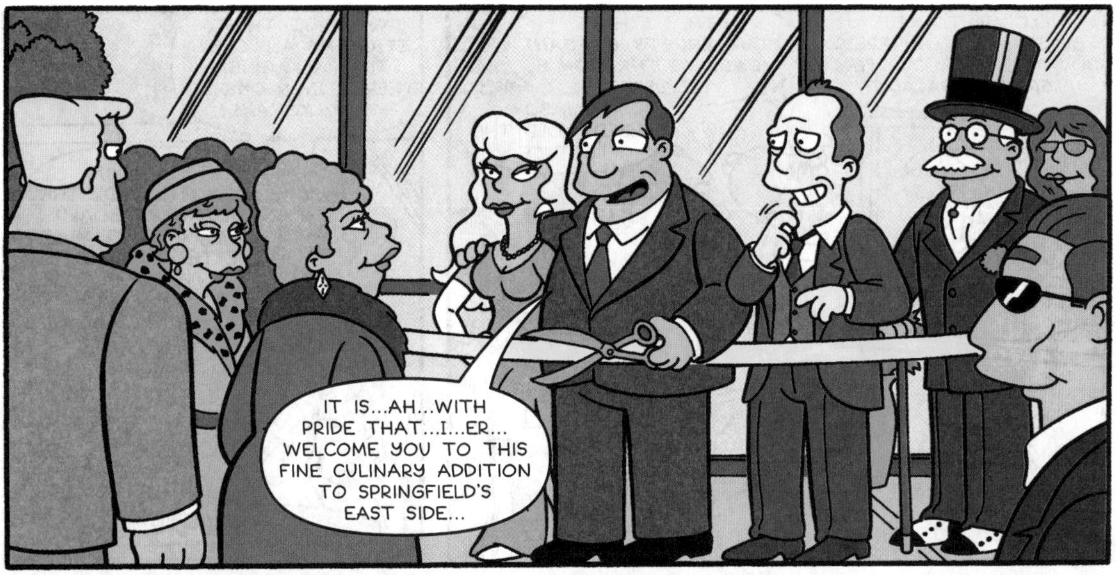
IT IS...AH...WITH PRIDE THAT...I...ER... WELCOME YOU TO THIS FINE CULINARY ADDITION TO SPRINGFIELD'S EAST SIDE...

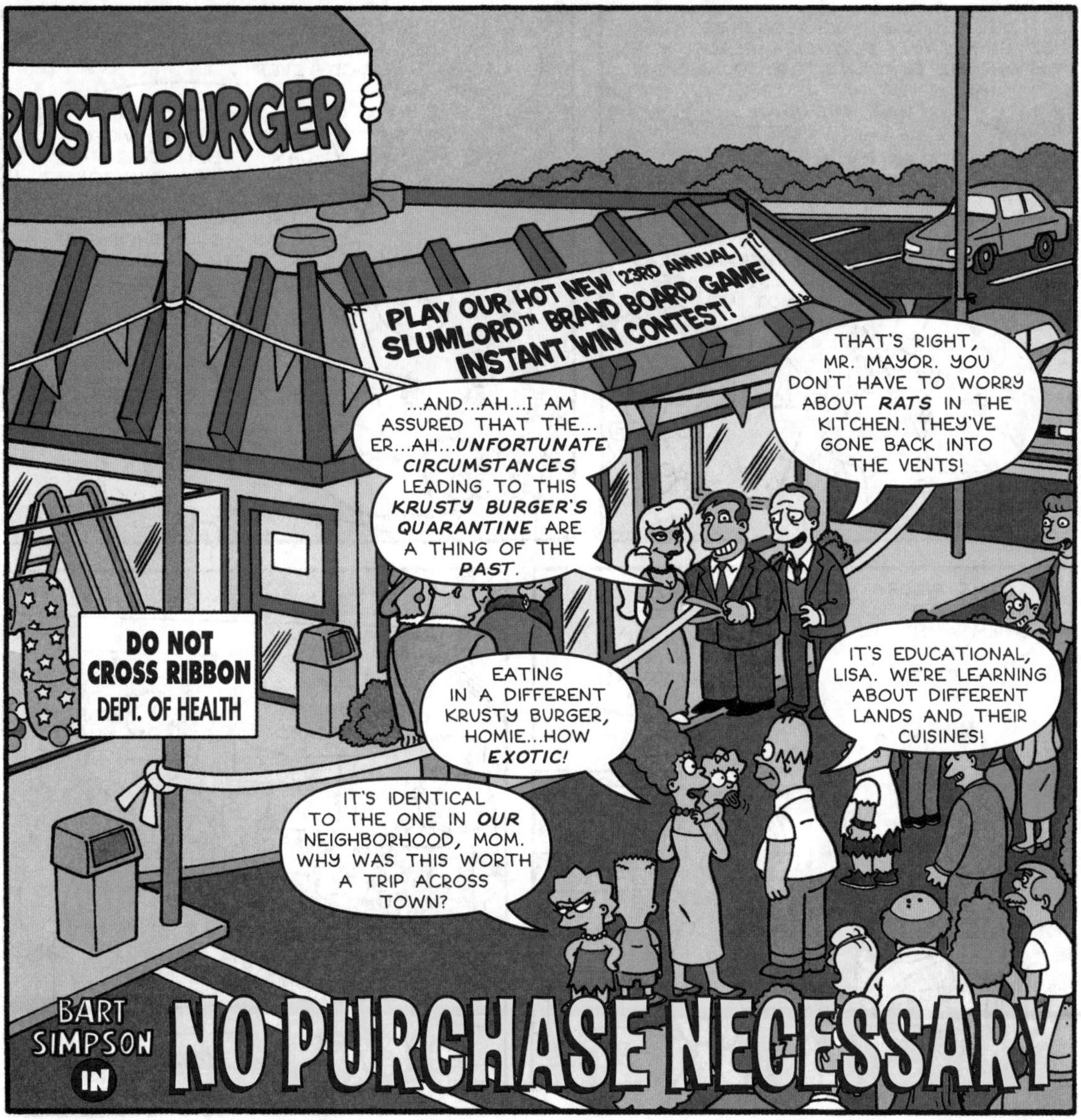
KRUSTYBURGER
PLAY OUR HOT NEW (23RD ANNUAL) SLUMLORD™ BRAND BOARD GAME INSTANT WIN CONTEST!
...AND...AH...I AM ASSURED THAT THE... ER...AH...UNFORTUNATE CIRCUMSTANCES LEADING TO THIS KRUSTY BURGER'S QUARANTINE ARE A THING OF THE PAST.
THAT'S RIGHT, MR. MAYOR. YOU DON'T HAVE TO WORRY ABOUT RATS IN THE KITCHEN. THEY'VE GONE BACK INTO THE VENTS!
DO NOT CROSS RIBBON DEPT. OF HEALTH
EATING IN A DIFFERENT KRUSTY BURGER, HOMIE...HOW EXOTIC!
IT'S EDUCATIONAL, LISA. WE'RE LEARNING ABOUT DIFFERENT LANDS AND THEIR CUISINES!
IT'S IDENTICAL TO THE ONE IN OUR NEIGHBORHOOD, MOM. WHY WAS THIS WORTH A TRIP ACROSS TOWN?
BART SIMPSON IN
NO PURCHASE NECESSARY

JOHN JACKSON MILLER SCRIPT · *PHIL ORTIZ* PENCILS · *MIKE DECARLO* INKS · *NATHAN HAMILL* COLORS · *KAREN BATES* LETTERS · *BILL MORRISON* EDITOR

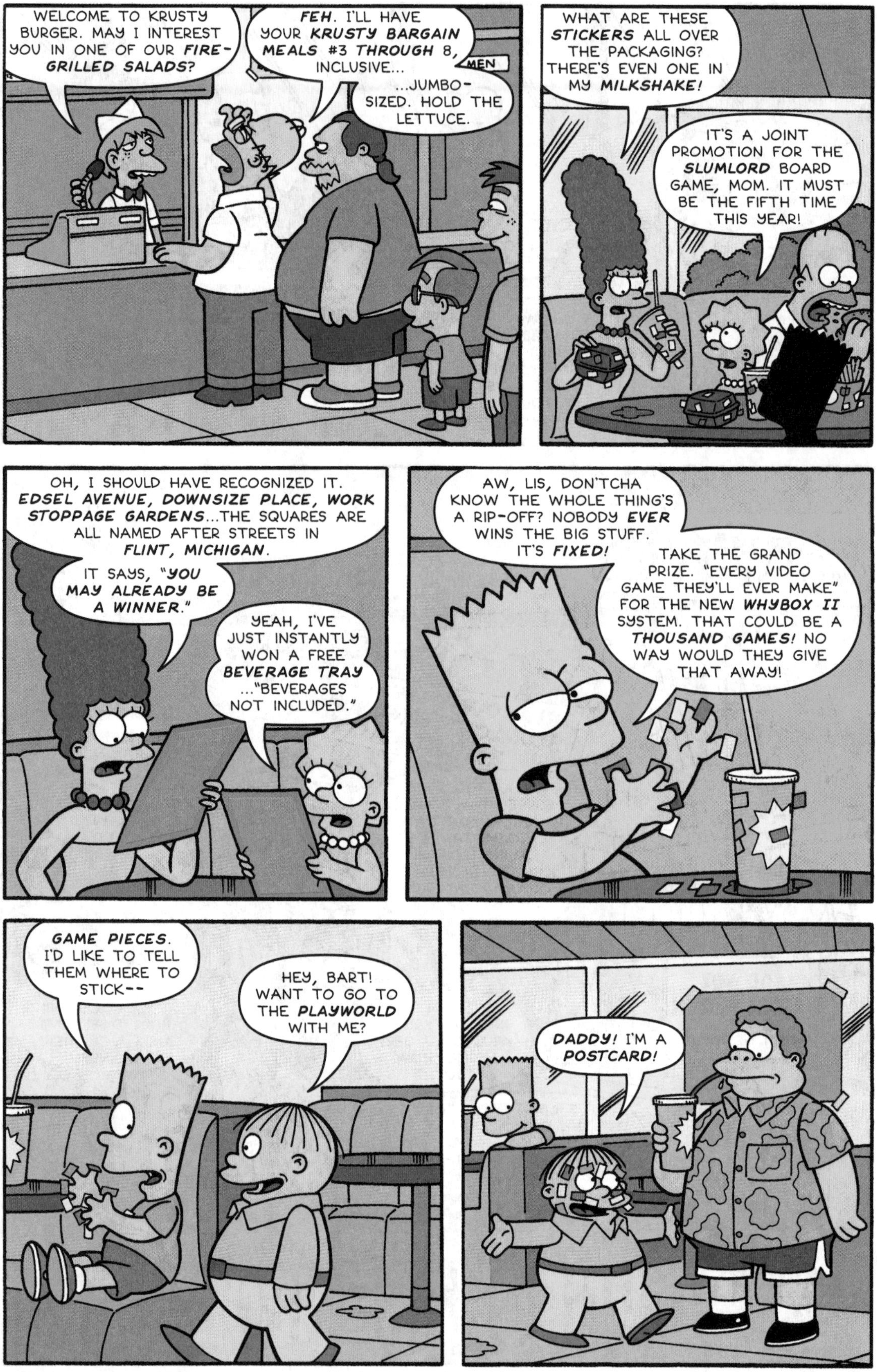
WELCOME TO KRUSTY BURGER. MAY I INTEREST YOU IN ONE OF OUR FIRE-GRILLED SALADS?
FEH. I'LL HAVE YOUR KRUSTY BARGAIN MEALS #3 THROUGH 8, INCLUSIVE...
...JUMBO-SIZED. HOLD THE LETTUCE.
MEN
WHAT ARE THESE STICKERS ALL OVER THE PACKAGING? THERE'S EVEN ONE IN MY MILKSHAKE!
IT'S A JOINT PROMOTION FOR THE SLUMLORD BOARD GAME, MOM. IT MUST BE THE FIFTH TIME THIS YEAR!
OH, I SHOULD HAVE RECOGNIZED IT. EDSEL AVENUE, DOWNSIZE PLACE, WORK STOPPAGE GARDENS...THE SQUARES ARE ALL NAMED AFTER STREETS IN FLINT, MICHIGAN.
IT SAYS, "YOU MAY ALREADY BE A WINNER."
YEAH, I'VE JUST INSTANTLY WON A FREE BEVERAGE TRAY ..."BEVERAGES NOT INCLUDED."
AW, LIS, DON'TCHA KNOW THE WHOLE THING'S A RIP-OFF? NOBODY EVER WINS THE BIG STUFF. IT'S FIXED!
TAKE THE GRAND PRIZE. "EVERY VIDEO GAME THEY'LL EVER MAKE" FOR THE NEW WHYBOX II SYSTEM. THAT COULD BE A THOUSAND GAMES! NO WAY WOULD THEY GIVE THAT AWAY!
GAME PIECES. I'D LIKE TO TELL THEM WHERE TO STICK--
HEY, BART! WANT TO GO TO THE PLAYWORLD WITH ME?
DADDY! I'M A POSTCARD!

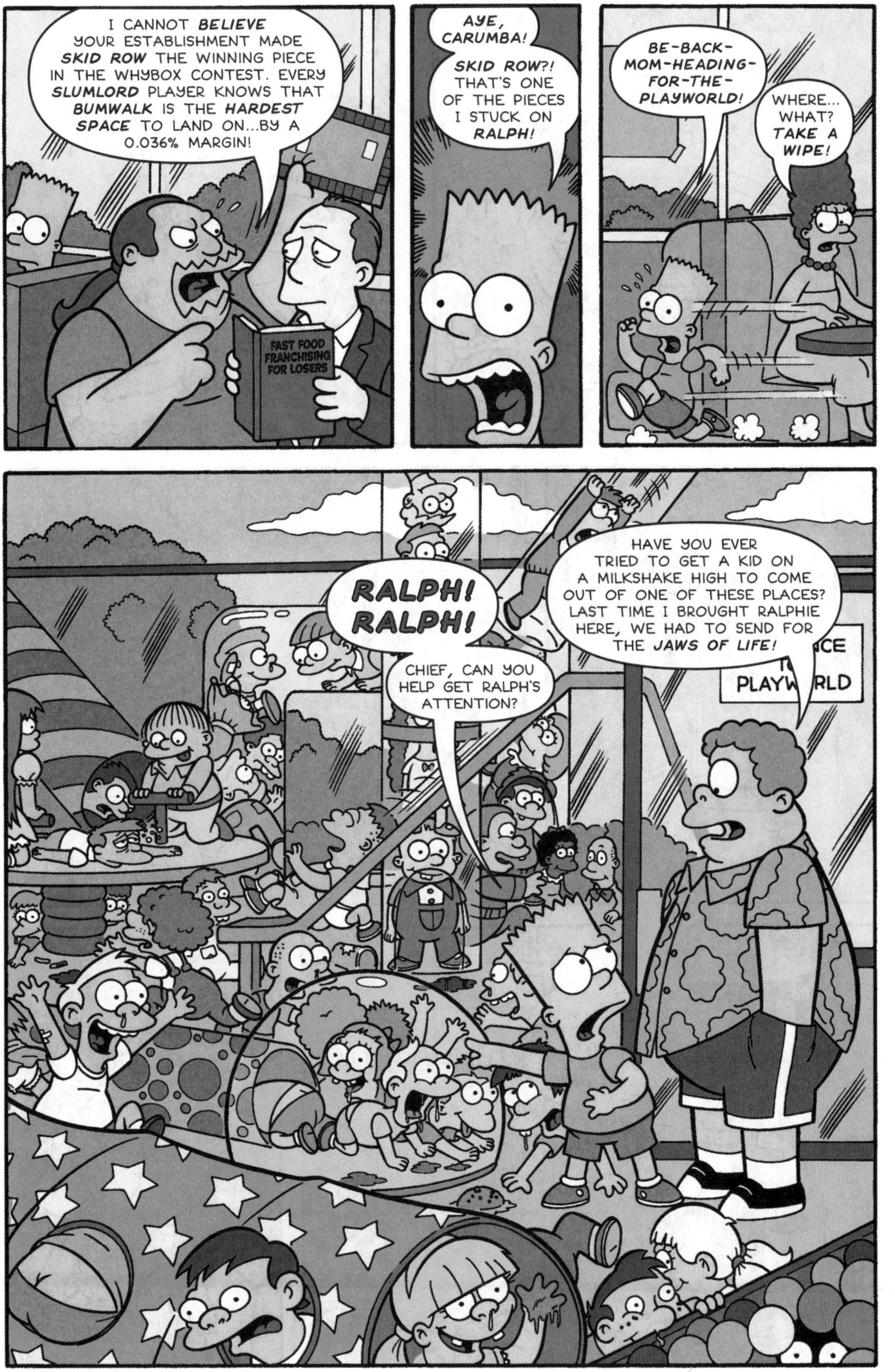
I CANNOT *BELIEVE* YOUR ESTABLISHMENT MADE *SKID ROW* THE WINNING PIECE IN THE WHYBOX CONTEST. EVERY *SLUMLORD* PLAYER KNOWS THAT *BUMWALK* IS THE *HARDEST SPACE* TO LAND ON...BY A 0.036% MARGIN!
FAST FOOD FRANCHISING FOR LOSERS
AYE, CARUMBA!
SKID ROW?! THAT'S ONE OF THE PIECES I STUCK ON *RALPH*!
BE-BACK-MOM-HEADING-FOR-THE-PLAYWORLD!
WHERE... WHAT? *TAKE A WIPE!*
RALPH! RALPH!
CHIEF, CAN YOU HELP GET RALPH'S ATTENTION?
HAVE YOU EVER TRIED TO GET A KID ON A MILKSHAKE HIGH TO COME OUT OF ONE OF THESE PLACES? LAST TIME I BROUGHT RALPHIE HERE, WE HAD TO SEND FOR THE *JAWS OF LIFE!*

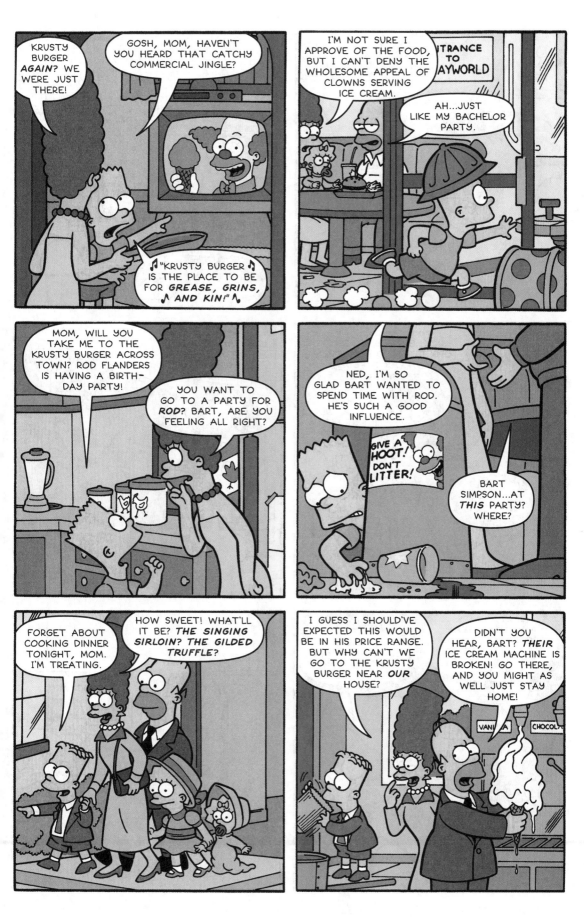

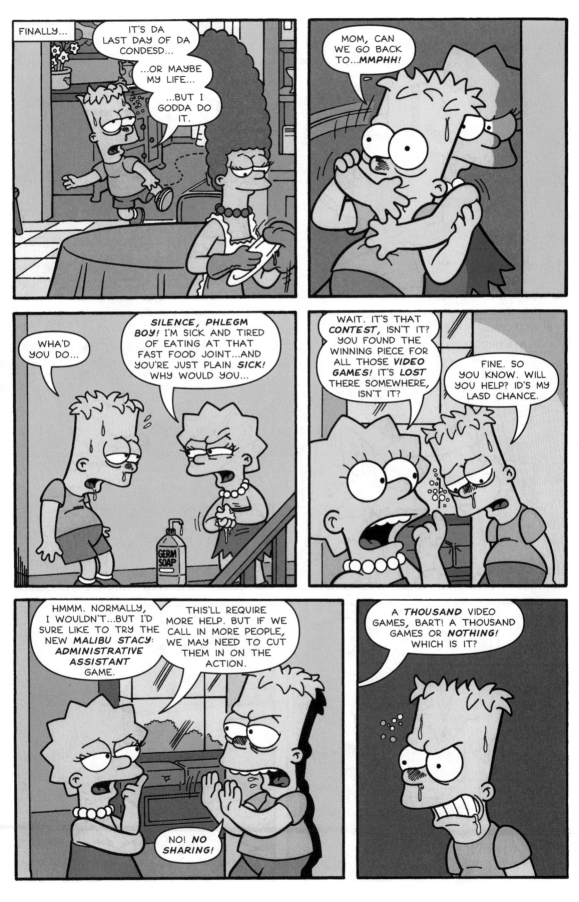

89

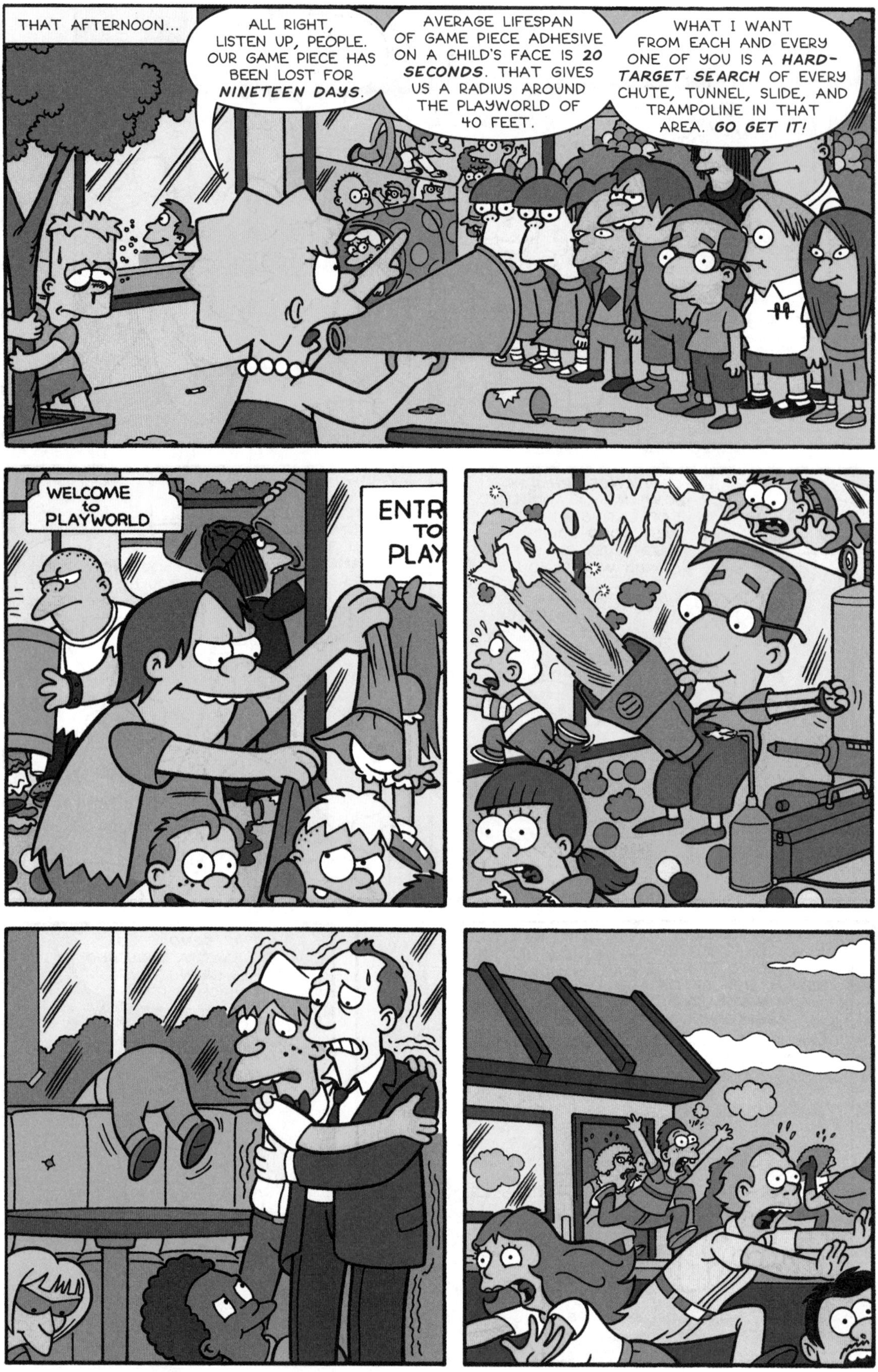
THAT AFTERNOON...
ALL RIGHT, LISTEN UP, PEOPLE. OUR GAME PIECE HAS BEEN LOST FOR NINETEEN DAYS.
AVERAGE LIFESPAN OF GAME PIECE ADHESIVE ON A CHILD'S FACE IS 20 SECONDS. THAT GIVES US A RADIUS AROUND THE PLAYWORLD OF 40 FEET.
WHAT I WANT FROM EACH AND EVERY ONE OF YOU IS A HARD-TARGET SEARCH OF EVERY CHUTE, TUNNEL, SLIDE, AND TRAMPOLINE IN THAT AREA. GO GET IT!
WELCOME to PLAYWORLD
ENTR TO PLAY
BOWM!

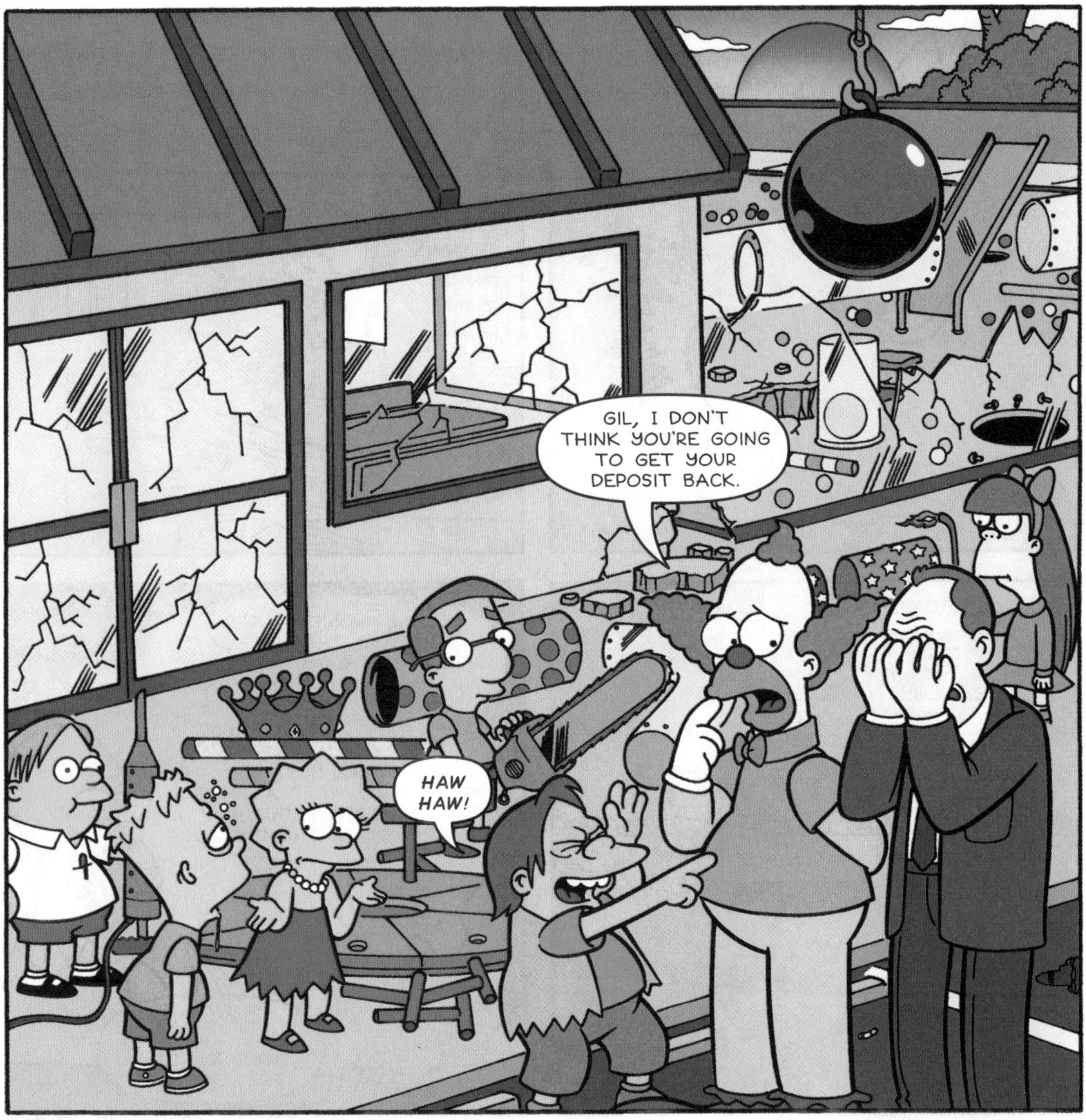
GIL, I DON'T THINK YOU'RE GOING TO GET YOUR DEPOSIT BACK.
HAW HAW!

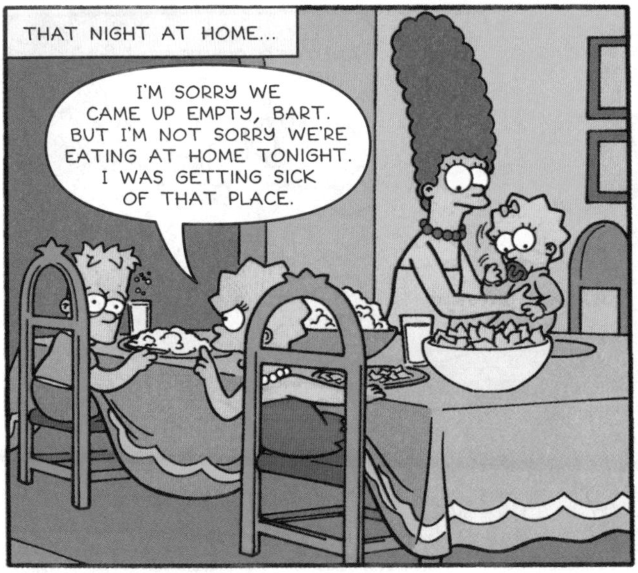
THAT NIGHT AT HOME...
I'M SORRY WE CAME UP EMPTY, BART. BUT I'M NOT SORRY WE'RE EATING AT HOME TONIGHT. I WAS GETTING SICK OF THAT PLACE.

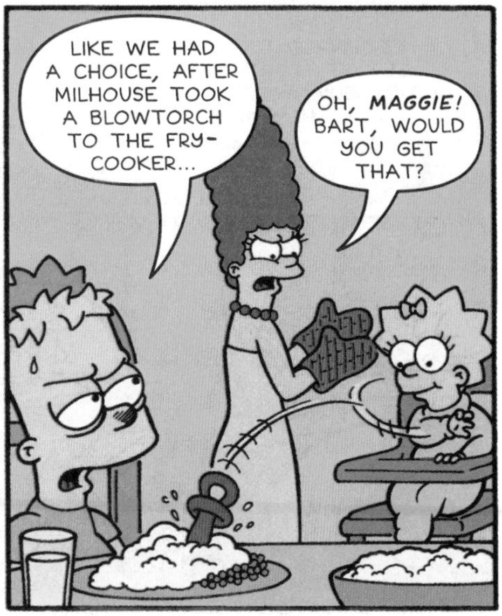
LIKE WE HAD A CHOICE, AFTER MILHOUSE TOOK A BLOWTORCH TO THE FRY-COOKER...
OH, **MAGGIE!** BART, WOULD YOU GET THAT?

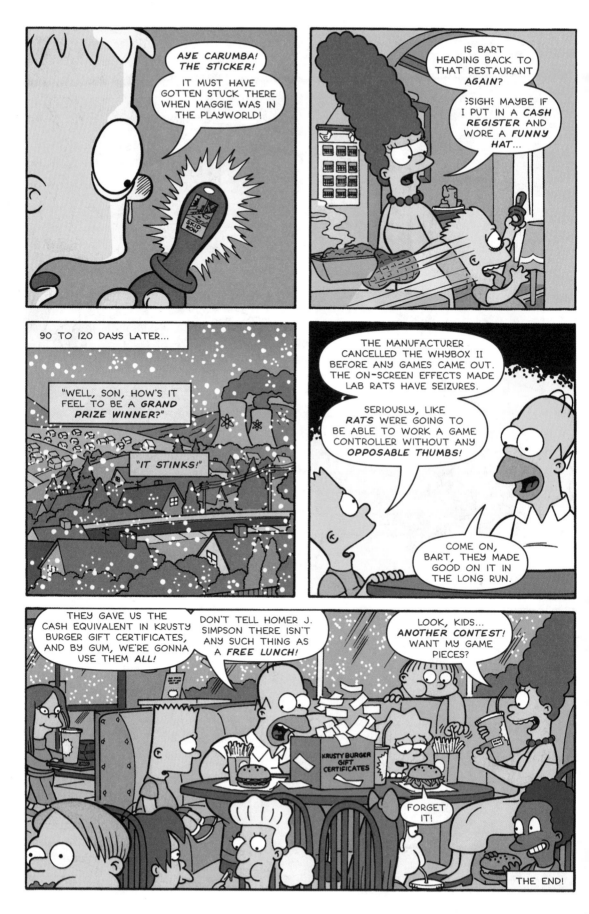

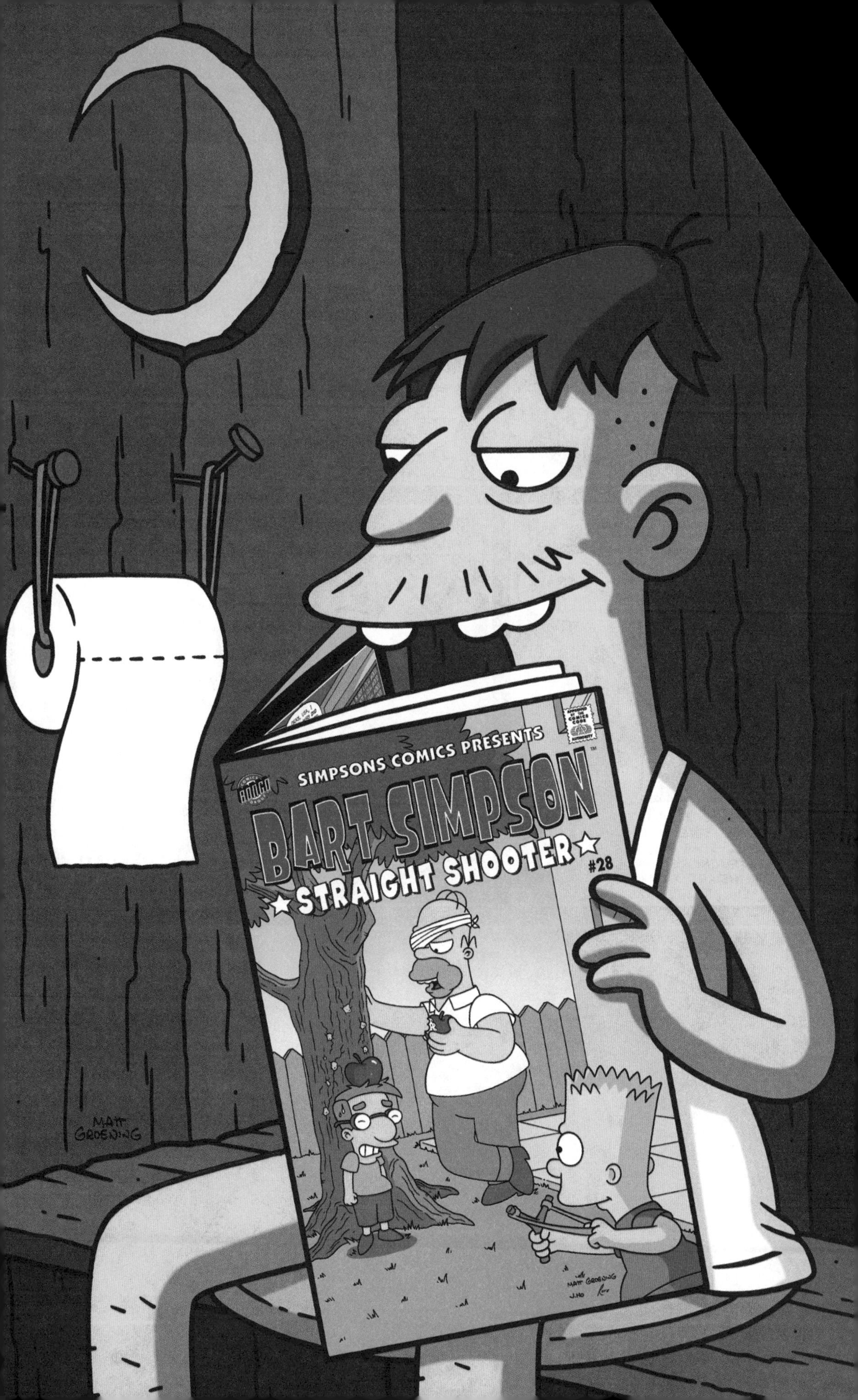

SIMPSONS COMICS PRESENTS
BART SIMPSON
STRAIGHT SHOOTER
#28
MATT GROENING

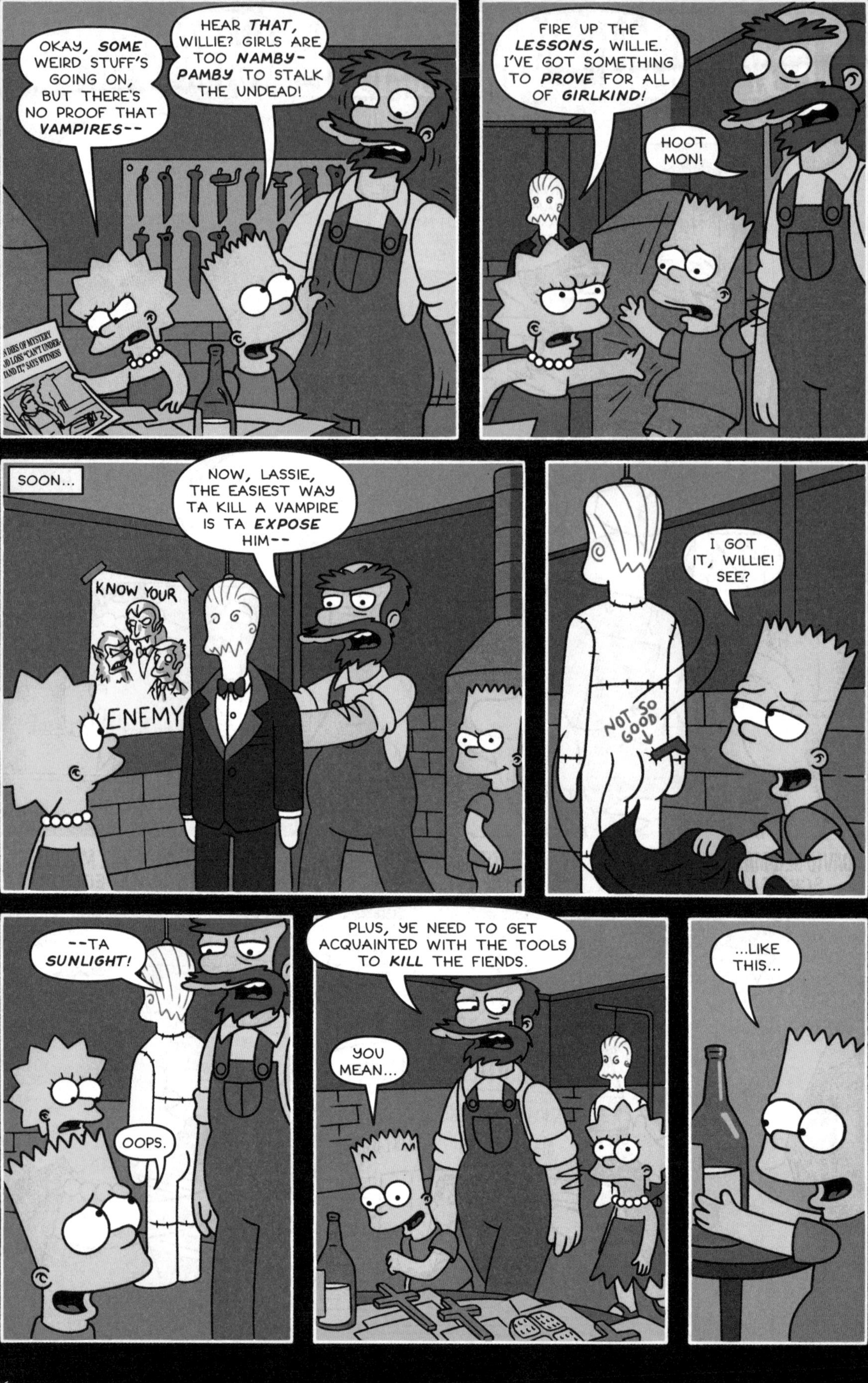
OKAY, SOME WEIRD STUFF'S GOING ON, BUT THERE'S NO PROOF THAT VAMPIRES--
HEAR THAT, WILLIE? GIRLS ARE TOO NAMBY-PAMBY TO STALK THE UNDEAD!
FIRE UP THE LESSONS, WILLIE. I'VE GOT SOMETHING TO PROVE FOR ALL OF GIRLKIND!
HOOT MON!
SOON...
NOW, LASSIE, THE EASIEST WAY TA KILL A VAMPIRE IS TA EXPOSE HIM--
KNOW YOUR ENEMY
I GOT IT, WILLIE! SEE?
NOT SO GOOD
--TA SUNLIGHT!
OOPS.
PLUS, YE NEED TO GET ACQUAINTED WITH THE TOOLS TO KILL THE FIENDS.
YOU MEAN...
...LIKE THIS...

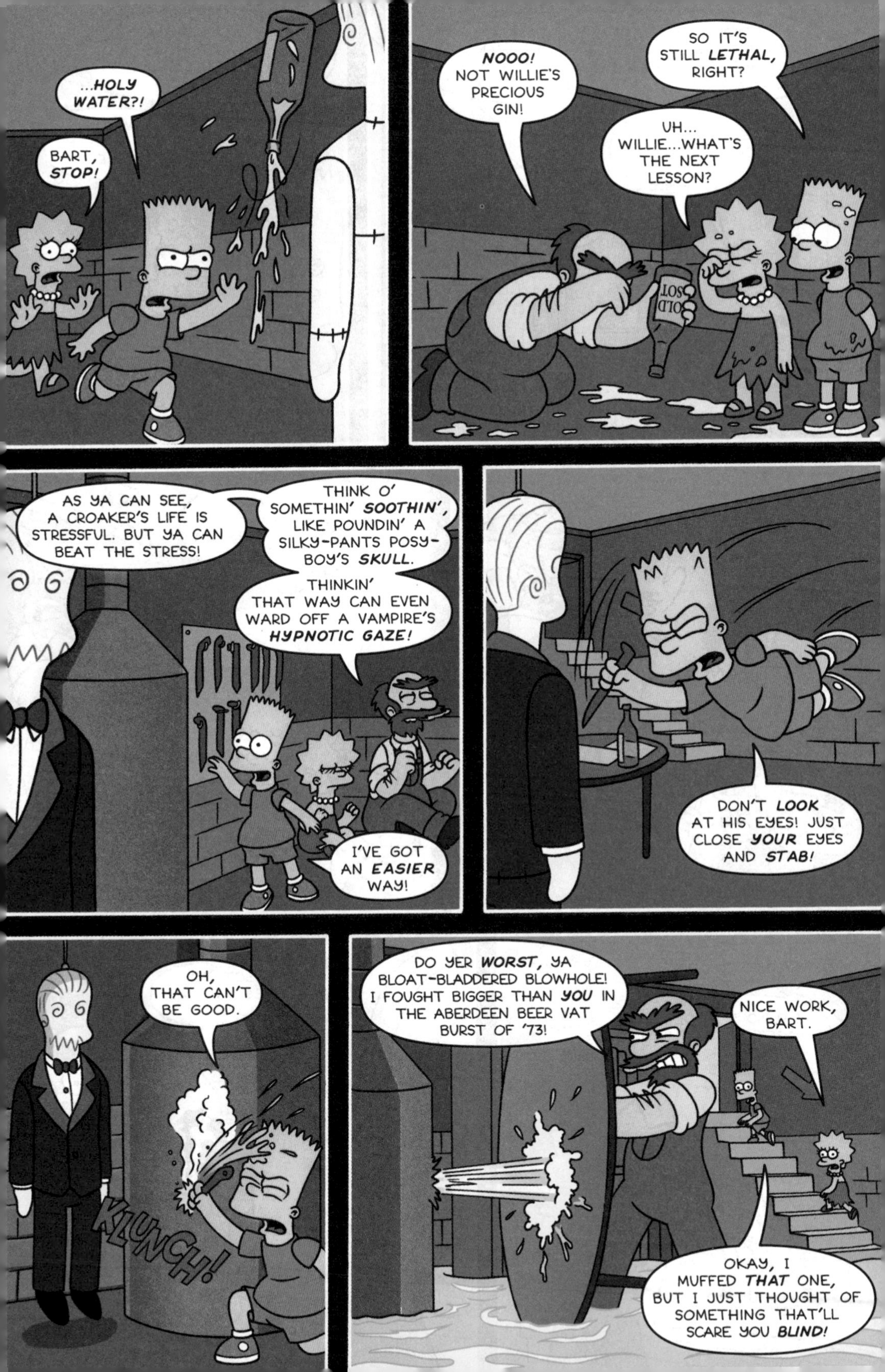
...HOLY WATER?!
BART, STOP!
NOOO! NOT WILLIE'S PRECIOUS GIN!
SO IT'S STILL LETHAL, RIGHT?
UH... WILLIE...WHAT'S THE NEXT LESSON?
AS YA CAN SEE, A CROAKER'S LIFE IS STRESSFUL. BUT YA CAN BEAT THE STRESS!
THINK O' SOMETHIN' SOOTHIN', LIKE POUNDIN' A SILKY-PANTS POSY-BOY'S SKULL.
THINKIN' THAT WAY CAN EVEN WARD OFF A VAMPIRE'S HYPNOTIC GAZE!
I'VE GOT AN EASIER WAY!
DON'T LOOK AT HIS EYES! JUST CLOSE YOUR EYES AND STAB!
OH, THAT CAN'T BE GOOD.
KLUNCH!
DO YER WORST, YA BLOAT-BLADDERED BLOWHOLE! I FOUGHT BIGGER THAN YOU IN THE ABERDEEN BEER VAT BURST OF '73!
NICE WORK, BART.
OKAY, I MUFFED THAT ONE, BUT I JUST THOUGHT OF SOMETHING THAT'LL SCARE YOU BLIND!

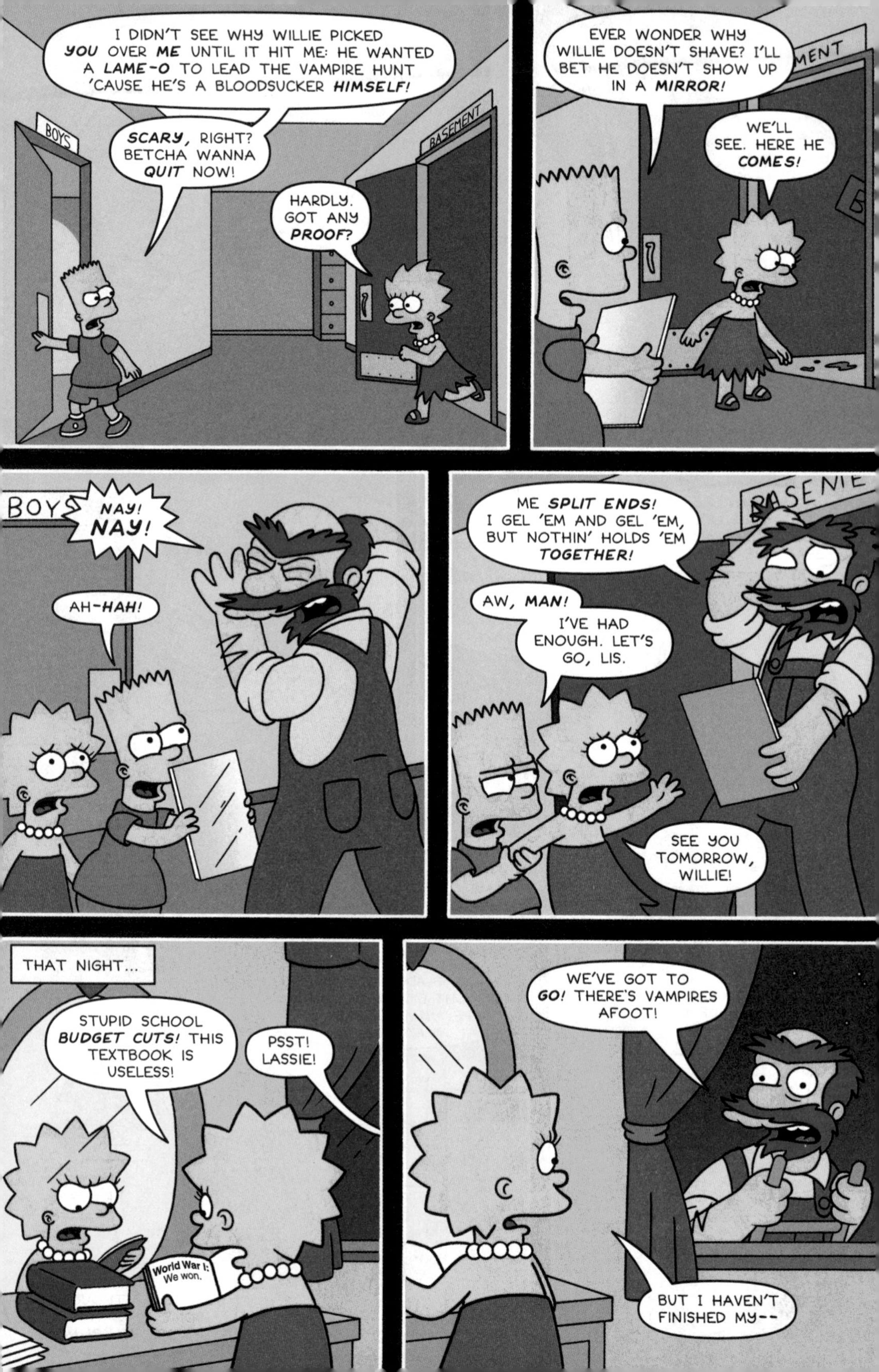
I DIDN'T SEE WHY WILLIE PICKED **YOU** OVER **ME** UNTIL IT HIT ME: HE WANTED A **LAME-O** TO LEAD THE VAMPIRE HUNT 'CAUSE HE'S A BLOODSUCKER **HIMSELF!**
BOYS
BASEMENT
SCARY, RIGHT? BETCHA WANNA **QUIT** NOW!
HARDLY. GOT ANY **PROOF?**
EVER WONDER WHY WILLIE DOESN'T SHAVE? I'LL BET HE DOESN'T SHOW UP IN A **MIRROR!**
WE'LL SEE. HERE HE **COMES!**
BOYS
NAY! **NAY!**
AH-**HAH!**
ME **SPLIT ENDS!** I GEL 'EM AND GEL 'EM, BUT NOTHIN' HOLDS 'EM **TOGETHER!**
AW, **MAN!**
I'VE HAD ENOUGH. LET'S GO, LIS.
SEE YOU TOMORROW, WILLIE!
THAT NIGHT...
STUPID SCHOOL **BUDGET CUTS!** THIS TEXTBOOK IS USELESS!
PSST! LASSIE!
World War I: We won.
WE'VE GOT TO **GO!** THERE'S VAMPIRES AFOOT!
BUT I HAVEN'T FINISHED MY--

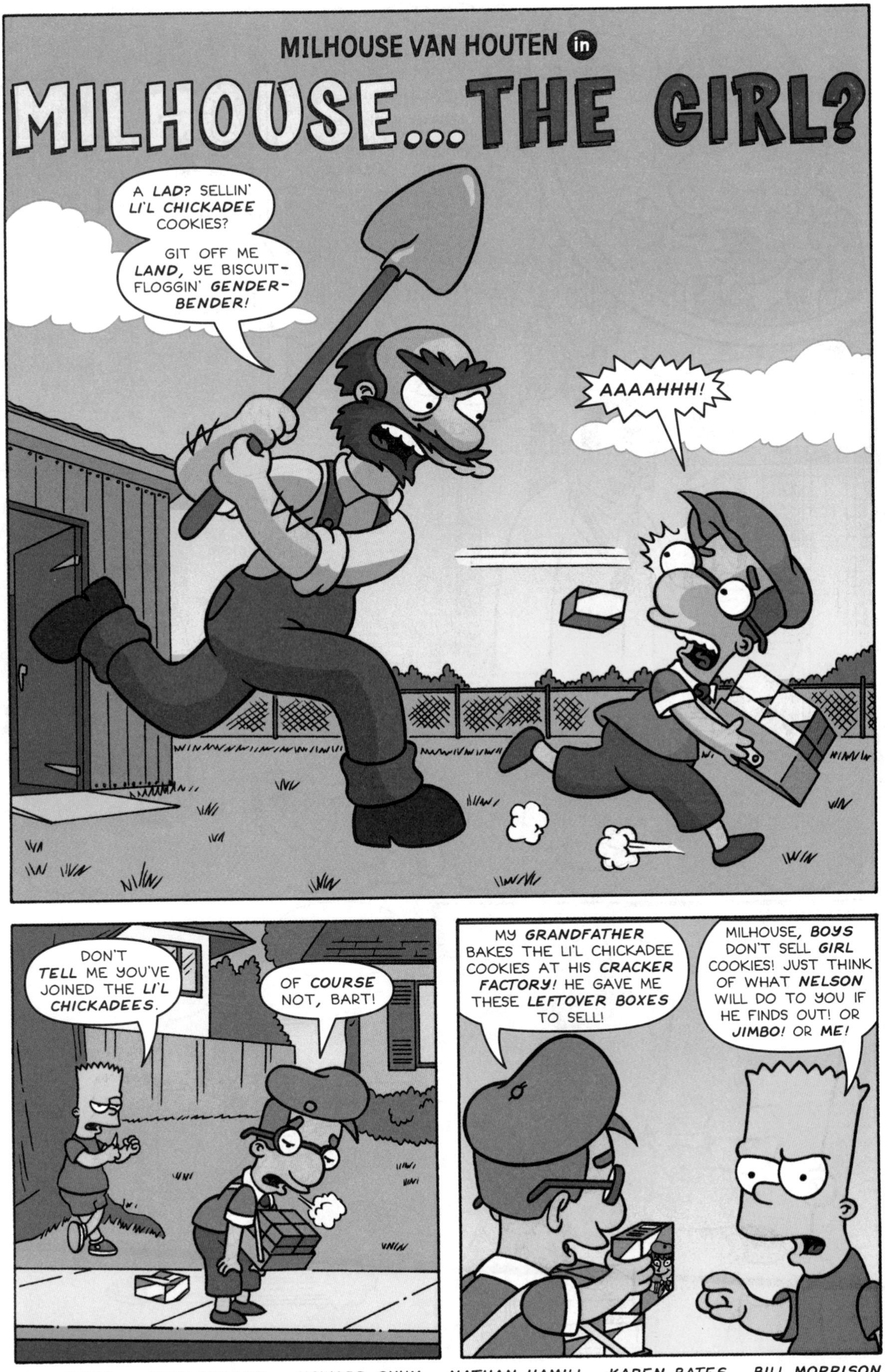
MILHOUSE VAN HOUTEN in
MILHOUSE...THE GIRL?
A LAD? SELLIN' LI'L CHICKADEE COOKIES?
GIT OFF ME LAND, YE BISCUIT-FLOGGIN' GENDER-BENDER!
AAAAHHH!
DON'T TELL ME YOU'VE JOINED THE LI'L CHICKADEES.
OF COURSE NOT, BART!
MY GRANDFATHER BAKES THE LI'L CHICKADEE COOKIES AT HIS CRACKER FACTORY! HE GAVE ME THESE LEFTOVER BOXES TO SELL!
MILHOUSE, BOYS DON'T SELL GIRL COOKIES! JUST THINK OF WHAT NELSON WILL DO TO YOU IF HE FINDS OUT! OR JIMBO! OR ME!

TOM PEYER	***MIKE WORLEY***	***HOWARD SHUM***	***NATHAN HAMILL***	***KAREN BATES***	***BILL MORRISON***
SCRIPT	PENCILS	INKS	COLORS	LETTERS	EDITOR

AFTER YOU CUT OUT THE LABELS, GLUE THEM IN THE APPROPRIATE PLACE--MAKE SURE YOU GET THOSE CORNERS AND EDGES FLAT--AND WATCH THE COMEDY HIJINX ENSUE.

D'OH! STUPID LABEL!

STICK THIS ONE TO A SOUP CAN.

Easy Casserole Recipe

1. Heat soup contents in frying pan

2. Add fish, poultry or beef, making sure you know which it is.

3. Mix in 2 cups white rice, some frozen vegetables, maybe a potato.

4. Simmer.

5. Pour into disposal and call for pizza delivery.

THIS ONE GOES ON YOUR FAVORITE SUGAR-FILLED CEREAL.

Nutrition Facts

Serving Size: One bowl

Amount	Cereal	with Milk
Calories	130	190
from Fat	30	50
from Head	25	45
	% Daily Value*	
Total Fat 4g	5%	3%
Saturated Fat .5g	3%	3%
Polyunsaturated Fat 1g		
Phonyunnatural Fat 1g		
Sodium 210mg	9%	11%
Potassium 45mg	1%	7%
Balonium 100mg	6%	18%
Total Carbohydrate 24g	8%	10%
Dietary Fiber 1g		
Carpet Fiber 2g		
Protein 1g		
Soylent Green 5g		
Vitamin A	10%	15%
Vitamin B12	10%	15%
Vitamin B52	10%	15%
Calcium	10%	15%
Niacin	10%	15%
Thiamin	10%	15%
Ropethemin	10%	15%
Vitamin G	10%	15%
Vitamin PG13	10%	15%
Vitamin R	10%	15%
Phosphorus	10%	15%
Magnesium	10%	15%
Gamma Rays	10%	15%
Iron	10%	15%
Copper	10%	15%
Aluminum	10%	15%
Gold	0%	0%
Riboflavin	10%	15%
Frinkinhoiven	10%	15%
Chemical X	10%	15%

*Percentages based on a 2,000 calorie diet. If intake is higher, numbers should be adjusted down, though you probably don't care about nutrition anyway, so why waste time on a fat pig like you?

BRYAN UHLENBROCK
SCRIPT

MIKE DECARLO
PENCILS

PHYLLIS NOVIN
INKS

NATHAN HAMILL
COLORS

KAREN BATES
LETTERS

BILL MORRISON
EDITOR

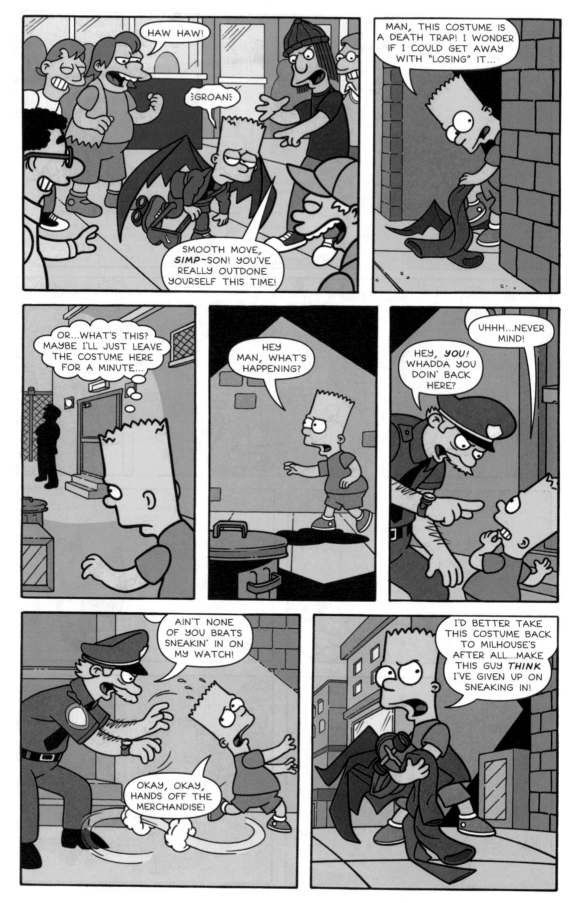

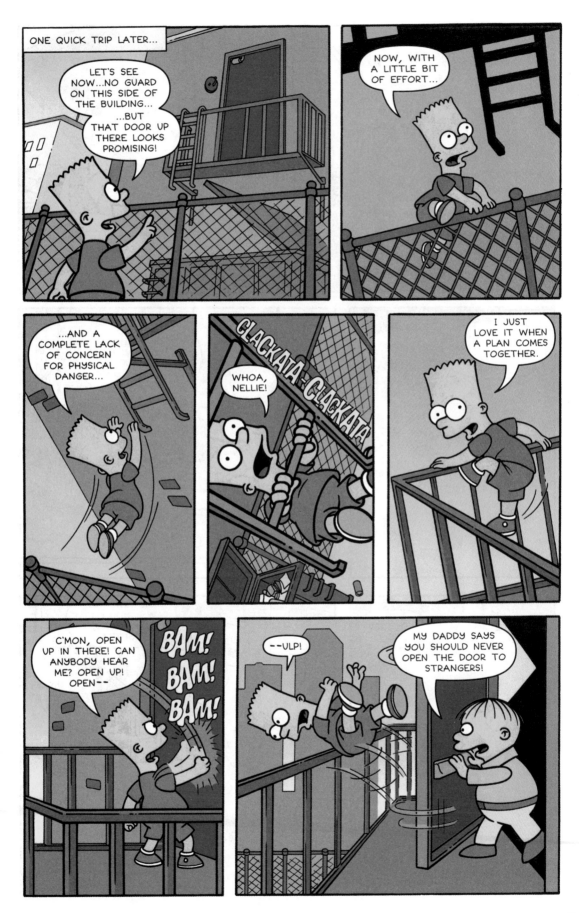

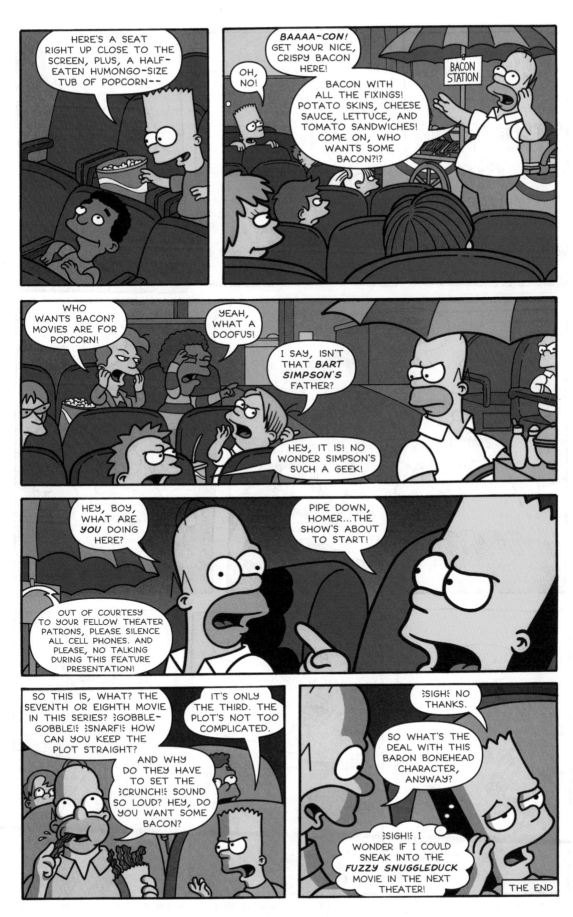

TONY DIGEROLAMO
SCRIPT

JASON HO
PENCILS

MIKE ROTE
INKS

NATHAN HAMILL
COLORS

KAREN BATES
LETTERS

BILL MORRISON
EDITOR

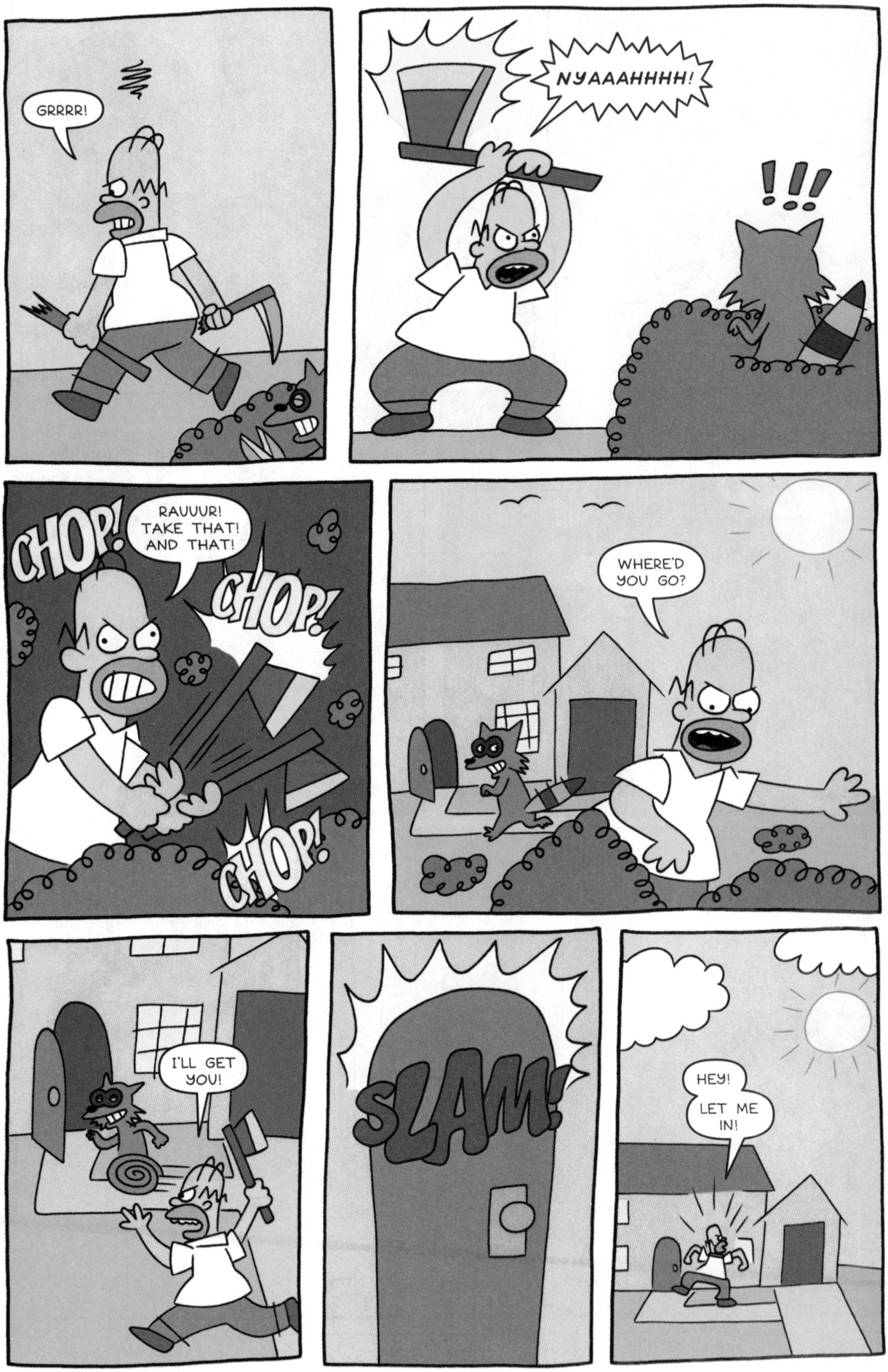
GRRRR!
NYAAAHHHH!
!!!
CHOP!
RAUUUR! TAKE THAT! AND THAT!
CHOP!
CHOP!
WHERE'D YOU GO?
I'LL GET YOU!
SLAM!
HEY!
LET ME IN!

Bill Morrison
CREATIVE DIRECTOR

Robert Zaugh
OPERATIONS

Serban Cristescu
SPECIAL PROJECTS

Karen Bates, Art Villanueva, Nathan Hamill
PRODUCTION/DESIGN

Matt Groening
PUBLISHER

Terry Delegeane
MANAGING EDITOR

Nathan Kane
ART DIRECTOR

Christopher Ungar
PRODUCTION MANAGER

Jason Ho, Mike Rote
STAFF ARTISTS

Sherri Smith, Pete Benson
ADMINISTRATION

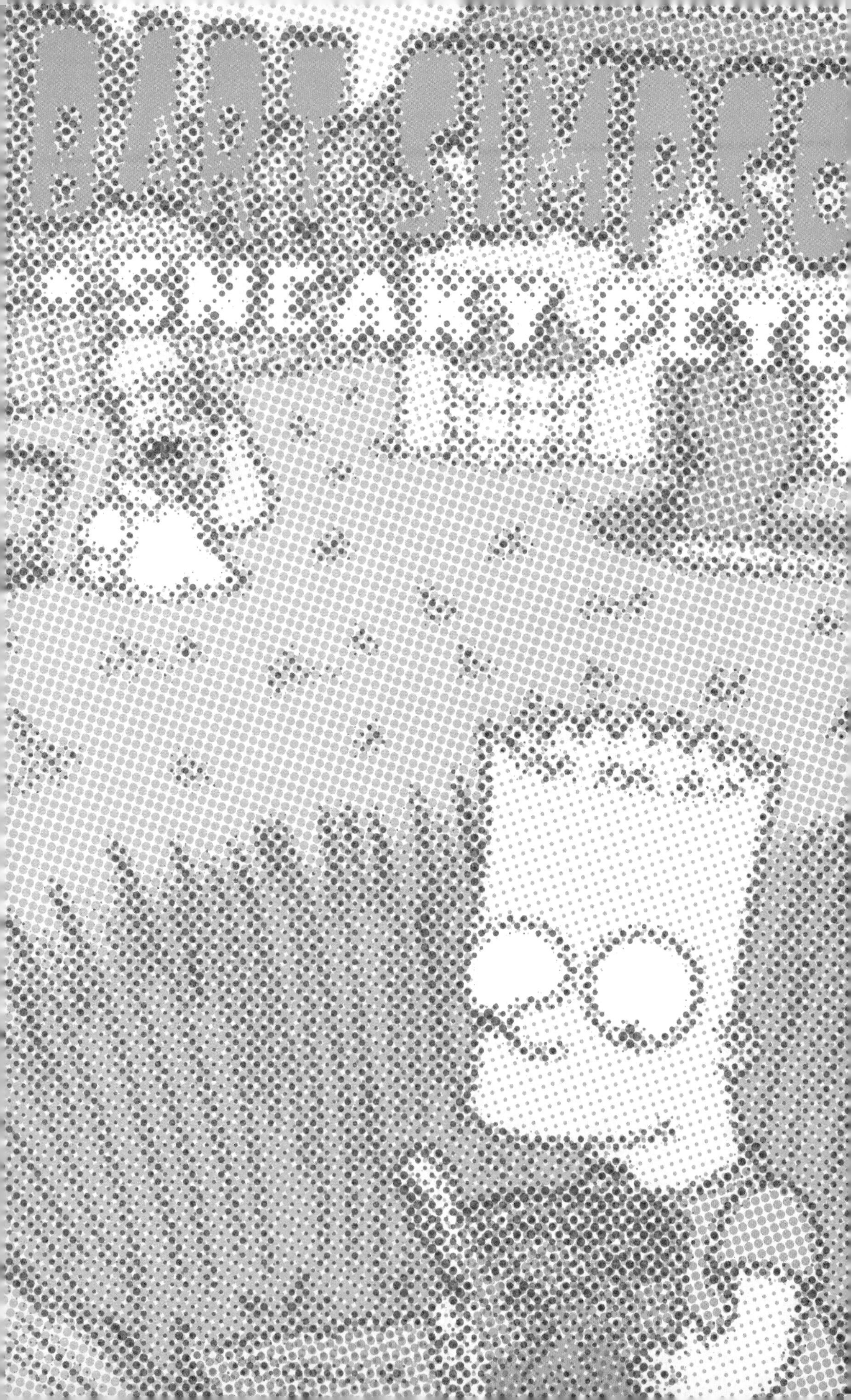